Studies in European Thought

From Piltdown Man
to Point Omega

Studies in European Thought

E. Allen McCormick
General Editor

Vol. 18

PETER LANG
New York • Washington, D.C./Baltimore • Boston • Bern
Frankfurt am Main • Berlin • Brussels • Vienna • Oxford

Noel Keith Roberts

From Piltdown Man to Point Omega

The Evolutionary Theory of Teilhard de Chardin

PETER LANG
New York • Washington, D.C./Baltimore • Boston • Bern
Frankfurt am Main • Berlin • Brussels • Vienna • Oxford

Library of Congress Cataloging-in-Publication Data

Roberts, Noel Keith.
From piltdown man to point omega: the evolutionary theory
of Teilhard de Chardin / by Noel Keith Roberts.
p. cm. — (Studies in European thought; vol. 18)
Includes bibliographical references and index.
1. Teilhard de Chardin, Pierre. 2. Human evolution. I. Title. II. Series.
B2430.T37R63   194—dc21   99-34226
ISBN 0-8204-4588-6
ISSN 1043-5786

Die Deutsche Bibliothek-CIP-Einheitsaufnahme

Roberts, Noel Keith:
From Piltdown man to point Omega: the evolutionary theory
of Teilhard de Chardin / Noel Keith Roberts.
–New York; Washington, D.C./Baltimore; Boston; Bern;
Frankfurt am Main; Berlin; Brussels; Vienna; Oxford: Lang.
(Studies in European thought; Vol. 18)
ISBN 0-8204-4588-6

The paper in this book meets the guidelines for permanence and durability
of the Committee on Production Guidelines for Book Longevity
of the Council of Library Resources.

Printed in the United States of America

Arise Mortal Man by Carmelita Clohesy

Acknowledgments

My deepest gratitude is due to Page, Anton, Gerard and Emma and their friends, without whose presence this book would not have been written; and to Betty, my wife, for her unfailing love and inspiration. My thanks is also due to the State Library of Tasmania for obtaining numerous interlibrary loans, to St. John Fisher College, University of Tasmania, for the use of its collection of the works of Teilhard de Chardin, and to the library of the University of Tasmania. Selwyn Grave and John Colman read the manuscript and made valuable suggestions. Mrs Carmelita Clohesy gave permission to use a copy of her painting "Arise Mortal Man", which was inspired by the writings of Teilhard de Chardin.

Also I acknowledge permission from the following publishers to quote from the works of Teilhard de Chardin:

Editions du Seuil:
Authorization given for reproduction in English in all territories:
Science et Christ, © Editions du Seuil. 1965 (*Science and Christ*)
La Vision du passé, © Editions du Seuil, 1957 (*The Vision of the past*)
Comment je crois, © Editions du Seuil, 1969 (*Christianity and Evolution*)
L'Energie humaine, © Editions du Seuil, 1962 (*Human Energy*)
Le Coeur de la matière, © Editions du Seuil, 1976 (*The Heart of Matter*)
L'Apparition de l'homme, © Editions du Seuil, 1962 (*The Appearance of Man*)
La Place de l'homme dans la nature, © Editions du Seuil, 1963 (*Man's Place in Nature*)

Authorization given for reproduction in English in Great Britain and the Commonwealth:
L'Activation de l'energie, © Editions du Seuil, 1963 (*Activation of Energy*)
L'Avenir de l'homme, © Editions du Seuil, 1959 (*The Future of Man*)
Le Coeur de la matière, © Editions du Seuil, 1976 (*The Heart of Matter*)
Le Milieu divin—Essai de vie intérieure, © Editions du Seuil, 1957 (*The Divine Milieu*)
Les Directions de l'avenir, © Editions du Seuil, 1973 (*Towards the Future*)

Authorization given for reproduction in English in Canada:

CONTENTS

INTRODUCTION

Teilhard de Chardin (1881–1955) was a French paleontologist and Jesuit priest, who claimed to have found scientific evidence for a new theory of evolution which in turn required a new theology. Bernard Towers, professor of anatomy at the University of Cambridge, reviewed the English translation of Teilhard's major work, *The Phenomenon of Man*, in 1960, and hailed it as 'the most outstanding book of the year, probably of the century, perhaps of the millennium'[1]. Though Teilhard's theory of evolution is at the center of his thought in science, philosophy and theology, it is hardly ever examined in the huge literature that has grown up about him. Recent studies, *Interpreting Evolution. Darwin and Teilhard de Chardin*[2] (1991) and *Theology of Creation in an Evolutionary World*[3] (1997), make no attempt to evaluate Teilhard's scientific ideas.

Teilhard is by no means simply a figure of historical importance. Issues fundamental to Teilhard's thought are still debated by scientists, notably the nature and evolution of consciousness, the relationship between the science of thermodynamics and biological evolution, genetic improvement of the human species, and the existence of extra-terrestrial beings. In *The Phenomenon of Man* Teilhard's major criticism of science was its failure to give due consideration to the phenomenon of consciousness in its description of the world. In recent times, however, the phenomenon of consciousness has become an important issue in scientific debate. As a prominent scientist remarked recently, in language reminiscent of Teilhard's: 'Consciousness is part of our universe, so any physical theory which makes no proper place for it falls fundamentally short of providing a genuine description of the world'[4].

There has been a resurgence of interest in evolutionary ideas in recent years, in the areas of philosophy, psychology, theology, and more generally of the history of ideas. Karl Popper, a famous critic of the theory of evolution as a *scientific* hypothesis, came to have a deep interest in evolutionary ideas in relation to the growth of human knowledge[5]. Quite generally, in philosophical discussion the apparent implications of the theory of evolution have become weighty considerations.

Teilhard welcomed the attempt to wed biology and sociology. 'Only recently, and yet timidly, sociology has ventured to set up the first bridges between biology and itself'[6], he remarked. And he made his own attempt to explain human society in biological terms[7]. Morality for Teilhard was 'nothing less than the higher development of mechanics and biology'[8]. In many ways he anticipated more recent efforts in sociobiology to provide a biological basis for social behavior and to derive ethical norms from evolutionary theory[9].

In the field of theology, the foremost Catholic theologian of our time, the Jesuit Karl Rahner, has examined an evolutionary understanding of the world. As part of his discussion of evolution and Christian theology he refers in *Theological Investigations* to the views of Teilhard[10] and urges theologians to take up the ideas of Teilhard on the nature of Christ and 'elaborate them with more precision and clarity, even though in his work it is not easy to find an intelligible connection between Jesus of Nazareth and the cosmic Christ, the Omega Point of world evolution' (p.227).

Following a brief biographical sketch, chapter 2 of this study is devoted to Teilhard's conception of science, and in particular it investigates Teilhard's involvement with the Piltdown forgery. Among fossil discoveries near Piltdown in the south of England between 1908 and 1915 was a human skull and ape-like jaw, apparently of great age. The combination of skull and jaw was accepted by many scientists and became known as Piltdown Man. In 1953 it was shown that the Piltdown Man was a forgery. The Piltdown skull was crucial to Teilhard's formulation of his theory of biological evolution. Among those suspected of the forgery was Teilhard[11]. The real importance of Piltdown Man, however, is not, Did Teilhard do it? but, What did Teilhard do with it? From the Piltdown skull Teilhard concluded that evolution was 'convergent' in contrast to other theories that saw it as divergent. Divergence as envisaged by Darwin meant that organisms continued to depart increasingly from their original type, whereas Teilhard maintained that after the appearance of Homo sapiens no further differentiation took place, and was replaced by convergence, the increasing interbreeding between all human variants. From the premiss of convergence he concluded that there was a culmination of the evolutionary process, which he named point Omega. The key concept of his theory of evolution, 'convergence', arose from his involvement with the discoveries at Piltdown.

Teilhard's approach to biological evolution, in particular his evidence for the fact of evolution and its direction, is examined in Chapter 3. In Chapter 4 an examination is made of Teilhard's reformulation of the science of thermodynamics, and his postulate of a single energy in the universe with two aspects, one of which, radial energy, he sees as responsible for the driving of the evolutionary process. Particular attention is given to Towers' claim that Teilhard's fundamental pioneering achievement 'was to make sense of the two most famous, but apparently contradictory, scientific ideas to come out of the nineteenth century: the theory of biological evolution on the one hand, and the second law of thermodynamics on the other'[12].

Teilhard's theory of evolution is related to the theories of Lamarck, Darwin and Wallace in Chapter 5. Great Teilhardian themes—'the law of complexity-consciousness', the 'noosphere' and 'point Omega'—are the topics of Chapter 6. The 'Reach of Evolution' is the subject of Chapter 7. In this chapter Teilhard's little known views on the genetic control of 'the products of human generation' and on the ethical basis of bringing about the 'ideal human type' are considered. The chapter concludes with Teilhard's attitude to the existence of extra-terrestrial intelligences, and it is shown that he considered their existence important for his theory. The place of sin and evil in Teilhard's evolutionary world is the subject of Chapter 8, along with his reformulation of the traditional view of the work of Christ in the light of his theory of biological evolution.

The book concludes with an account of Teilhard's 'cosmic optimism' and how this optimism is to be explained. Teilhard's phenomenal influence is a question kept in mind throughout the book.

NOTES

1 B. Towers, Blackfriars, Vol.41. 1960, pp.119–126. Reprinted in *Concerning Teilhard*, (London: Collins, 1969) p.53.

2 H. James Birx, *Interpreting Evolution: Darwin and Teilhard de Chardin*, (Buffalo: Prometheus Books, 1991).

3 K. Schmitz-Moormann, *Theology and Creation in an Evolutionary World*, (Pilgrim Press, 1997).

4 R. Penrose, *Shadows of the Mind*, (Oxford University Press, 1994) p.8.

5 K. Popper, *Objective Knowledge. An Evolutionary Approach*, (Oxford University Press, 1975) p.145.

6 Teilhard de Chardin, *The Future of Man*, trans. N. Denny, (London: Collins, 1964) p.131.

7 Ibid., p.238.

8 Teilhard de Chardin, *Human Energy*, trans. J.M. Cohen, (London: Collins, 1969) p.105.

9 E.O. Wilson, *Sociobiology: The New Synthesis*, (Cambridge, Massachusetts, and London: Harvard University Press, 1975).

10 K. Rahner, *Theological Investigations*, trans. H.M. Riley, (London: Darton, Longman and Todd, 1988) p.25.

11 The hoaxer was recently unmasked. *Nature*, Vol.381, No. 6580 (1996) pp261–262.

12 B. Towers, *Concerning Teilhard*, (London: Collins, 1969) p.93.

CHAPTER ONE

TEILHARD DE CHARDIN: THE MAN

In the eyes of many Teilhard is seen as a martyr for science and a new religion, a modern Galileo and secular saint all wrapped into one. Even the Jesuit Father General, Peter-Hans Kolvenbach[1], takes up the martyr image used by Jesus and applies it to Teilhard: "Unless a grain of wheat falls to the earth and dies, it remains but a grain of wheat". Teilhard de Chardin is an enigmatic figure who has eluded the clutches of all his biographers. We never have the feeling that we know the man. He appears remote and elusive, even in his love letters[2] to Lucile Swan. Reading their letters we sympathize with her complete failure to understand him. On one occasion her annoyance with Teilhard caused a "deep feeling of depression". She ascribes her inability to communicate with him to his living "on a different plane", and to his God who "seems so cold, so far away" (p.139). His "frankness" could also be offensive. Pierre Leroy S.J., Teilhard's close friend, records two occasions; one of which caused an Ambassador to leave the table in the middle of a meal[3]. Throughout his life Teilhard suffered from bouts of severe depression which, on occasions, brought him to the brink of despair[4]. There is also a touch of arrogance and insensitivity in his personality, as evidenced in his attitude to war and suffering, and especially in his estimate of the role assigned to him by "Providence". In view of these personality features, why has his influence been so pervasive, and why has he attracted such esteem? Perhaps the reason is that given the author by the Editor of the influential English Catholic paper *The Tablet*: "I think myself that Teilhard is one of the spiritual masters of the twentieth century, warts and all"[5]. The title of the Bampton Lectures at Oxford University for 1996, *Christ in All Things: Exploring Spirituality with Teilhard de Chardin*[6] expresses this commonly held opinion of him.

The late 19th century was a period in which the Catholic Church suffered from intellectual stagnation and more than a touch of complacency. Pierre Leroy S.J., comments that the religious instruction which Teilhard received was "still wrapped up in conventional phraseology and its presentation to children was dry and stodgy"[7]. The complacency of the times was soon shattered by the First World War, the rise of Communism and the intellectual ferment arising from the surge in scientific discovery. Prescient spirits like John Henry Newman, whose life spanned the 19th century, saw the storm clouds gathering. In a letter he wrote in 1882, a year after Teilhard's birth, he foresaw the political attacks on the church in France, and forecast that "the first and second generation after us will have a dreadful time. Satan is almost unloosed"[8]. Teilhard lived through these times. His response to the gathering storm clouds was to reformulate Christian belief in the light of the theory of evolution, confident that it would be accepted: "We are experiencing to-day an increasing necessity of readjusting the fundamental lines of our Christology to a new universe"[9]. It is ironic that Teilhard appealed to Newman's ideas on the development of Christian doctrine to support his evolutionary Christianity. Newman would have had little sympathy with Teilhard's ideas.

Many influential Jesuits are sympathetic to Teilhard's views. One of his staunchest supporters was the Cardinal Henri de Lubac. S.J., a peritus at the Vatican II Council. The first English translation of the Council documents edited by Walter Abbott S.J. refers to a passage in *The Pastoral Constitution on the Church in the Modern World (Gaudium et Spes)*: "Let [the faithful] blend modern science and its theories ... with Christianity and doctrine"[10] and in a footnote makes the comment that: "Here, as elsewhere, it is easy to recognize the compatibility of the insights developed by thinkers such as Teilhard de Chardin". Leading Australian bishop at the Council, Archbishop Guilford Young[11] of Hobart, Tasmania, once expressed to me his conviction that Teilhard's thought was "essentially Pauline", and he welcomed the contribution that Teilhard's insights had made to the Council's deliberations.

These comments from prominent Churchmen go some way towards validating Teilhard's orthodoxy, but fail to explain the attraction of his teaching. Prominent Jesuit philosopher, Frederick Copelston, ascribes Teilhard's popularity to his meeting a "felt need" among Christians.

Unfortunately, severe editing by the French editors of his complete works, Editions du Seuil, has made assessment of Teilhard difficult. In 1950 Teilhard wrote a short autobiographical essay, *The Heart of Matter*[12], which presents an idealized view of his intellectual and spiritual progress, notable for its omission of any reference to his involvement in the discovery of Piltdown Man. Another important account of his life is by his Jesuit friend Pierre Leroy S.J.[13]. Since his death in 1955 hundreds of books and articles, inspired by his ideas, have appeared, with no sign of abatement. His message has been applied to such diverse areas as drug addiction, co-dependency, ecology, Taoism, Hinduism, Eastern mysticism and Marxism. Teilhard's influence continues to be strong and pervasive. Teilhardian scholar, Karl Schmitz-Moormann, has recently published *Theology and Creation in an Evolutionary World*[14], which relies to a great extent on Teilhard's ideas.

Marie Joseph Pierre Teilhard de Chardin was born on 1 May 1881. He was the fourth of 11 children. Teilhard was reared in a pious, well-to-do French family. "I was an affectionate child, good, and even pious", Teilhard remarks. In childhood Pierre experienced the death of 7 of his siblings. This had a profound effect on him and contributed to his sense of insecurity. He admits that his whole life was a search for permanence.

> A Memory? My very first! I was five or six. My mother had snipped of[f] a few of my curls. I picked one up and held it close to the fire. The hair was burnt up in a fraction of a second. A terrible grief assailed me; I had learnt that I was perishable... What used to grieve me as a child? This insecurity of things. And what used I to love? My genie of iron! With a plowhitch I believed myself, at seven years, rich with a treasure incorruptible, everlasting. And then it turned out that what I possessed was just a piece of iron that rusted. At this discovery I threw myself on the lawn and shed the bitterest of tears of my existence.[15]

Teilhard admits that while others of his age "experienced their first 'feeling' for a person, or art, or for religion"[16] he felt drawn to matter. His search for permanence led him from iron to rocks, and ultimately to an abiding interest in geology and paleontology. Teilhard recalls that from the ages of 10 to 30 his secret delight lay 'in the solid state'[17].

Teilhard was sent to the Jesuit school at Villefranche where he was a good pupil, often at the top of his class, except in religious instruction. At 18 he entered the Jesuit novitiate at Aix-en-Provence. Two years later in 1902 he went to Laval to continue his studies in French, Latin and Greek. In the same year the religious orders were expelled from France, and Teilhard was forced to go abroad with the community to seek refuge in Jersey. While there he studied scholastic philosophy and was able to give some time to his favorite subject, geology. His fellow seminarians recall that Teilhard never went for a walk without his geologist's hammer and magnifying glass. In an article he wrote in 1905 for *Quodlibeta*[18], the organ of the Jesuit Scholasticate at Jersey, he grapples for the first time with the nature of scientific method.

After 3 years as a scholastic, he was sent to teach physics and chemistry at the Holy Family College in Cairo. He was there for 3 years. From Egypt he was sent to England for the last stages of his training as a priest. The year 1908 was momentous for Teilhard in several respects. In that year he became profoundly aware of Evolution or Transformism, as the French are wont to call it, through the reading of Bergson's *Creative Evolution*, and more importantly through his meeting with Charles Dawson and the discovery of Piltdown Man[19]. He makes no mention of the latter event in his autobiographical essay. But the evidence is clear enough; it was in the "Wealden clay" of Sussex, he writes, that "a sort of universal being was about to take shape suddenly in Nature before my very eyes". Teilhard left instructions, after the discovery in 1953 that Piltdown Man was a forgery, to delete all references to it from his writings. Although Leroy lauds, at length, Teilhard's "keen powers of observation" in the discovery of Peking Man (Sinanthropus)[20], he makes no mention of Piltdown Man.

In the First World War Teilhard was a stretcher-bearer with the 8th regiment of Moroccan Tirailleurs with the rank of corporal. He was decorated twice, receiving the Médaille Militaire and the Légion d'Honneur. Teilhard's attitude to war has shocked his most ardent admirers. The Editor of *The Tablet* in a letter to the author in 1992 acknowledges that Teilhard's "attitude to war in particular can be scandalously optimistic"[21]. Few have plumbed the reasons for his attitude.

In 1919 Teilhard returned to his scientific career. In 1922 he completed his doctoral thesis under Marcellin Boule at the Natural History Museum in Paris on the mammals of the Lower Eocene period in France and their strata. As a result of an article he wrote on Original Sin, he was asked by his superiors to confine his writings to scientific topics. His life took an unexpected turn in 1923; he went to China to work with a fellow Jesuit, Émile Licent, who had been there since 1914 engaged in paleontological research. It was in China that he produced his most influential writings. In 1929 he made the acquaintance of the Sculptor Lucile Swan, who typed the manuscript of his best known work, *The Phenomenon of Man*. Apart from brief visits to other countries he remained in China until 1946.

From 1946 to 1951 Teilhard was in Paris and in 1948 he was offered the chair at the Collège de France, as successor to Abbé Breuil. Teilhard made his involvement in the discovery of Piltdown Man a prominent aspect of his application for the position. He was directed by his superiors to decline the offer, which he did. In 1951 Teilhard left France for a visit to South Africa, after which he traveled to New York where he remained until his death in 1955. Lucile Swan was among the few mourners who attended his funeral Mass at St. Ignatius Church in New York. During his lifetime Teilhard disseminated his writings widely to his associates but declined to publish them, in accord with the wishes of his superiors.

Teilhard concludes his autobiographical essay, *The Heart of Matter*, with a section entitled 'The Feminine, or the Unitive'. It was dedicated to Beatrice, the woman who by her glance alone had inspired Dante to make his journey from the Inferno, through Purgatorio to Paradiso.

> Ever since my childhood I had been engaged in the search for the Heart of Matter, and so it was inevitable that sooner or later I should come up against the Feminine. The only curious thing is that in the event it was not until my thirtieth year that this happened: so powerful was the fascination the Impersonal and the Generalized held for me. .... I have experienced no form of self-development without some feminine eye turned on me, some feminine influence at work.

Many women had a profound influence upon Teilhard. He met his second cousin once removed, Marguerite Teillard-Chambon, shortly before he entered military service in December 1914 and his many letters to her from the Front appeared as *The Making of a Mind*[22]. The next important influence was Lucile Swan, a divorcee, whom he met in China in 1929. Unlike Marguerite, Lucile did not share Teilhard's Catholic faith. Other significant women in Teilhard's life were Ida Treat, an American and pro-Communist activist, whom he met in the laboratory of Marcellin Boule (Professor of National History Museum in Paris), and the ex-wife of his colleague Helmut de Terra, Rhoda de Terra. Letters to these two women were published as *Letters to Two Friends: 1926–1952*. Another was Léontine Zanta, a Catholic Feminist and devotee of Henri Bergson. During 1920's and 1930's Teilhard frequently attended her literary salons.

His letters to her were also published[23]. Jeanne Mortier, with whom he also corresponded[24], was initially an ardent student of scholastic philosophy. She was enthralled with *Le Milieu Divin*, and dedicated herself to spreading Teilhard's message. Teilhard appointed her his literary executor and, following his death, she arranged for publication of his works[25] and wrote a glowing account of him in *Pierre Teilhard de Chardin, penseur universel*[26].

It is not surprising that Teilhard advocated a "third way", a union for man and woman, which involved the development of a spiritual bond between them that excluded conjugal privileges. He regarded this union as a higher spiritual level than celibacy. Some 12 years after Teilhard's death the Father General of the Jesuit order was asked if young Jesuits "seeking personal growth might follow the 'Third Way'"[27]. He declined to give consent.

In spite of his gratitude for the influence of many women, Teilhard, at the end of his life, wept at "the memory of all the reproachful 'Beatrices' he knew and had hurt unwittingly"[28].

NOTES

1 *Der Spiegel*, December 1986, p.80.
Spiegel: Der Naturwissenschaftler und Jesuit Teilhard de Chardin war ein sehr authentischer Mann. Alle Welt hat das anerkannt, nur mit dem Vatikan hatte er seine Probleme.
Kolvenbach: Das ist das Gesetz der Geschichte. Ausserdem sagt das Evangelium: "Wenn das Weizenkorn nicht in die Erde fällt und stirbt, bleibt es allein, stirbt es hingegen, so bringt es reiche Frucht."

2 T.M. King and Mary Wood, *The Letters of Teilhard and Lucile Swan*, (Washington: Georgetown University Press, 1993).

3 P. LeRoy, "The Man" in Teilhard, *Letters from a Traveller*, trans. R. Hague et al., (London: Collins,1962) p.35.

4 P. Leroy, *Letters from my Friend Teilhard de Chardin*, trans. M. Lukas, (New York: Paulist Press, 1980) pp 10, 26–27, 28, 94, 163–165.

5 John Wilkins, Editor, *The Tablet*, to Dr Noel Roberts, 21 August 1992.

6 U. King, *Christ in all Things: Exploring Spirituality with Teilhard de Chardin*, (Orbis, 1997).

7 P. LeRoy, "The Man" in Teilhard, *Letters from a Traveller*, p.21.

8 J.H. Newman to Sister Maria Pia (Maria Biberne), 3 July 1882.

9 Teilhard, *Christianity and Evolution*, trans. R Hague, (London: Collins, 1969) p.139.

10 W. Abbott, *The Documents of Vatican II*, (London/Dublin: Geoffrey Chapman, 1966) p.269–270.

11 Ibid., Most Reverend Guilford C. Young, *Introduction to Presbyterorum Ordinis*, p.526–531.

12 "Incidentally, the Graham Greene title (*The Heart of the Matter*) would be wonderful for me (although with a quite different meaning) for an essay I am dreaming to write ..."

13 P. LeRoy, "The Man" in Teilhard, *Letters from a Traveller*.

14 K. Schmitz-Moormann, *Theology and Creation in an Evolutionary World*, (Pilgrim Press, 1997).

15 C. Cuénot, *Teilhard de Chardin, A Biographical Study*, trans. V. Colimore, (London: Burns and Oates: 1965) p.3.

16 Teilhard, *The Heart of Matter*, trans. R. Hague, (London: Collins, 1978) p.17.

17 Ibid., p.23.

18 Teilhard, *De l' Arbitraire dans les lois, théories, et principes de la physique*, Quodlibeta, 2, 1905.

19 Teilhard, *The Heart of Matter*, p.25.

20 P. LeRoy, "The Man" in Teilhard, *Letters from a Traveller*, p.33.

21 John Wilkins, Editor , *The Tablet*, to Dr Noel Roberts, 21 August 1992.

22 Teilhard, *The Making of a Mind*, trans. R. Hague, London: Collins,1965.

23 Teilhard, *Letters to Leontine Zanta*, trans. Bernard Wall, (London: Collins 1969).

24 Teilhard, *Letttres à Jeanne Mortier*, Paris: Seuil, 1984.

25 T.M. King and Mary Wood, *The Letters of Teilhard and Lucile Swan*, p.297.

26 J. Mortier, *Pierre Teilhard de Chardin, penseur universel* , (Paris: Éditions du Seuil, 1981).

27 T.M. King and Mary Wood, *The Letters of Teilhard and Lucile Swan*, p.295.

28 M. and E. Lukas, *Teilhard*, (London: Collins, 1977) p.319.

CHAPTER TWO

TEILHARD THE SCIENTIST

> My first stroke of good fortune in this area of ancient human paleon-
> tology was to be included, when still young, in the excavation of
> Eoanthropus dawsoni [Piltdown Man] in England.
> —Teilhard de Chardin, in S. Gould, *Hen's Teeth and Horse's Toes*

Among Teilhard's admirers the scientists regard him as a great
theologian and the theologians see him as a great scientist. The
scientific admirers of Teilhard tend to emphasize his spiritual
contribution to humanity while the theologians eulogize his scientific
prowess and his success in reconciling science and religion. The
noted Jesuit historian of philosophy, Frederick Copleston, in his
many-volumned *A History of Philosophy*[1], remarks on the wide appeal
of Teilhard's vision.

> A world vision of this kind, which synthesizes in itself science, a meta-
> physics of the universe and Christian belief and is at the same time
> markedly optimistic, is just the sort of thing which many people have
> looked and hoped for and have not found elsewhere. It has been able
> to appeal even to some, such as Sir Julian Huxley, who feel themselves
> unable to go all the way with Teilhard de Chardin ...there can be no
> doubt of its meeting a felt need.

Most works dealing with Teilhard's views confine their attention
to his theological speculations. However, from the beginning there
have been those who accorded him great status as a scientist and
those for whom he was of small account as a scientist. The theologian, John Macquarie in his book on twentieth century religious
thought describes him as 'a scientist of high distinction'[2] and *The
Oxford Dictionary of the Christian Church* refers to his 'notable
reputation as a paleontologist' and his 'remarkable effort to relate
Christian tradition to the contemporary understanding of nature'[3].
The historian of science, Joseph Needham, hailed the *Phenomenon of
Man* as 'the work of a first-rate evolutionary biologist who knew the
facts ...a brilliant physical anthropologist'[4]. Scientists have expressed
a similar attitude. The eminent geneticist, Theodosius Dobzhansky,
speaks of him as a 'great scientist'[5]. Julian Huxley, a close friend,
describes Teilhard as 'a distinguished paleontologist'[6]. A fellow
Jesuit, Robert O'Connell, equates his scientific achievements with

those of Copernicus, Darwin and Freud. 'Teilhard's view of reality' O'Connell writes, 'like any revolutionary hypothesis [is] as strange and shocking as their hearers found Copernicus' proposal, or Darwin's, or Freud's'[7]. H. James Birx in *Interpreting Evolution: Darwin and Teilhard de Chardin* (1991), although hostile to 'the blind dogma of religious faith', praised Teilhard as 'a truly great scientist' whose 'lasting contribution [was] his serious introduction of the fact of evolution into modern theology'[8]. But Peter Medawar, director of the National Institute for Medical Research, describes Teilhard as practicing 'an intellectually unexacting kind of science in which he achieved a moderate proficiency. He has no grasp of what makes a logical argument or of what makes for proof'[9]. In reply to Medawar's assessment, Bernard Towers, professor of anatomy at the University of Cambridge, hails Teilhard as 'a seminal force of great significance to science' and points out that 'the initial opposition to Copernicus and Galileo came, not from theologians, but ...from the scientific establishment of the period'[10]. Stephen Gould of Harvard University referred to *The Phenomenon of Man* as 'a cult book of the 1960's' and Teilhard 's 'florid and mystical writing [as] more difficult to decipher than his role at Piltdown', but accepted that his technical works in paleontology 'are sound and solid' [existing] in a world of discourse quite separate from his anthropocentric vision of cosmic evolution'[11]. George Gaylord Simpson[12] of The American Museum of Natural History, rejects Teilhard's claim that his most important work *The Phenomenon of Man* is a scientific treatise. Simpson in that review points to a contradiction of this claim in *The Phenomenon of Man*. At the conclusion of the book Teilhard says:

> Man will only continue to work and to research so long as he is prompted by a passionate interest. Now this interest is entirely dependent on the conviction strictly undemonstrable to science, that the universe has a direction and that it could—indeed, if we are faithful, it *should*—result in some sort of irreversible perfection'[13]

Whereas, says Simpson, 'the direction of evolution toward an irreversible perfection is the whole theme, and not merely a philosophical appendage, of the book'[14]. Furthermore, Simpson remarks that 'It has been claimed, and Teilhard himself seems to have believed at times, that he was reasoning from scientific premises to theological conclusions. In plain fact, he did exactly the opposite.'[15]

Eoanthropus Dawsoni (Piltdown Man)

Teilhard's involvement with the discovery of *Eoanthropus Dawsoni*, more commonly known as Piltdown Man, has been the subject of intense scrutiny ever since the hoax was unearthed. As recently as 1993, in the journal *Current Anthropology*[16], the possible identity of the forger was still being debated, with Teilhard among the suspects. While Teilhard was correct in refusing to assign the jaw and the skull to the same creature, he accepted both as genuine fossils, dating from the Pleistocene period. The skull of *Eoanthropus Dawsoni* led him to formulate his theory of human evolution, a theory from which he never departed. After returning from Egypt to continue his priestly studies at Hastings in England, Teilhard became deeply interested in the subject of evolution from reading Henri Bergson's *L'évolution créatrice* (1907) in 1908[17]. While he was at Hastings in 1909 he became friendly with Charles Dawson, the discoverer of Piltdown Man, and became involved with him in the subsequent finds at Piltdown. Tobias[18] has prepared a useful timetable of the Piltdown discoveries. Teilhard saw his meeting with Dawson as providential coming so soon after his reading of Bergson.

At the conclusion of *The Phenomenon of Man* Teilhard admits that without his acquaintance with the writings of St. Paul and St. John he would 'never have ventured to envisage or formulate the hypothesis [of point Omega] rationally, if in my consciousness as a believer, I had not found not only its speculative model but also its living reality'[19]. His Christian belief only awaited the discovery of the Piltdown skull to elicit his theory.

Once he had concluded that human evolution was 'convergent' and must come to focus at some distant point in time, he proceeded to formulate a theory of mechanism to account for the 'paleontological evidence'. Already in 'L'évolution'[20] (1911) Teilhard rejects Darwinian natural selection and inclines to Lamarckism complemented by a vital force. His colleague, Helmut de Terra, voices this feeling in referring to Teilhard's concept of evolutionary convergence. 'The concept of convergence', De Terra writes,

> in the evolution of the human race was so essential to Teilhard's account of Man's origin that it is easy to understand why he was so greatly encouraged in that idea by his new-found knowledge of extinct types of primitive man in Java. With the disappearance of typal diversity within the Java and Peking Man group, modern man emerged as the sole surviving species and the one which dominated the whole

world. What others saw as a chance phenomenon of survival became, for Teilhard, a manifestation of some deeper meaning underlying the evolution of man.[21]

But de Terra seems unaware that Teilhard had formulated the idea of convergence much earlier from his involvement with Piltdown Man.

Teilhard formulated a theory of evolution, from which he never departed, and provided a mechanism for it, based primarily on his reaction to the Piltdown skull. In 1948 in an application for the prestigious chair of Paleontology at the College of France, Teilhard, at the age of 67 years, writes, 'My first stroke of good fortune in this area of ancient human paleontology was to be included, while still young, in the excavation of Eoanthropus Dawsoni in England'. Not even the discovery of the forgery in 1953 caused him to alter his mind about the nature of human evolution.

Between 1908 and 1915 a skull and a jaw with two molar teeth were discovered by Charles Dawson, the lawyer and amateur archeologist, in close proximity at a gravel pit at Piltdown. Dawson did not bring the specimens to Arthur Smith Woodward, keeper of paleontology at the British Museum, until 1912, three years after the first finds. Teilhard who was completing his theological training at Hastings not far from Piltdown met Dawson in 1909 while hunting for fossils and they soon became firm friends. Teilhard became part of the group in the first joint excavations at Piltdown along with Dawson and Arthur Smith Woodward. In what appeared to be a remarkable piece of luck, Teilhard picked up a canine tooth of the lower jaw in 1913 during a brief return journey to England for a religious retreat. 'In the earth', Teilhard writes to his parents, 'dug up from the previous excavations and now washed by the rain I found the canine tooth from the jaw of the famous Piltdown Man'[22]. The tooth was apelike in appearance but worn in human fashion, appearing to confirm that the jaw and skull belonged to the same creature. Dawson and the majority of English paleontologists accepted the integrity of the creature and gave it the taxonomic name Eoanthropus Dawsoni. The Piltdown discovery became public knowledge in 1912. No one suspected fraud, but a few scientists, including Teilhard, had doubts about ascribing the jaw and skull to the same creature. Further fossil discoveries were made at another site two miles from Piltdown in 1915 and seemed to confirm Dawson's contention that the jaw and skull were indeed from the same creature. By this time Teilhard was back in France serving as a medical orderly in the First World War. His association with the Piltdown discovery had preceded him; for one day in the summer of 1915 he was greeted by a friend, 'you're the Piltdown man'[23].

Teilhard's wrote a short article, 'Le cas de l'homme de Pilt-down'[24] (1920), on the Piltdown discoveries in which he rejects the integrity of the skull and jaw, but accepts that both are genuine prehistoric fossils. His paper draws two important conclusions. Firstly the chimpanzee existed in western Europe in the Pleistocene age. Secondly and of the greatest importance for Teilhard's theory of evolution, the skull belongs to a legitimate new genus, ancestral to Heidelberg Man and to modern human beings.

> Above all, it is henceforth proved that even at this time [of Piltdown] a race of men existed, already included in our present human line, and very different from those that would become Neanderthal, and also probably very different from those who were then Mauer Man. Thanks to the discovery of Mr. Dawson, the human race appears to us even more distinctly, in those ancient times, as formed of strongly differentiated bundles, already quite far from their point of divergence. For anyone who has an idea of paleontological realities, this light, tenuous as it appears, illuminates great depths.[25]

Two years later in a review of a book he refers to the Piltdown skull alone: 'the bony fragments of pre-glacial man (the jaws of Mauer and of Taulach and the Piltdown skull) although highly suggestive, are miserably fragmentary'. Teilhard then repeats his view of evolution given in the 1920 essay on Piltdown Man.

> Evolution is no more to be represented in a few simple strokes, for us than for other living things: but it resolves itself into innumerable lines which diverge at such length that they appear parallel. These lines are certainly bound together in some way (we are more and more sure of that) but so far down the scale that we are not able to see.[26]

That Teilhard never departed from this assessment can be seen from the unexpurgated essays 'Fossil Men—Recent Discoveries and Present Problems' (1943) and 'The Idea of Fossil Man' (1953), both of which are reproduced as facsimiles by Schmitz-Moormann in his collection of Teilhard's scientific writings. (The first essay also appears in the Éditions du Seuil, L'Apparition de l'homme with all references to Eoanthropus deleted at Teilhard's request to his editor, Wildiers; see pp.16 and 17). Interestingly, the English translation still shows on figure 13 Eoanthropus as an ancestor of modern man. This figure once again illustrates Teilhard's theory of different human lineages, diverging and becoming parallel. Teilhard refers to Eoanthropus by the skull alone and maintains that the association of the skull and jaw is impossible: 'The lower jaw is extraordinarily Chimpanzee-like ...most of the anthropologists (although unable to explain the presence of a Chimpanzee in Pleistocene England!) regard the association of the skull and of the jaw as anatomically impossible ...Eoanthropus has been tentatively placed (according to the characters of *the skull)* at the root of the Homo sapiens group, its age being assumed to be middle Pleistocene'[27]. Teilhard also placed the skull of Eoanthropus on the tree of human evolution at a meeting of the New York Academy of Sciences on 23 February 1952[28]. In 'The Idea of Fossil Man' (1953), two years before his death, Teilhard refers to the most recent paleontological research as confirming his evolutionary theory and Piltdown Man as an ancestor of Homo Sapiens and belonging to a new evolutionary line which underwent no further differentiation. Whereas the sheets running parallel to the Homo Sapiens containing Neanderthal man and others became extinct.

> The first, but oversimplified, idea of the early human paleontologists, as I mentioned above, was to connect Homo sapiens genetically, and in a direct line, with each newly discovered fossil man, either with the Neanderthal man or with Pithecanthropus and Sinanthropus.

> To-day as a franker recognition and better understanding of such pre-Neanderthal, 'sapientoid' forms as the men of Palestine, the Swanscombe man, the Steinheim man, and Piltdown man[29], we are beginning to realize (1) that the formation and rise of Homo Sapiens has apparently been a long and complicated process ...and (2) that the process of 'sapientization', which the most central portion of the primordial human stock had to undergo in order to become fully hominized, is itself controlled by two main types of antagonistic morphogenetic forces: (a) the divergent forces of speciation, which work continuously to produce Human subspecific types, and (b) the convergent forces of aggregation ('totalisation'), which (through interbreeding and socialization) continually compel the newborn types of men into a most remarkable and, so far badly understood, single superarrangement of a biological nature—man as a planetary unit.[30]

It was not until 1953 that it was proven that the Piltdown bones had been chemically stained to mimic great age, the teeth artificially filed to simulate human wear, the associated mammal remains all brought in from elsewhere, and the flint 'implements' recently carved. The skull bones were those of a modern human, most likely female, and the jaw and teeth were from an orangutan. When Dr. Oakley, one of those who uncovered the fraud, wrote to Teilhard on 19 November 1953 informing him that he and Woodward had been 'hoodwinked' at Piltdown. Teilhard replied, in a puzzling manner; for he had always regarded the Eoanthropus skull as providing support for his theory of evolution and had never expressed any doubt, until the fraud was uncovered, about the genuineness of the fossils.

> I congratulate you most sincerely on your solution of the Piltdown problem. Anatomically speaking 'Eoanthropus' was a kind of monster. And, from a paleontological point of view, it was equally shocking that a 'dawn-Man' could occur in England.[31]

The phrase 'anatomically speaking' refers to the association of skull and jaw, as indicated by his essay 'Fossil Men—Recent Discoveries and Present Problems' (1943), an association which Teilhard had always rejected. But to express shock at the notion that 'dawn-Man' could occur in England is surprising, as he had never cast doubt on that aspect of the discovery and had always accepted the skull as a genuine Pleistocene fossil and an ancestor of Homo sapiens.

The search was then on for the culprit(s). Was it a hoax or a conspiracy, a serious attempt at fraud? The answer to this question would determine the perpetrator and his motive. From the beginning Dawson was a prime suspect, but did he act in consort with others? In 1980 Gould presented a strong case implicating Teilhard as a hoaxer.[32]

Gould's case against Teilhard relies on three points. Firstly Teilhard's correspondence with Kenneth Oakley, one of those who uncovered the forgery, shows 'his fatal error', according to Gould, when confronted with the forgery. Teilhard described a visit with Dawson to a second Piltdown site and the discovery of another fossil combination of ape jaw and human skull. Gould argues that Teilhard could not have visited the site with Dawson as Dawson had found the fossils in 1915, whereas Teilhard had been mustered into the French army in December 1914. For Gould this inconsistency suggests that Teilhard had manufactured the fossils with Dawson before he left. Teilhard's defenders argue that he was not referring to the second Piltdown site. Secondly the virtual silence about Piltdown Man in Teilhard's publications. According to Gould Piltdown Man provided

> proof, *the only available proof* [my emphasis], of multiple parallel linea-ges within human evolution itself—for its skull belonged to an advanced human older than primitive Neanderthal. Piltdown was the most sublime argument that Teilhard possessed, and he never breathed it again after the 1920 article.[33]

> And Piltdown furnished the best available support that the fossils could provide for the most important argument of Teilhard's cosmic and mystical views about evolution, the dominant theme of his career and the source of his later fame. Teilhard never availed himself of his own best weapon, partly provided by his own hand. (p.216)

Gould exaggerates Teilhard's silence. There are references in Teilhard's writings to Piltdown Man. They are not numerous but they are significant, as seen above.

Gould's third consideration implicating Teilhard as the hoaxer is that, although Teilhard was present at the discovery of Peking Man he made no comparison with Piltdown Man when others did. Gould writes:

> When Peking man was discovered, its cranium was reconstructed in-correctly to yield a capacity lying, like Piltdown's, in the modern human range. This unleashed a flurry of commentary about the rela-tionship between Piltdown and Peking. Now Teilhard was in China where he was contributing (as a geologist) to the original Peking finds. He was the only one there with personal knowledge of Piltdown. Yet, so far as I can tell, he said nothing at all. His own mentor, Marcellin Boule, published a paper comparing the Peking and Piltdown crania. It included long quotations from Teilhard about the geology of the Pe-king site, but not a word about the crania. (p.238)

Presumably Gould is referring to the paper[34] by Marcellin Boule, a life-long friend of Teilhard and Director of the Institut de Paléon-tologie Humaine, published in 1929 and commenting on the discovery of Peking man in 1928. Boule refers to the comments of Davidson Black, Professor of Anatomy at the Peking Union Medical College, that Sinanthropus was 'a large brained form'. These comments led to speculation in the English press, especially from Elliot Smith, that the remarkable association in both Sinanthropus and Eoanthropus of a skull, clearly human (nettement humain) and a jaw clearly simian (mandibule nettement simienne) removed the doubts of continental paleontologists regarding the integrity of Eoanthropus dawsoni. Boule then quotes at length from a letter of Teilhard who had seen the skull encased in a block of very hard travertine. 'In summary', Teilhard writes, 'Sinanthropus appears at this moment to represent an extremely precise morphological transition between Pithecanthropus and Neanderthal man'[35] (En somme, le Sinanthropus se présente en ce moment comme faisant une transition morphologique extrêmement précise entre le Pithécanthrope et l'Homme de Néanderthal[36]). In a brief note, 'Homo Pekinensis' 1929, Teilhard repeats the same opinion: 'Le crâne est à peu prés aussi petit et étroit que celui du *Pithécanthrope* de Java; mais il est plus humain. Sa région frontale, par exemple, distinctement bombée, a sensiblement la même forme que chez les Hommes fossiles de la race de Néanderthal'[37]. In view of Teilhard's own words it is not surprising that he did not consider comparing Peking with Piltdown, as the latter had a cranial capacity close to modern man, and moreover he had never associated the skull and jaw in Eoanthropus. Gould's comments on Teilhard's failure to compare the two finds, therefore, do not argue for a guilty silence on his part. At both Piltdown and Peking Teilhard had judged correctly, namely that the skull and jaw did not belong to the same creature, Eoanthropus dawsoni, and that Sinanthropus fills a 'harmonious interval between the Neanderthal type and Pithecanthropus'[38]

Stephen Gould does, however, make a very important observation, in his article, 'The Piltdown Conspiracy'. The editor of Teilhard's *The Heart of Matter*[39], N.M. Wildiers, has deleted one crucial sentence from Teilhard's curriculum vitae for the chair of Paleontology at the College of France in 1948 without any indication of having done so. Gould found a copy of this unpublished, mimeographed document in a reprint collection of a friend, A.S. Romer. Under the heading, List of Most Notable Investigations or Results, Teilhard mentions, general geology, paleontology of mammals, and last and most importantly, Human Paleontology. Under the last heading the original document, as Gould ascertained, reads:

My first stroke of good fortune in this area of ancient human paleontology was to be included, when still young, in the excavation of Eoanthropus dawsoni [the official taxonomic designation of Piltdown

man] in England. The second was, in 1923, to be able to establish, with
Emile Licent...(p.214)

Whereas Wildiers has printed:

My first stroke of good fortune in this field of human paleontology excavation came in 1923, when, with Emile Licent...(p.162)

Gould presents a well-argued case to implicate Teilhard in the
Piltdown hoax along with Dawson, and ascribes Teilhard's involvement to the natural exuberance of a young, playful and intelligent
mind. If so, it is difficult to imagine why Teilhard, at the age of sixty-
seven, should refer to the discovery in an application for a chair in a
prestigious institution in 1948. Whatever the involvement of Teilhard
in the Piltdown forgery, it is clear that his association with Charles
Dawson, lawyer and amateur archeologist, the finder of the first
specimens, and Arthur Smith Woodward, keeper of paleontology at
the British Museum, launched him into a very successful career in
paleontology. All references to Piltdown Man had been expurgated
by the editor of Teilhard's writings, N.M.Wildiers, which were
published by Editions de Seuil, Paris. Fortunately a more extensive
facsimile reprint of Teilhard's professional publications[40] preserves
the originals in some instances. But why would Teilhard and his
editors wish to make such expurgations? Gould takes the view that
'In trying to spiff up Teilhard's record, they [the editors] made him
appear even more culpable by accentuating the impression of guilty
silence'[41].

Even if the combination of skull and jaw, Piltdown Man, presented 'an insoluble classification problem', as Wildiers correctly
reports, Teilhard had never indicated at any stage that he accepted
the skull and jaw as belonging to the same creature. Blinderman in
The Piltdown Inquest admits that Teilhard's reticence would be even
more suspicious if Piltdown Man were a good example of [his]
philosophy of evolution'[42], but then dismisses the possibility on the
basis by a statement of a 'Teilhard partisan', claiming that the
sequence of Piltdown skull followed by smaller skulls argued
precisely for what Teilhard rejected in his philosophy: 'the domination of matter over spirit' (p.129). This Teilhardian partisan has
obviously misunderstood Teilhard's evolutionary mechanism. For an
essential aspect of Teilhard's theory, as we have seen, is the concept
of a series of lineages, evolving along separate paths which allows for

the very possibility rejected as being opposed to Teilhard's theory, namely, the simultaneous presence of both ancestral and primitive forms of man. Blinderman's conclusion that Piltdown Man does not support Teilhard's theory of evolution and that

> Whatever gambit one tries to open an understanding of whether Piltdown Man did or did not exemplify Teilhard's cosmic philosophy, the game ends in stalemate. (p.129)

is not justified by the evidence. Teilhard used Eoanthropus (the skull alone) to support his evolutionary ideas until the forgery was uncovered in 1953 shortly before his death in 1954. It is therefore surprising to find a recent paper, 'On Piltdown: The French Connection Revisited' (1993), expressing the view that Teilhard rejected Piltdown on scientific grounds, when he only rejected the association of the jaw with the skull, and until the end of his life he accepted the Eoanthropus skull as being of crucial significance to his theory of human evolution. 'It could be argued', the writer of this paper maintains,

> that on scientific grounds, Teilhard had rejected the Piltdown remains as being of any relevance to the questions in which he was interested, namely, those centering on the origin and evolution of life and, especially, of mankind.[43]

Ian Langham, who unfortunately died before he could complete the work, carried out the most authoritative study on the Piltdown forgery. Frank Spencer has published Langham's findings in *Piltdown, A Scientific Forgery*[44]. Spencer considers that Teilhard did not take part in the deception and it would be difficult to disagree with his finding in the light of the extensive documentary evidence he provides. It seems most likely, according to the evidence presented by Spencer, that Teilhard was duped by Sir Arthur Keith, Conservator of the Hunterian Museum of the Royal College of Surgeons, and Charles Dawson. (A recent appraisal of the case against Sir Arthur Keith was published in1992 by Phillip Tobias[45], along with comments by other paleontologists.)

But in the 23 May, 1996, issue of *Nature*[46] Brian Gardiner, professor of paleontology at King's College, London, reported the discovery of a canvas travelling trunk under the roof of London's Natural History Museum containing bones stained and carved in the same way as the Piltdown fossils and associated artifacts, and more importantly containing iron and manganese in the same proportions. The bag belonged to Martin Hinton, curator of zoology in the Natural History Museum at the time of the Piltdown discoveries, and an expert on the geology of the Weald area of Sussex, in which Piltdown is located. It seems that Hinton had a disagreement with Arthur Smith Woodward, keeper of paleontology at the museum, over payment for employment, and sought to 'get back at the pompous, stuffy keeper of paleontology'. Smith Woodward remained convinced of the authenticity of Eoanthropus Dawsoni until the day he died, and his book *The Earliest Englishman*[17], published in 1948, was dictated from his death bed. One of the artifacts found at Piltdown was 'piece of elephant bone carved to look like a cricket bat (a fitting accoutrement for the "first Englishman")'. The findings certainly incriminate Hinton but they do not clarify whether he acted alone in the forgeries.

Spencer does not comment on Teilhard's instruction to Wildiers to delete all reference to Eoanthropus in his published works after the discovery of the forgery. The reason for Teilhard's instruction to Wildiers is most likely the fact that the skull provided the best evidence for his theory of evolution, and when it proved to be a forgery it became an embarrassment and a threat to his status as a paleontologist. But by this stage of his life Teilhard's fame was assured and his theory of cosmic evolution had found a congenial home in the theological sphere seemingly immune to the paleontological facts.

In summary, Teilhard judged correctly in not assigning the jaw and cranium to the same creature. Of much more interest, however, is that the Piltdown skull was the paleontological evidence which prompted Teilhard to advance his concept of convergence in human evolution.

Teilhard's language and style

Anyone attempting to assess Teilhard's scientific status needs to take into account his unusual style. Medawar expresses the opinion that 'it is the style which creates the illusion of content, and which is in some part the cause as well as merely the symptom of Teilhard's alarming apocalyptic seizures' (p.81). Although Medawar has been accused of exaggeration, even a writer who is sympathetic to Teilhard makes a similar observation. 'There are other difficulties in the obscurities of Teilhard's style and the exuberance of thought which forces it on under the compulsion of an almost manic excitement.'[48]

Emile Rideau's comprehensive book on Teilhard's thought, *Teilhard de Chardin: A Guide to His Thought*[49], celebrates Teilhard's style and characterizes a number of its features. Rideau remarks in an appendix, 'Vocabulary and Language', that 'Teilhard's thought cannot be understood without a study of his language'. He mentions that 'in 1951, Teilhard realizing that there were a number of neologisms in his vocabulary, and anxious to make his meaning perfectly clear, started to plan a dictionary of his principal terms'. Rideau admits that 'Teilhard may not have fully appreciated the philosophical significance of his terms and imagery', but claims that Teilhard's thought is stated with perfect clarity. Teilhard 'attributed great importance to language and its power to express ideas. That language is animated by an individual style that reflects the soul of the person ....The thought is expressed with perfect clarity and sharpness ...A continual illumination, a joy to the mind, emerges from the lucidity of the text'. Teilhard 'loves what he is expressing; he is passionately excited by his vision of the universe' ....His lyricism, though sometimes restrained or muted, constantly breaks through'. 'Although there are normally no signs of an attempt to achieve a melodious effect, Teilhard's style sometimes acquires a deep musical charm in the ordered balance of his sentences and his choice of words' (pp. 274–6). 'Teilhard adapts his style to the different types of literary work he was successively engaged in: scientific papers, essays in general cosmology, theology, spirituality, prayer, correspondence'. But Rideau concedes that as Teilhard grew older 'He seemed to become aware of his tendency to pile words one upon another. His wartime essays, and even *Le Milieu Divin* show a certain prolixity and over-amplification that were later corrected in his masterpiece, *The Phenomenon of Man*'. Rideau also acknowledges 'a certain narrowness, even poverty, in Teilhard's use of symbols. 'Fire' is given so much prominence that it excludes others less striking and dynamic...Teilhard made little use of the richness of biblical language'. A clue to Teilhard's motivation for the particular mode of expression he chose for his thought is found in Rideau's assertion that 'no-one in future, can afford to neglect the line marked out by

Teilhard. A world in genesis must become an integral part of our thought' (p.258). This passage points to a very significant feature of the expression of Teilhard's thought, namely a language, vocabulary and style adapted to promoting an acceptance of his particular evolutionary ideas.

Surprisingly, Teilhard found the first World War a setting in which to state his views on literary style. In a letter[50], dated 14 August 1917, he says; 'I should go back and breathe again the heady atmosphere of the firing line. As always after a long rest, I feel overcome again by nostalgia for the front'. Then he proceeds to discuss the art of writing, 'A literary piece, if it is really felt and expressed, should be like a piece of music, with shades of emphases, silences, themes, an over-all harmony ...a completely individual typographic arrangement'.

The willingness of some to accept Teilhard's world-view without understanding it appears to be due in large part to his style and language. For example, one contributor to a book, *The Human Search*, writes referring to the Omega Point: 'Exactly what this means it is not easy to say, but for our purposes here we can note one thing: Teilhard's conviction that the points to which the human and the religious developments were working were in fact one and the same'[51].

As a defender of Teilhard, Bernard Towers makes a very interesting comment on Teilhard's euphoria:

> There is something about Teilhard's euphoria, both of thought and style, that encourages readers to let themselves be carried away and lose their heads in a wave of passion. Any imbalance that results is bound to produce, in time, a reaction. There have been those who, after feeling the first flush of enthusiasm, have subsequently wondered, disappointed, how it was that they ever allowed themselves to be 'taken in'. Actively hostile critics are then quick to seize the chance, and belabour the former idol in a way that incenses those devotees for whom the light has far from failed.[52]

But Towers also castigates the

> relatively few, hostile critics, who have let emotion run away with them in denouncing what they interpret as theological betrayal, or scientific nonsense, or philosophical naiveté, or downright rubbish.

To Copleston's explanation of the wide appeal of Teilhard's vision—'a world vision which synthesizes in itself science, a metaphysics of the universe and Christian belief and is at the same time markedly optimistic'—should be added the influence of Teilhard's style and language. The language and style are not those of a scientist but of a seer. One of Teilhard's scientific admirers, the eminent biologist Theodosius Dobzhansky, does not hesitate to call him an 'inspired seer' and a 'prophet'[53]. Indeed, Teilhard's mode of expression bears all the marks of prophetic utterance.

In the essay, 'The Spiritual Power of Matter'[54] (1919) Teilhard displays an ecstasy which recalls some of the Old Testament prophets. The essay begins with a quotation from *The Second Book of The Kings* referring to the taking up to heaven of the prophet Elijah in a fiery chariot. Teilhard identifies himself with an Elijah-like figure in his description of a man who gains an insight into the spiritual power of matter. The 'Thing ' swoops down on the man as he walks in the desert with a companion. It penetrates his soul and 'an irresistible rapture' takes possession of the man. But 'at the same time the anguish of some superhuman peril oppressed him, a confused feeling that the force which had swept down on him was equivocal, turbid, the combined essence of all evil and all goodness'. The 'Thing' says to the man,

> Never, if you work to live and grow, never will you be able to say to matter, 'I have seen enough of you; I have surveyed your mysteries and have taken enough food for my thought to last me for ever'. (p.71)

The man in submitting to the 'Thing' is enlightened.

> And then the frenzy of battle gave place in his heart to an irresistible longing to submit: and in a flash he discovered, every-where present around him, the one thing necessary.

> Once and for all he understood that like the atom, man has no value save that part which passes into the universe ....He saw before his eyes, revealed with pitiless clarity, the ridiculous pretentiousness of human claims to order the life of the world, to impose on the world the dogmas, the standards, the conventions of man. (pp.72–73)

The seer-like quality of Teilhard's utterances is evident but one is surprised to find that the 'Thing', 'the combined essence of all evil and all goodness', could be identified with any Biblical concept of divine possession.

Not surprisingly, then, even in his major 'scientific treatise' (p.29) *The Phenomenon of Man*, the foreword is entitled 'Seeing' (p.31). 'This work', it says, 'may be summed up as an attempt to see and to show what happens to man, and what conclusions are forced upon us, when he is placed fairly and squarely within the framework of phenomenon and appearance'. (p.31)

Hemut de Terra, a geologist, who worked with Teilhard on several expeditions, questions Teilhard's claim that *The Phenomenon of Man* is 'purely and simply a scientific treatise'. De Terra remarks that 'It was only to be expected that as believer and as a scientist, Teilhard would qualify his conception of science. This he did by commending seeing and contemplation as aids to a deeper understanding of the human being'[55].

In 'The Christic', completed a month before his death on 10 April 1955, Teilhard again claims to be seer, but the assurance of *The Phenomenon of Man* has gone:

> How is it, then, that as I look around me, still dazzled by what I have seen, I find that I am almost the only person of my kind, the only person to have seen? And so I cannot, when asked, quote a single writer, a single work, that gives a clearly expressed description of the wonderful 'Diaphany' that has transfigured everything for me?[56]

Teilhard's paleontology

As mentioned previously in connection with the Piltdown forgery, Teilhard's scientific papers appear in two different editions. The standard edition of Teilhard's writings appears in *Oeuvres de Pierre Teilhard de Chardin*[57] Éditions du Seuil. K. Schmitz-Moormann has collected all of Teilhard's scientific works and a few others of general interest in *Pierre Teilhard de Chardin L'Oeuvre Scientifique*[58]. All papers are facsimiles. There is a remarkable difference in the content of papers appearing in both editions. Those appearing in the Éditions du Seuil have been severely edited. Consequently, any comments relating to Teilhard's scientific standing should be based on the facsimiles reproduced by Schmitz-Moormann. All English translations of Teilhard's scientific papers published by Collins (London), Harper and Row (New York), and Harcourt Brace Jovanich Inc. (New

York), have been made from the edited versions and so are unreliable for an assessment of Teilhard's scientific status. Only in *L'apparition de l'homme* of Éditions du Seuil is any mention made by the editor N.M.Wildiers that the works in that volume have been edited to remove any reference to Piltdown Man. But even there it is more than a simple deletion of all references to Piltdown. The importance of the Piltdown skull in Teilhard's theory of evolution is lost. In other volumes of the series deletions and editing are not mentioned.

Teilhard's paleontological work is generally acknowledged to be sound, but it is often accompanied by a claim that other ideas enable him to make scientific comment about human evolution, that there is a tendency to move from paleontology to scientifically unfounded remarks about the direction of evolution. Teilhard's prime concern is about the future of man rather than the past. A characteristic statement appears in his scientific paper, 'Sinanthropus Pekinensis' (1930).

> Human paleontology is only striving, after all, to rediscover the embryogenesis of the human species ...But to appreciate, *even scientifically* [my emphasis], the prodigious event represented by the appearance of thought in the earth's history, we must look in another direction. The scientific solution of the human problem will never be attained by the study of fossils, but by a more careful consideration of the properties and possibilities that permit us to foresee in man of today the man of tomorrow.[59]

The question is whether there is a science of the future: Teilhard's answer is an emphatic yes. In a scientific publication, 'Fossil Men. Recent Discoveries and Present Problems' (1943) Teilhard remarks:

> Since the days of Lamarck and Darwin, the question has been and still is bitterly debated whether there is any definite trend in biological evolution. Here, however, in the particular case of Man, and owing to the fact that in Man psychical properties reach their maximum, a definite drifting of organic matter toward increasing cerebralization associated with increasing consciousness is clearly registrable. Why not extend and generalise this law from Man to the rest of the living world?[60]

Even so, Teilhard sees support for his faith in human progress in the paleontological evidence: 'Thus are justified and directed, on scientific ground, our modern hopes and expectations for human progress'.

Teilhard now advances another of his favorite themes. 'It is possible', he says,

> (although by no means sure) that, the human brain having reached by now the maximum of complexity allowed by physico-chemical laws for a single molecular fabric, we cannot proceed any further. ....But in the direction of collective organization (on which it seems that anthropogenesis has been concentrating the best of its efforts since the dawn of *Homo sapiens*) we have scarcely begun to advance. In this matter, therefore, our physical and spiritual future is almost unlimited, and lies largely in our heads and hands. ....Too many people believe that Prehistory dangerously bends our eyes down and back toward some sort of 'under-Mankind'. Its quite opposite effect ...is to force our vision up and ahead, in the direction of an 'upper-Humanity'[61]

Teilhard claims that although the direction of human evolution is inferable on sound scientific grounds, this direction must not be left to purely natural forces. Superhumanity 'will only come about if we develop to the end, within ourselves, the extremely powerful forces of organization released by sympathy between men and the forces of religion'. In effect man will determine the direction of the evolutionary process. But is it possible to view evolution as a scheduled journey, and at the same time open to us whether or not we intervene in the process? Teilhard's attempt to effect a reconciliation between human freedom and the play of predetermined natural forces will be examined in Chapter 3.

Teilhard's claim that paleontological evidence supports the view that life in its various forms is moving towards increasing consciousness, and that mankind is evolving into a super-organism is a difficult one to find evidence for. This latter aspect of his thought is referred to often in his scientific papers and is a crucial to his system. For example, in one of his last scientific papers, 'The Singularities of the Human Species" published in *Annales de Paléontologie* (1954) Teilhard is in no doubt that 'a peak of hominisation must necessarily exist ...which must certainly lie very far above in consciousness, if not so far from us in time as we might at first be tempted to suppose'[62]. The existence of a peak of hominisation relies on a supposed scientific extrapolation involving Teilhard's 'law of complexity-consciousness' and his view that no further differentiation occurs in the human species after Homo sapiens.

Indeed there is no longer any possible doubt that the play of the planetary forces of complexity-consciousness, normally extended, summons
us to and destines us for this peak of hominisation (or, as I have become accustomed to calling it the point Omega) (p.246)

The Phenomenon of Man

Although Teilhard's scientific publications reveal him as a competent
paleontologist, with, however, a tendency to go beyond the scientific
evidence, the question of his scientific greatness rests on his book *The
Phenomenon of Man* (1940), published in English in 1959, four years
after his death, and exactly one hundred years after the appearance
of Darwin's, *The Origin of Species*. At the outset Teilhard states that, 'If
this book is to be properly understood, it must be read ....purely and
simply as a scientific treatise'.[63] And again in the Appendix written
some 8 years after the original manuscript, this view is reaffirmed.
'My aim in this book has been limited to bringing out the positive
essence of the biological process of hominisation' (p.311). Bernard
Towers reviewing *The Phenomenon of Man* comments:

> The world, of which we form a part, can be known and understood.
> Man can arrive at truths about it, if only by degrees and primarily by
> the use of the scientific method. Teilhard, as befits a great scientist, is a
> great champion of science and the scientific method, related as it al-
> ways is to phenomena[64].

Julian Huxley, who wrote the introduction for the English translation to *The Phenomenon of Man*, sees it as 'the most important of
Teilhard's published works', and praises him for achieving 'a
threefold synthesis—of the material and physical world with the
world of the mind and the spirit; of the past and the future; and of
variety with unity, the many and the one' (p.11). Furthermore,
Huxley accepts that

> With this approach he is rightly and indeed inevitably driven to the
> conclusion that, since evolutionary phenomena (of course including
> the phenomenon known as man) are processes, they can never be
> evaluated or even adequately described solely or mainly in terms of
> their origins: they must be defined by their direction, their inherent
> possibilities (including of course also their limitations), and their de-
> ducible future trends. (p.13)

Huxley appears to accept Teilhard's belief in the possibility of foreseeing the future of evolution, but he is careful to speak of 'future trends' rather than predicting the culmination of the evolutionary process. And he then begins to express reservations with regard to Teilhard's scientific achievement with a series of 'If I understand him aright[s]'. Huxley is doubtful about Teilhard's linking of the evolution of mind with the concept of energy: 'If I understand him aright, he envisages two forms of energy...[one of] which increase[s] with the complexity of organized units' (p.16). Huxley also expresses difficulty with Teilhard's extrapolation of biological evolution to 'point Omega', the culmination of the evolutionary process: 'If I understand him aright, he considers that two factors as co-operating to promote this further complexification of the noosphere' (p.18). And the hyperpersonal organization of Omega 'is not fully clear' to him (p.19). Teilhard's law of complexity-consciousness, hailed by Towers[65] as a pioneering achievement, causes Huxley some puzzlement, introduced by 'As I understand it' (p.15)

While George Gaylord Simpson rejects *The Phenomenon of Man* as being a scientific treatise (see Chapter 2), the Dutch philosopher, Bernard Delfgaauw, argues that Teilhard

> develops the theory of an integral evolution, according to which life emerges from dead matter, so called, and man from animal. Teilhard is emphatic in presenting his book solely as a piece of scientific theory. He does not offer any philosophy—still less any theology[66].

Debate between Bernard Towers and Peter Medawar

Two prominent scientists, Bernard Towers and Peter Medawar, represent opposing views of Teilhard's scientific standing. It is of interest to examine their views in some detail since many other writers reflect their positions and it was the debate between them that influenced public opinion. Although Towers admits that his thinking was 'enormously deepened ' by Teilhard, he is not enamoured of the 'emotional advocacy of some of Teilhard's "devotees"'[67]. Towers makes remarkable claims for Teilhard:

> For myself, I would go so far as to say that Teilhard's vision—he writes like a visionary, but a visionary whose feet are always planted firmly on or in terra firma—marks the most significant achievement in syn-

thesis since that of Aquinas. (p.43) ....*The Phenomenon of Man* is certainly the outstanding book of the year, probably of the century, perhaps even of the millennium. (p.53)

Towers remarks that Teilhard's views are more likely to be censured by the scientific community than by theologians because he is an affront to the prevailing scientific positivism. In particular, Towers attacks Medawar as being among the ablest of their number who 'ignore metaphysical questions about truth or value in any significant sense' (p.45). But Towers is more concerned about the motivation required for science to progress than about the disregard of metaphysical questions: 'I think it unlikely that science will be able to progress if its only source of inspiration is positivism' (p.45). This remark picks up a constant theme of Teilhard's and Julian Huxley's that only evolutionary humanism is capable of motivating modern man.

Towers discusses Teilhard's scientific prowess in his BBC Third Programme Talk, 'Scientific Master versus Pioneer: Medawar and Teilhard', in which he compares the pioneering scientific achievement of Teilhard with the lowly bread-and-butter science of Medawar: 'advances made by the master—and they are often big and important ones—are always in limited fields, and they fall within the accepted framework of ideas' (p.91). In Towers' eyes there is no doubt where Medawar stands in scientific relationship to Teilhard. Medawar is the master of his subject but he is no pioneer. Towers goes on to remark that the first to criticize the pioneer in any field is usually the master in that field:

> The initial opposition to Copernicus and Galileo came not from the theologians but from the university professors, master astronomers and mathematicians, the scientific establishment of the period. So too with Darwin. When his book was published in 1859 it was no less a person than Professor Sir Richard Owen, the most knowledgeable anatomist of his day and a distinguished pillar of academic society, who was behind what William Irvine called 'the venomous and confused counter-attacks' against the theory of evolution (p.92)

Towers applauds Teilhard's charting of the future course of evolution.

> Much of his life was spent in the study of the far distant past. But he became increasingly conscious that the patterns displayed throughout

the course of evolutionary history are of the greatest significance if we
are to appreciate what paths might be open to mankind in the future.
(p.44)

And he mentions two other outstanding scientific contributions made
by Teilhard to our scientific heritage. 'The fundamental pioneering
achievement of Teilhard', he writes,

was to make sense out of the two most famous, but apparently contradictory ideas to come out of the nineteenth century: The theory of
biological evolution on the one hand, and the second law of thermodynamics on the other. (p.93)

How the Teilhardian harmonization was effected will be indicated in a moment. With regard to the other of Teilhard's pioneering
scientific achievements Towers writes:

Of all the original hypotheses invented by Teilhard, the central one is
that which he stated as the 'law of increasing complexity-
consciousness ....Teilhard takes a historical view of the world, as only
an expert geologist and paleontologist can. He backs his law with a
wealth of scientific evidence ...The theory obviously allows, for instance, for the probability—indeed virtual certainty—of intelligent
beings on other planets. ....The law of increasing complexity-
consciousness is far more than an unreasoned hope for the future. The
law is scientific in the real sense, that it is open to verification. If it is
tested and found to be valid, and if its implications are accepted, then
the ultimate physical death postulated by the second law of thermodynamics will be seen to have lost its sting (p.96–98)

Towers is particularly impressed with this 'law' and has no doubt
that in due course it will become known "as is customary in science,
as 'Teilhard's Law'".

These are important claims and if substantiated would confirm
Teilhard as a truly great scientist. Teilhard makes great play of what
he sees as the apparent contradiction between the second law of
thermodynamics and biological evolution. He regards the second law
of thermodynamics as postulating that the normal movement of
matter over time is from an ordered to a less ordered state, that is, the
disintegration of organized matter, such as complex biological forms,
into simpler units; whereas the theory of evolution postulates the
opposite, that is, the organization of matter over time from simple
elements of matter, such as atoms and molecules, into cells and

ultimately higher and higher organisms, culminating in man. To reconcile the apparent conflict Teilhard assumes a new form of energy, 'radial energy', hitherto unobserved by scientists, which drives evolution without infringing the second law of thermodynamics. Towers sees Teilhard's approach as 'a pioneering achievement'. But Medawar maintains that Teilhard has misunderstood the second law and that there is no contradiction between it and biological evolution. As for the law of complexity-consciousness which Towers asserts to be 'scientific in the real sense, that it is open to verification', Medawar denies that there is such a law.

Medawar attacks Teilhard's thought in an attack on his style. 'Teilhard habitually and systematically cheats with words', Medawar writes,

> His work, he has assured us, is to be read, not as a metaphysical system, but 'purely and simply as scientific treatise' executed with remorseless' or 'inescapable' logic; yet he uses in metaphor words like energy, tension, force, impetus, and dimension as if they retained the weight and thrust of their special scientific usages. Consciousness, for example, is a matter upon which Teilhard has been said to have illuminating views. For the most part consciousness is a manifestation of energy ...but elsewhere we learn that consciousness is a dimension, or is something with mass, or is something corpuscular and particulate which can exist in various degrees of concentration, being sometimes infinitely diffuse. (p.84)

Medawar also rejects Teilhard's assertion that love in humans would be impossible were it not for the attraction between atoms at the beginnings of the evolutionary process.

> Nothing is wholly new: there is some primordium or rudiment or archetype of whatever exists or has existed. Love for example,—'that is to say, the affinity of being with being'—is to be found in some form throughout the organic world, and even at the 'prodigiously rudimentary level', for if there were no such affinity between atoms when they unite into molecules it would be 'physically impossible for love to appear higher up, in 'hominized' form' (p.85)

Teilhard's concept of science

A fellow Jesuit, Robert O'Connell, in *Teilhard's Vision of the Past, The Making of a Method* (1982), mounts a spirited defense of Teilhard's concept of science against his scientific critics. 'Medawar's and Simpson's approach' to *The Phenomenon of Man*, he writes, 'is so thoroughly misguided as to make the majority of their criticisms a series of irrelevancies'[68]. Even those scientists who are sympathetic to Teilhard, in particular the noted biologist, Dobzkansky, are chided for failing to identify 'the method-spine which gives the work its bone structure' (p.2). O'Connell makes much of an early essay Teilhard wrote as a seminarian at the age of 24, 'On the Arbitrary [Element] in the Laws, Theories, and Principles of Physics'[69] (1905). In particular, O'Connell points to Teilhard's acquaintance with the thought of the physicist, Pierre Duhem, whose view was that

> the entire realm of scientific knowledge [is restricted] to the 'phenomenal' order. The business of science was not that of 'explaining' the workings of the real world ...that task belonged to philosophy, and more particularly to metaphysics. ...Hence physics must content itself with proposing, not causal, but 'phenomenal' laws; with discovering and bringing into order the ways in which the real world 'appeared' to act'.[70]

Thus science must not pose as a philosophy 'proposing the underlying 'causes' which explain why things act, and indeed must act, the way they do'. Duhem claimed that the history of science provided abundant proof for this assertion. Another question arises: how do scientists choose one theory as against another? Duhem's answer comes in stages. Firstly, the procedure is governed by an 'instinct for simplicity'. 'Aesthetic emotion is not the only sentiment inspired by the theory brought to a high degree of perfection. A theory in this state 'persuades us of more: persuades us to view it as *natural classification*'. Here O'Connell comes to the heart of his thesis: 'natural classification' becomes central to Teilhard's subsequent thinking and writing[71].

The important question is whether Teilhard's view of science conforms to Duhem's, as O'Connell claims; or proceeds beyond offering a natural classification, a series of phenomenal antecedents and consequents, and provides a theory of mechanism. O'Connell has no doubt that Teilhard is a true disciple of Duhem: the competence of science, 'Teilhard tirelessly repeats, is limited to establishing the sequence of phenomenal antecedents and consequents' (p.31). But Teilhard *did* propose an evolutionary mechanism. As O'Connell admits, Teilhard chose 'brains and nervous systems as the 'Ariadne's thread' through evolution's labyrinth' and by implication accepted 'the corollary of that choice: the 'psychic' character of that evolution'[72]. But Teilhard not only accepted psychism as the essential evolutionary phenomenon: more importantly he saw it as the driving force of evolution. A new form of energy, radial energy, psychic in nature, was responsible for matter assuming ever-increasing forms of complexity; and this increasing complexity was associated with higher forms of consciousness. Also, Teilhard postulated that evolution proceeded by a mechanism of groping or 'directed chance'. He replaced Darwinian natural selection by psychic selection which, he considered, drove evolution in a pre-programmed direction.

Furthermore, Teilhard invoked theological arguments drawn from St. Paul's Epistles to confirm the existence of point Omega (which he identified with Christ), the climax of the evolutionary process. How O'Connell could think that Teilhard confined himself to the phenomenal level in his account of evolution is difficult to understand.

What scientists as well as non-scientists have felt as Teilhard's scientific appeal is due, in no small part, to his 'synthetic' approach. Teilhard was disenchanted with what he saw as the extremely narrow view of the scientific enterprise; and the warmth with which many scientists greeted his message reveal that he struck a responsive chord with them. Even those who found his scientific account 'dated' responded to his 'synthesis'[73]. While Teilhard viewed the scientific enterprise as of immense value he felt the time had come to move from the analytical approach of the past to a synthetic one. 'Modern man ' he writes,

> is obsessed by the need to depersonalise (or impersonalise) all that he admires. There are two reasons for this tendency. The first is *analysis*, that marvellous instrument of scientific research to which we owe all our advances but which, breaking down synthesis after synthesis, allows one soul after another to escape, leaving us confronted with a pile of dismantled machinery, and evanescent particles. The second lies in the discovery of the sidereal world, so vast that it seems to do away with all proportion between our own being and the dimensions of the cosmos around us. Only one reality seems to survive and be capable of succeeding and spanning the infinitesimal and the immense: energy— the floating, universal entity from which all emerges and into which all falls back as into a ocean; energy, the new spirit; the new god. So, as the world's Omega, as at its Alpha, lies the Impersonal.[74]

Earlier, Teilhard expressed the same thoughts at greater length in the essay 'Science and Christ' (1921). The essay is an incisive rebuttal of the claim of many scientists that truth lies in tracking matter back to its ultimate components, that is by the method of analysis. But analysis is understandable, for 'if we want to know what is inside a house'

> we open the door—in a watch, we strip it down—in a walnut, we crack it. The first step taken by the mind that wants to know what something is made of, is to take it to pieces and analyse it. The whole of science is derived from this instinctive act. Science is essentially analysis. Its method of enquiry and its conclusions are governed by the principle that the secret of things lies in their elements, so in order to understand the world all we have to do is to arrive at the most simple terms from which it has emerged.[75]

Teilhard then proceeds to look at some of the extraordinary achievements of science using the method of analysis. But what is the end result of such an approach?

> The first thing a man thinks when scientific analysis has led him to the extreme lower limits of matter is that in these ultimate particles of matter he really holds the very essence of the riches of the universe. 'The elements contain in themselves the virtue of the whole: to hold the elements is to possess the whole'. That is the principle implicitly accepted by a number of scientists and even philosophers. Were that principle true, we should have to say that science forces us into materialism. (p.27) ....Consider for a moment what, when finally weighed up, science has left us with which to reconstruct the world—atoms more or less dissolved in formless energy. (p.28)

Still it was necessary, says Teilhard, to reach this impasse in order to realize an important truth: 'in our analysis we have allowed what constitutes the value and solidity of beings to escape from us. The only consistence beings have comes to them from their synthetic element, in other words from what, at a more perfect or less perfect degree, is their soul, their spirit'. He then proceeds to describe what he means by the synthetic element or soul. In analysis we proceed by a series of successive fragmentations:

> At each operation we separated two elements: an ordering principle, which is imponderable, cannot be analysed, and is synthetic—and ordered (ponderable) elements. On every occasion, as a direct result of

analysis, that ordering principle disappeared. We accordingly concentrated our attention on the ordered elements, which seemed to be of a stable nature. These in turn yielded to analysis, sacrificing a fresh order and being reduced to sub-elements. And so the process continued. ...It was a hopeless search. We did, it is true, discover a certain law on which reality is built up, a hierarchical law of increasing complexity in unity. But reality itself, the supreme Thing we were trying to reach, eluded us and with each new analysis continued to move even further away. (p.29–30)

Teilhard expresses the concern of many scientists and his appeal can be traced in no small part to the manner in which he emphasizes the deficiency of the analytical tendency in some areas of science. But: 'Can we still ask science to guide us on this new journey? It has already led us up to the pole at which they are supremely dissociated; can it now lead us to the pole at which they supremely associated?'. Only 'Christian views', he says, can 'supply what we are looking for' in a synthesis; yet science is capable of showing the existence of a unifying center needed for synthesis.

Science by the very impotence of its analytical efforts has taught us that in the direction in which things become complex in unity, there must lie a supreme centre of convergence and consistence, in which everything is knit together and holds together. We should be overcome with joy (which is not putting it too strongly) to note how admirably Jesus Christ ...fills this empty space. (p.34)

But ten years later in the essay 'The Spirit of the Earth' (1931) his estimate of science has grown enormously. He now exalts science to the pinnacle of human activity. 'The moment is approaching when we shall perceive' that scientific research 'is the highest of human functions. It will absorb the spirit of war and shine with the light of religions'.[76] In the light of this comment it is not surprising that Teilhard in 'The Mysticism of Science''(1939) sees the Christian scientist as the ideal human type and the nucleus around which a new society must grow.

It remains (and is the least one can say) that the Christian scientist seems to everyone the best situated and the best prepared to develop in himself and foster around him the new human type seemingly awaited at present for the further advancement of the earth.[77]

Not a claim that would be readily accepted by 'everyone'; not a claim that anyone could be readily supposed to accept.

Teilhard's criticism of the scientific enterprise has grown well beyond a call for a synthesis in the face of the predominately analytical approach. Now he sees science, in particular the biological theory of evolution, as an all-encompassing worldview embracing every field of human activity. Teilhard's synthesis is to extend the purely biological theory of evolution to all reality. His often quoted words from The *Phenomenon of Man* express the belief that evolution alone is capable of illuminating all reality.

> Is evolution a theory, a system or a hypothesis? It is much more: it is a general condition to which all theories, all hypotheses, all systems must bow and which they must satisfy henceforward if they are to be thinkable and true. Evolution is a light illuminating all facts, a curve that all lines must follow. (p.219)

No aspect of reality escapes an evolutionary interpretation.

Furthermore even though Teilhard dismisses the proposition that Christian dogmas can be deduced from science—'I would never dream, my friends, of deducing Christian dogmas solely from an examination of the properties our reason attributes to the structure of the world'[78]—he came close to this very position later in life, in his essay 'Christ the Evolver' (1942). It is obvious from this essay that he wants a reformulation of traditional doctrine about Christ in the light of biological evolution.

There is a clear message to emerge from Teilhard's concept of science. His understanding of science and Christianity cannot be separated. One must either accept or reject both. In few other writers is the connection between science and religion so intimate. Even this matrix is not enough to explain Teilhard's wide appeal. Frederick Copleston explained Teilhard's appeal as due to an optimistic world vision embracing science and Christian belief. But beyond this is a further factor alluded to in a symposium to mark the centennial of the birth of Teilhard de Chardin. Strange as it may seem the convenors of the meeting gave the following reason for the symposium.

> We decided not to gather Teilhard experts to explore again [Teilhard's] writings. Beyond the writings there is something else that could best be described as spirit. It is an adventuresome spirit that looks forward with openness and expectation.[79]

As it happened not many of the participants were particularly favorable to Teilhard's evolutionary views, so perhaps it is no wonder that the writings of Teilhard were not the subject of discussion. The major evolutionist at the meeting, Richard Leakey, dismisses Teilhard's the thesis in *The Phenomenon of Man* that man is the pinnacle of evolution, and in a recent book, *Origins Reconsidered* admits that he himself has fallen into the same trap as Teilhard in seeing evolution 'as a scheduled journey'[80] which, however, is only revealed as such in hindsight.

> I find it difficult to visualize ourselves as the inevitable consequence of evolution. We are the consequence of a series of events, and it is possible to study those events and document them. ...we are not an inevitability, we are merely the end of a particular branch on a bush rather than at the pinnacle of a tree.[81]

In the course of its exposition and examination of various aspects of Teilhard's theory of evolution this book tries to make manifest the Teilhardian spirit.

NOTES

1 F. Copleston, *A.History of Philosophy*, (New York Image, 1977) Vol.9 part 2, p.113–114.

2 J. Macquarie, *Twentieth Century Religious Thought*, (London: SCM Press, 1971,) p 271.

3 F.L. Cross and E.A. Livingstone (eds.), *The Oxford Dictionary of the Christian Church*, (Oxford: Oxford University Press, 1983) p.1344.

4 J. Needham, *New Statesman*, 7 November 1959, pp.632–3.

5 T. Dobzhansky, F. Ayala, G. Stebbins, J. Valentine, *Evolution*, (San Francisco, Freeman, 1977) p.450.

6 Teilhard de Chardin, *The Phenomenon of Man*, revised trans. B. Wall, (London: Collins, 1959 revised 1965) p.11.

7 R. O'Connell, *Teilhard's Vision of the Past*, (New York: Fordham University Press, 1982) p.128.

8 H. James Birx, *Interpreting Evolution: Darwin and Teilhard de Chardin*, (Buffalo: Prometheus Books, 1991,) p.218.

9 P. Medawar, *Critical Review of 'The Phenomenon of Man'*, Mind, 70 (1961) pp 99–106.

10 B. Towers, *Concerning Teilhard*, (London: Collins, 1969) p.89.

11 S. Gould, *Hen's Teeth and Horse's Toes* , (New York and London: W.W. Norton, 1983) p 245, 249.

12 G.G. Simpson, *Scientific American*, April 1960, p.201.

13 Teilhard, *The Phenomenon of Man*, p.284.

14 Simpson, *Scientific American*, April 1960, p.202.

15 G.O. Browning, J.L. Alioto and S.M. Farber (eds.), *Teilhard de Chardin: In Quest of the Perfection of Man*, (Cranbury: Associated University Presses, 1973,) p.88.

16 P.V. Tobias, *Current Anthropology*, Vo.34, number 1, February 1993, p.65.

17 Teilhard, *The Heart of Matter*, trans. R. Hague, (London: Collins, 1978) p.25.

18 P.V. Tobias, *Current Anthropology*, Vo.33, number 3, June 1992, p.278.

19 Teilhard, *The Phenomenon of Man*, p.294.

20 K. Schmitz–Moormann, *Pierre Teilhard de Chardin: L'Oeuvre Scientifique*, 10 Vols (Olten und Freiburg im Breisgau: Walter Verlag, 1971) Vol 1 p.69.

21 H. de Terra, *Memories of Teilhard de Chardin*, trans. J.M. Brownjohn, (London: Collins, 1964) p.120.

22 Teilhard, *Letters From Paris 1912–1914*, trans. M. Mazzarese, (New York: Herder and Herder, 1967).

23 R. Speaight, *Teilhard De Chardin*, (London: Collins, 1967) p.59.

24 K. Schmitz–Moormann, *Pierre Teilhard de Chardin: L'Oeuvre Scientifique*, 10 Vols (Olten und Freiburg im Breisgau: Walter-Verlag, 1971) Vol 1 pp.208–214.

25 Ibid., Vol 1, p.214.

26 Ibid., Vol 1, p.405.

27 Ibid., Vol IX, p.3921.

28 C. Blinderman, *The Piltdown Inquest,*, (New York: Promethus 1986) p.141–142.

29 Schmitz–Moormann, Vol.1X p.3932, Fig.12, for a similar description.

30 Ibid., Vol X, p.4483.

31 Ibid., Vol X, p.4561.

32 S. Gould 'The Piltdown Conspiracy' and 'A Reply to Critics' in *Hen's Teeth and Horse's Toes*, p.201 and p.227.

33 Ibid., p.218.

34 Schmitz–Moormann, Vol 111, p.1162.

35 my translation.

36 Schmitz–Moormann, Vol 111, p.1164.

37   Ibid., p.1160.

38   Teilhard, *The Appearance of Man*, trans. J.M. Cohen, (London: Collins, 1965) p.64.

39   Teilhard, *The Heart of Matter*, trans. R. Hague, (London: Collins, 1978).

40   reference 21.

41   Gould, *Hen's Teeth and Horse's Toes*, p.214.

42   C. Blinderman, *The Piltdown Inquest*, (New York: Promethus 1986) p.129.

43   P. V. Tobias, *Current Anthropology*, Vol 34, 1993, p.65.

44   F. Spencer, *Piltdown, A Scientific Forgery*, (London: Oxford University Press, 1990).

45   P. Tobias, *Current Anthropology*, Vol.33, number 3, June 1992, p.243.

46   *Nature*, Vol.381, No 6580, 1996, pp261–262.

47   A. Smith Woodward, *The Earliest Englishman*, (London: Watts and Co. 1948).

48   A. Hanson (ed.), *Teilhard Reassessed*, (London: Darton, Longman and Todd, 1979) p.9.

49   E. Rideau, *Teilhard de Chardin—A Guide to His Thought*, trans. R. Hague, (London: Collins, 1967) p.257.

50   Teilhard, *The Making of a Mind*, trans. R. Hague, (London: Collins, 1965) pp.201–202.

51   G. Appleton, M.Le Morvan, J. Newson, M. Thompson, *The Human Search*, (Glasgow: Collins, 1979) p.13.

52   B. Towers, *Teilhard de Chardin*, (London: Lutterworth Press, 1966) p.viii.

53   T. Dobzhansky, *The Biology of Ultimate Concern*, (London: Rapp and Whiting, 1969) pp.114–115.

54   Teilhard, *The Heart of Matter*, p.67.

55   H. de Terra, *Memories of Teilhard de Chardin*, trans. J.M. Brownjohn, (London: Collins, 1964) pp.123–124.

56 Teilhard, *The Heart of Matter*, p.100.

57 *Oeuvres de Pierre Teilhard de Chardin*, Paris, Éditions du Seuil, 1955–1976.

58 K. Schmitz-Moormann, *Pierre Teilhard de Chardin: L'Oeuvre Scientifique*, 10 Vols(Olten und Freiburg im Breisgau: Walter Verlag, 1971).

59 Teilhard, *The Appearance of Man*, p.67.

60 Schmitz-Moormann, Vol.IX, p.3935, This paper was originally published in English. It was then translated into French for inclusion in the collected writings published by Éditions du Seuil and then retranslated into English for the edition produced by Collins! The quotations above are from the original English paper produced as facsimile by Schmitz–Moormann.

61 Ibid., p.3936.

62 Teilhard, *The Appearance of Man*, p.246.

63 Teilhard, *The Phenomenon of Man*, p.29.

64 Towers, *Concerning Teilhard*, p.47.

65 Ibid., p.96.

66 B. Delfgaauw, *Evolution—The Theory of Teilhard de Chardin*, trans. H. Hoskins, (London: Collins, 1969) p.28.

67 Towers, *Concerning Teilhard*, p.19.

68 R. O'Connell, *Teilhard's Vision of the Past, The Making of a Method*, (New York: Fordham University Press, 1982) p.1.

69 Teilhard, *De l' Arbitraire dans les lois, théories, et principes de la physique*, Quodlibeta, 2, 1905, 247–274, A facsimile appears in K. Schmitz–Moormann, *Pierre Teilhard de Chardin, L'Oeuvre Scientifique*, (Olten und Friburg im Breisgau: Walter-Verlag, 1971) vol 1, p.1.

70 R. O'Connell, *Teilhard's Vision of the Past*, p.14.

71 Ibid., p.20.

72 O'Connell, *Teilhard's Vision of the Past*, p.165.

73   T. Dobzhansky, 'Pierre Teilhard de Chardin as a Scientist' in *Letters to Two Friends, 1929 –1952*, p.226.

74   Teilhard, *The Phenomenon of Man*, pp.257–258.

75   Teilhard, *Science and Christ*, trans. R. Hague, (London: Collins, 1968) p.24.

76   Teilhard, *Human Energy*, trans. J.M. Cohen, (London: Collins, 1969) p.38.

77   Ibid., p.180.

78   Teilhard, *Science and Christ*, p.33.

79   T.M. King and J.F. Salmon (eds.), Teilhard *and the Unity of Knowledge*, (New York: Paulist, 1983) p.3.

80   R. Leakey and R. Lewin, Origins *Reconsidered,,* (New York: Doubleday 1992) p.346.

81   King and Salmon (eds), *Teilhard and the Unity of Knowledge*, p 53.

CHAPTER THREE

BIOLOGICAL EVOLUTION: FACT AND THEORY

Even if all the specific content of the Darwinian or Lamarckian explanation of life were to be demolished, the fundamental fact of evolution would remain.

—Teilhard de Chardin, *Vision of the Past*

Teilhard alternates between two terms, transformism and evolution, to describe the progressive biological organization of matter over time from inorganic material to the cell and eventually to man. Gould maintains that Teilhard makes a distinction between the two terms:

> I realize that Teilhard used the term evolution in a metaphysical sense to identify the laws of cosmic progress, not in our usual sense to specify the mechanics of organic change (which Teilhard recognized and studied, but called *transformisme*). Teilhard's technical works in paleontology are sound and solid, but deal with *transformisme* and exist in a world of discourse quite separate from his anthropocentric vision of cosmic evolution.[1]

But in 'How the Transformist Question Presents itself Today' (1923) Teilhard writes:

> Transformism, we must tirelessly repeat, imposes no philosophy. Does this mean that it does not hint at one? Of course not. But here, strangely enough, we notice that the systems of thought which suit it best are, perhaps, precisely those that thought themselves the most threatened.[2]

Teilhard is referring to Christianity which he sees as 'essentially founded on the double belief that man is an object specially pursued by the divine power throughout the creation, and that Christ is the end supernaturally but physically marked out as the consummation of humanity'. At the conclusion of *The Phenomenon of Man* he admits that without his acquaintance with the writings of St. Paul and St. John he would 'never have ventured to envisage or formulate the hypothesis [of point Omega] rationally, if in my consciousness as a believer, I had not found not only its speculative model but also its living reality'[3]. It is no wonder then that it is not possible to make the clear distinction proposed by Gould. It will become obvious that

Teilhard's technical work in paleontology is not separate from his anthropocentric vision of cosmic evolution, and indeed that it is inextricably interwoven with it.

Teilhard insists that one must accept evolution as a scientific fact if one is to be classified as a 'modern' man, and he shows dismay at the lack of acceptance of this scientific fact by many minds. 'One might well become impatient or lose heart', he writes,

> at the sight of so many minds (and not mediocre ones either) remaining today still closed to the idea of evolution. ....What makes and classifies a 'modern' man (and a whole host of our contemporaries are not yet 'modern' in this sense) is having become capable of seeing in terms ...of biological space time.[4]

The fact of evolution

There has been considerable debate in recent times about the distinction between fact and theory in regard to evolution. While many postulate evolution as a theory, Teilhard regards it as a fact. He states his attitude with particular force in his 1942 essay, 'Christ the Evolver, or a Logical Development of the Idea of Redemption':

> Using the word 'evolution' in its most generally accepted meaning, and in a purely experiential context, I would say that man's origin by way of *evolution* is now an *indubitable* fact for science. There can be no two ways about it: the question is settled so finally that to continue to debate it in the schools is as much a waste of time as it would be to go on arguing whether or not the revolution of the earth is an impossibility.[5]

But in the first paper he wrote on evolution, 'L'Évolution' (1911), Teilhard accepts that no invincible proof has been provided for the mutation of one species into another[6], although he accepts, as morally certain, that species of the same genus have passed into each other. But when it comes to genera, families orders, in fact to life as a whole, he asserts that transformism is and will always remain, no doubt, an hypothesis ('surtout à la vie totale, le transformisme ...est, et restera, sans doute, toujours une hypothèse'[7]). But by 1922 in a review of a book *Hommes fossiles* by M. Boule, professor of paleontology at the Paris museum, Teilhard moves from viewing evolution as a hypothesis to accepting it as a fact. In an endeavor to reconcile evolution with the biblical account he writes: 'The letter of the Bible shows us the Creator fashioning the body of man from the earth. Conscientious observation of the world tends to make us understand today that by the 'earth' must be understood a substance slowly elaborated by the totality of things,—in the sense that man, we should say, has been evolved not exactly of [sic] a little shapeless matter, but by a prolonged effort of the whole 'Earth''[8]. By 1926 Teilhard accepts evolution as a 'fundamental fact'.

Teilhard makes a distinction between the 'fact' of evolution and the mechanism of evolution. In the essay 'The Basis and Foundations of the Idea of Evolution'[9] (1926) Teilhard, while admitting that the mechanism is still largely undetermined—'All these questions still remain without definite answers'—stresses that the mechanism of evolution is of secondary importance; the fact of evolution remains certain:

> Even if all the specific content of the Darwinian or Lamarckian explanation of life were to be demolished (and it is precisely this content that the enemies of transformism are attacking), the fundamental fact of evolution would remain imprinted as deeply as ever on our whole experience of life. It no longer seems possible to defend our vision of the living universe, so far as its phenomena are concerned, without assuming the existence of a perceptible (enregistrable) biological development. This is the factual and very firm position that the defenders of evolution must never abandon; they must never let themselves be deflected into secondary discussions of the scientific 'hows' and the metaphysical 'whys'.[10]

Here he is equating the fact of evolution with the 'existence of a perceptible biological development'. But what meaning can be attributed to 'perceptible'? This question becomes all the more important upon reading the sentences following: 'Approached from this direction', he writes,

> and in this generalized form (that is to say as a universal and continuous testimony of systematics [the classification of fossils] the evolution of organic matter demands belief, independent of all direct perception of any transformation of life at the present time. In common with many observers I am convinced the modification of zoological forms continues to take place in exactly the same way as the folds and cracking of the earth's crust and that only the slowness prevents our seeing them. I am convinced, for example, that everywhere around us races are being formed at the present day, in preparation for the com-

ing of new species. But even if the contrary were to be established, that
is to say if the *present* immobility of the biosphere were to be scientifically proved, the necessity of movement in the past to explain the
present state of things would remain unchanged.[11]

In these passages Teilhard is discussing the biosphere, and
draws the conclusion that it presents itself as a 'constructed whole'.
'One conclusion is inevitable', he writes, 'that it took shape progres-
sively. Alter things and words as we may, so far we have found only
one way of explaining the structure of the world of life discovered by
systematics; we can see it only as the result of a development, of an
evolution' (p.122). In this context describing the fact of evolution as a
'perceptible biological development' can only refer to the fossil
record. In effect he is saying that the fact of evolution is an inescap-
able deduction from the classification of organisms. But referring to
the fossil record as a 'perceptible biological development ' is begging
the question. One can only do so on the assumption that evolution is
a fact. The indisputable fact is the fossil record, not a 'perceptible
biological development'.

Teilhard is prepared to accept evolution as a fact even if it were
to be shown that species are now biologically immobile, because an
explanation is required for 'movement in the past'. 'Movement in the
past' like 'perceptible biological development' refers to the evidence
of the fossil record. But does it follow that an evolutionary explanation is required for the past? Could not one argue equally well that
the perception that species are now immobile is strong argument that
all species were immobile in the past and that no evolution has taken
place? He anticipates this objection in a footnote to this passage. He
refers to a familiar objection against evolution that 'all attempts to
obtain stable variations of forms artificially generally fail'. Instead of
using the persuasive arguments against this proposition (see Chapter
5) advanced by Alfred Russel Wallace[12], co-proposer of the theory of
natural selection with Charles Darwin, Teilhard takes another tack.
He replies by noting that this objection 'proves nothing because *it
proves too much*. It would actually lead to the conclusion that the
hundreds of thousands of fixed species recognized by systematics
represent so many independent 'creations''.

Teilhard provides us with his own theory of how evolutionary
change takes place. As will be seen, he does not accept the Darwinian
or Lamarckian theories. With his insistence on the fact of evolution as
opposed to any particular theory, Teilhard approaches the current

view of Gould who likewise insists on the fact of evolution irrespective of whether any particular theory of evolution is correct. Gould expresses the relation between fact and theory with regard to evolution as follows:

> Evolution is a theory. It is also a fact. And facts and theories are different things, not rungs in a hierarchy of increasing certainty. Facts are the world's data. Theories are structures of ideas that explain and interpret facts. Facts don't go away when scientists debate rival theories to explain them. Einstein's theory of gravitation replaced Newton's in this century, but apples didn't suspend themselves in midair, pending the outcome. And humans evolved from ape-like ancestors whether they did so by Darwin's proposed mechanism or by some other yet to be discovered[13].

But is the comparison between gravitation and evolution legitimate? Teilhard makes a similar comparison[14]. We certainly observe the fact of the fall of apples and other effects of gravitation, but we do not observe the evolution of one species into another. What we observe is a sequence of fossils with geological time. The fact, among others, with regard to evolution is the fossil record not the fact of common ancestry.

Gould, however, introduces his own definition of 'fact':

> Moreover, 'fact' doesn't mean 'absolute certainty'; there ain't no such animal in an exciting and complex world. ...Evolutionists make no claim for perpetual truth, though creationists often do (and then attack us falsely for a style of argument they themselves favour). In science, 'fact' can only mean confirmed to such a degree that it would be perverse to withhold provisional assent. I suppose that apples might rise tomorrow, but the possibility does not merit equal time in physics classrooms.

The fact, however, is not the existence of the force of gravitation but the falling of apples and no-one doubts that apples fall; that fact is absolutely certain. True, the fossil record is compatible with and suggestive of an evolutionary process, but one can not identify the fact of evolution with the fossil record as some evolutionists do:

> Much of the evidence of large-scale evolutionary change comes from the fossil record. Only in the fossil record can we watch evolution for long enough to be able to detect large-scale patterns[15].

One can only claim to watch evolution if evolution is assumed as fact. What is actually viewed is the sequence of fossils. But simply pointing to the fact of evolution and conceding ignorance as to the means, approaches the position of the creationists who have always been chided for being unable to say anything about the mechanism of creation. By contrast a distinguishing feature of science is to provide a testable hypothesis to explain a particular phenomenon. Without such a hypothesis, the fact of evolution becomes somewhat akin to a religious belief, that is an act of faith, evidenced but not *established* by the evidence. Colin Patterson, a senior paleontologist at the British Natural History Museum and the author of that museum's general text on evolution, in a lecture to the American Museum of Natural History in 1981 warned that evolutionists increasingly talk like creationists in that they point to a fact but cannot provide an explanation of the means.[16]

What is needed to convert observations into a scientific fact of evolution is a theory that can be tested by experiment. Popper regarded evolution not as a scientific theory but as a metaphysical research program: 'I have come the conclusion that Darwinism is not a testable scientific theory, but a *metaphysical research programme* —a possible framework for testable scientific theories'[17]. The metaphysical is nonfalsifiable. 'Although it is metaphysical', Popper writes, the theory of evolution 'sheds much light upon very concrete and very practical researches. It allows us to study adaptation to a new environment in a rational way: and it allows us even to study in detail the mechanism at work. And it is the only theory so far which does all that'. But he held that Darwin's theory of evolution

> does not have sufficient explanatory power to *explain* the terrestrial evolution of a great variety of forms of life, [though] it certainly *suggests* it, and draws attention to it. And it certainly does *predict* that if such an evolution takes place, it will be *gradual*. ....Gradualness is thus, from a logical point if view, the central prediction of the theory. (It seems to me that it is its only prediction) (p.172).

Many scientists, such as Colin Patterson, a prominent zoologist of the British Museum, accept Popper's position on the theory of evolution. 'If we accept Popper's distinction between science and non-science', Patterson writes, we must ask first whether the theory of natural selection is scientific or pseudo-scientific (metaphysical). That question covers two quite separate aspects of evolutionary theory. The first is the general thesis that evolution has occurred—all animal and plant species are related by common ancestry—and the second is the idea of natural selection (in fact, Darwin arrived at the first idea about three years before the second).

Taking the first part of the theory, that evolution has occurred, it says that the history of life is a single process of species-splitting and progression. This process must be unique and unrepeatable, like the history of England. This part of the theory is therefore an historical theory, about unique events, and unique events are, by definition, not part of science, for they are unrepeatable and so not subject to test. Historians cannot predict the future (or they are deluded if they try), and they cannot explain the past, but only interpret it. ....The theory of evolution is thus neither fully scientific, like physics, for example, nor unscientific, like history.'[18].

But late in life Popper softened his earlier view that the theory of evolution is not a scientific theory, when he conceded that although evolution is a series of unique events, seemingly untestable, 'the description of unique events can very often be tested by deriving from them testable predictions or retrodictions'[19]. In view of Popper's position on the status of the theory of evolution it is puzzling that he is 'very ready to accept evolution as a fact'[20]. Gould in his essay, 'Evolution as Fact and Theory', also separates the fact of evolution from the mechanism of evolution and claims that Darwin did as much:

Evolutionists have been clear about this distinction of fact and theory from the very beginning, if only because we have always acknowledged how far we are from completely understanding the mechanisms (theory) by which evolution (fact) occurred. Darwin continually emphasized the difference between his two great and separate accomplishments: establishing the fact of evolution, and proposing a theory—natural selection—to explain the mechanism of evolution. He wrote in the *Descent of Man*:
'I had two distinct objects in view; firstly, to show that species had not been separately created, and secondly, that natural selection had been the chief agent of change. ...Hence if I erred in ...having exaggerated its [natural selection's] power ...I have at least, as I hope, done good service in aiding to overthrow the dogma of separate creations'. [21]

The fact of evolution from the time of Darwin has been the acceptance of the view that species were not separately created but evolved from a common ancestor.

Transitional forms

Teilhard points to the discoveries of transitional forms predicted by evolutionary theory as establishing the fact of evolution:

> Since the days of Darwin and Lamarck numerous discoveries have established the existence of the transitional forms postulated by the theory of evolution.[22]

At this juncture, he does not allude to any particular transitional forms or discuss what might constitute a transitional form. Strangely, this argument for the factuality of evolution is denied later on in *The Phenomenon of Man* where he admits that the transitional forms are absent from the fossil record and claims that evolutionary theory predicts as much: 'the favourite argument employed against the transformists has always lain in pointing out their incapacity to prove the *birth* of a species in terms of *material traces* ...[they point out that] your first mammalian is already a mammal, your first equine already a horse, and so on along the line. Accordingly, though there may well be evolution within a given type, we see no new type produced by evolution'. But Teilhard argues that:

> Nothing is so delicate and fugitive by its very nature as a beginning. ....There is nothing surprising in our finding, when we look back that everything seems to have burst into the world *ready made*. ....If our machines (cars, planes, etc) were swallowed up in some cataclysm and 'fossilised', future geologists, finding them, would get the same impression as we get from the pterodactyl. Represented only by the latest makes, these products of our invention would seem to have been created without any previous evolutionary groping—completed and 'fixed' at the first attempt.[23]

Again, in the essay 'The Basis and Foundations of the Idea of Evolution' (1926) Teilhard makes an equally clear admission that there is an 'absence of intermediate forms': 'the discontinuity of the genealogical trees drawn by systematics is beyond dispute'.[24] 'The anti-evolutionists', Teilhard writes, attach great importance to this discontinuity of phyla, and generally view it as a death-sentence on transformism. Not only does the disappearance of the zoological peduncles leave standing an undoubted total structure requiring a scientific explanation which the anti-evolutionists have never attempted to give; but also, properly understood, it provides one of the most reassuring signs that the evolutionary views are right. The lacunary character of phyletic lines, at first sight so disconcerting to transformists, is in reality, if carefully viewed, the most certain indication of a true movement of growth in life.[25]

No longer do transitional forms assure us of the reality of evolution, on the contrary, the very absence of transitional forms is a sure sign that evolution has taken place. In support of this latter proposition Teilhard appeals to archaeology, languages and law in which no expert would deny a development, an evolution, yet rarely can a line of descent be established even when there is no doubt. 'We ask the zoologists to show the first origin of horses, or of amphibians, or of reptiles. But have we ever thought of asking the archaeologists for the origins of the Semites, the Greeks and the Egyptians?'. 'In reality all that we can conclude in zoology,' Teilhard writes,

> from the absence of intermediate forms, is that since the biosphere reacts in exactly the same manner to the methods of historical analysis as everything that we know to be evolutionary, it is itself evolutionary by nature. By this statement, the objection is transformed into proof ...To shake transformism in its essence, would be to attack the whole of our science of past reality; would be to upset the whole of history.[26]

Teilhard draws a clear comparison between history and evolution in that they are both a series of unique, unrepeatable events which often fail to reveal transitional steps in the appearance of final forms.

'How the Transformist Question Presents itself To-day' (1921) devotes considerable space to the failure of the fossil record to furnish transitional forms. He begins by highlighting the simplistic explanations of the early evolutionists from Lamarck to Haeckel, 'Like all scientific theories in their origins, biological evolutionism began by being extremely simple in its explanations'. This simplicity according to Teilhard was to imagine that evolution should leave its traces in a continuous series of transitional forms in the fossil record:

> All living and fossil animals, it was thought, could be arranged on a small number of lines, along which increasingly complicated types re-

placed one another in the course of time ...The transformation of organisms on each line being continuous, and all the lines forming a
simple sheaf, it was easy to mark precisely the empty places, that is to
say, to count the missing links on each living chain[27]

Teilhard points out that at the time of his writing the picture is
much more complicated, 'It became necessary to renounce the idea of
a regular, continuous and total evolution' (p.10). For example some
creatures such as the cockroaches and the scorpions are

> true living fossils, which have not departed in a single important fea-
> ture from their type in the Secondary, the Carboniferous or even the
> Cambrian. While certain regions of the animal world were completely
> renewing themselves, others therefore remained strictly stationary.
> This is a curious fact. But what is even more disturbing is that the im-
> mobilised types which we find in nature are not only final twig ends,
> species squeezed in a sort of morphological blind alley ...[but also] if
> known only in their fossil state, quite easily assume the role of genea-
> logical intermediates. (p.10)

'These limitations', Teilhard writes, 'imposed by the facts on the
first conceptions of the transformists have been considered by the
anti-transformists as so many defeats by nature on their adversaries.
Their triumph is unjustified'. In answer to these objections Teilhard
adopts a position very similar to the recent 'punctuated equilibrium'
theory of Stephen Gould in which some species remain unchanged
for long periods of time and then undergo rapid periods of change.
'To-day', Teilhard writes,

> natural scientists have abandoned the conception of a too simple and
> regular development of life ...They now recognize that life, similar in
> this respect to a great tree or a great people, is transformed regionally
> and in jerks—here completely stuck for long periods, there brusquely
> awoken and beginning to grow again, and in another place fresh and
> still climbing. They know too that within a single geological group
> only certain individuals can begin to change while the rest remain sta-
> tionary, so that one sees the old types persisting for a long time beside
> the new. Because of the great number of species and the rarity of fos-
> sils, they despair of exactly reconstructing genealogies, line by line,
> and are content with approximate seriation, which is all that is possible
> with the elements at their disposal. (p.12)

Teilhard is aware that all this might sound like special pleading,
'But, it will perhaps be objected:', he writes, 'If we make all these

saving concessions, does it not thereby become unverifiable? To this objection we must reply with an unhesitating No. No.' He warns against turning one's attention to any random region of the organic world, for in doing so 'one is in danger of being impressed only by the leaps and gaps of life in movement, that is of perceiving only disorder' (p.13). Acceptance of evolution is for Teilhard an unshakeable conviction, 'a conviction that has grown beneath the surface arguments' (p.22).

In 'The Transformist Paradox' (1925) he returns to the issue of the absence of transitional forms in the fossil record. He maintains that the apparent fixity of species does not endanger the fact of transformism. 'Let us admit', he writes,

> that the contradictory appearances of supple movement and fixed rigidity, presented alternately by life according as one looks at it from far or near, as a whole or in detail, is not a simple play of light. Let us admit further that, in this contradiction between our experiences, reality is entirely on the side of the fixed and rigid, so that the sequence of living species, as we know them better, must always and increasingly reveal itself to us as series of compartments, arranged according to a pattern of movement, but each motionless and each walled off from the other.[28]

Teilhard is undismayed by this most unfavorable situation. He refers to it as a hypothesis but in reality it represents the true state of affairs, as he readily admits. Even so he mentions one fact, 'the natural distribution of living forms', which he thinks is alone sufficient to prove that evolution has occurred. 'Before all hypotheses'. Teilhard writes,

> from a simple inspection of the geometrical distribution of living things on the earth, one is forced to admit that no zoological species could have made its physical appearance at any other time or place than it did. In other words, by virtue of the total play of the astronomical, geological and biological factors of our world, each living form occupies an exact position; it has a *natural place*, from which it could not be uprooted without destroying the whole balance of the universe. (p.86)

On the basis of the concept of a 'natural place' for each living organism Teilhard argues that the absence of transitional forms does not support the fixity of species:

An illusion, the flowing of one zoological species into another? I grant it [Passe] ...An illusion, the general ascent of forms towards increasing consciousness and spontaneity? I grant this too [Passe encore] ...But an illusion, the ordered, organised ineluctable distribution of living beings through time and space? I deny this with all the strength of my palaeontological experience ....Even in a universe in which animal species succeed one another by leaps, without direct filiation, it would still be necessary to find a scientific explanation for the order followed by these discontinuities; that is to say, to find a law of evolution' (p.86–88).

He now admits that the gaps in the fossil record are truly enormous: 'I would go much further and say that the gaps in our palaeontological knowledge are so large that it requires a real effort of the imagination even to conceive of their hugeness' (p.93). This admission is at odds with an earlier remark in *The Phenomenon of Man* on the numerous discoveries of transitional forms since the time of Darwin and Lamarck. Teilhard's explanation for the huge gaps in the fossil record and the absence of transitional forms is, 'quite simply, that palaeontology (like all long-distance vision) only reveals *maxima*. Before an animal form *begins* to appear in the fossil record, it has to be already legion' (p.94). 'By all sorts of positive reasons and analogies', Teilhard writes,

we are led to think that the formation of zoological species takes a relatively short time. The period being brief, and the mutations no doubt affecting, at the beginnings of each species, only a relatively small number of representatives of the old species, the absolute quantity of individuals of a truly 'transitional' type is extremely small. Not only is the size of these individuals, who are of such supreme interest to zoology very slight, but their total number remains perforce extremely small also. In all their quantitative characteristics, the penduncles of phyla therefore stand as *minima* in biological evolution. By virtue of what we know about the difficulties of fossil preservation, they are condemned to disappear ...Once a phylum becomes perceptible to us, it cannot fail to be already entirely defined in its features and hardened in its characteristics. (p.94–95)

The chief assumptions in this argument are that the formation of new species from old takes a relatively short time, that the number of the transitional forms between the old and new species is small and that these transitional forms are small in size. Consequently, in view of the difficulty of fossil preservation the likelihood of finding transitional forms in the fossil record is minimal. It should be noted that these assumptions are contrary to those postulated by Darwin. Teilhard does acknowledge that Darwin was of the opposite opinion as regards the second assumption, for he saw 'in the great species the material for evolution' and thus postulated that there were a large number of transitional forms between species. But the important Darwinian assumption, the gradual change of one species into another over immense periods of long time, is at odds with the first assumption and is not alluded to by Teilhard. Regarding the third assumption Teilhard writes:

> It has been observed that the first known representatives of the various zoological families are much smaller than their descendants ...the often tiny dimensions of primitive zoological types are a very great obstacle, first to their fossilization and then to their discovery ...unless we presume that the number of mutated individuals was immediately very large ...this is very improbable. (p.93)

But the failure of transitional forms to fossilize relies on the validity of the first and second assumptions. The third assumption, the small size of the mutated individuals in a species, is only significant if the formation of new species takes a short time and the number of mutated forms is small. If the number of transitional forms between species is large and is spread over immense periods of time, as Darwin suggested, there is no particular reason why they should not be fossilized. Teilhard does not mention the 'reasons and analogies' which led him to accept the first and second assumptions apart from the lack of transitional forms in the fossil record. It seems that when there are transitional forms in the fossil record a Darwinian explanation is possible and when they are absent Teilhard's explanation is at hand.

Darwin postulated the existence of transitional forms and he saw the imperfection of the fossil record in his time as serious blow to his theory: 'I can give no satisfactory answer ...Nature may almost be said to have guarded against the frequent discovery of her transitional or linking forms'[29]. His hope was that these transitional forms would be found. Darwin's theory is not compatible with Teilhard's because the former postulates the presence of clear and numerous transitional forms between species whereas the later expressly denies their existence. As Popper observed, the one prediction of Darwin's theory is gradualness. In this respect Teilhard's ideas on evolution are a repudiation of Darwin's. Since both mechanisms are incompati-

ble it is difficult to see how the presence and the absence of transitional forms can both can be adduced by Teilhard for the fact of
evolution. His first piece of evidence in *The Phenomenon of Man* (1940)
for the fact of evolution is that 'numerous discoveries have established the existence of the transitional forms postulated by the theory
of evolution'. Here he appears to espouse the Darwinian gradualness. But earlier in 'The Transformist Paradox' (1925) he lays
emphasis on the absence of transitional forms. So Teilhard's remarks
in *The Phenomenon of Man* do not support the fact of evolution only a
particular theory of evolution. Only, particular theories of evolution
can explain either the presence or absence of transitional forms in the
fossil record. Both theories, of course, are incompatible with each
other. Teilhard introduces subsidiary hypotheses, which are not part
of the Darwinian picture, to explain why the expected transitional
forms are not observed in the fossil record. Transitional forms there
must be if evolution occurred, but Teilhard asserts that they are not
preserved because of their small number, physical size and the
difficulty of fossilization. Nonetheless this conviction did not prevent
him from searching for transitional forms in the evolution of man.
The real problem is ascertaining what counts as a transitional form.
One can only conclude that Teilhard was inconsistent or confused in
his discussion of the existence of transitional forms and that neither
of his positions can be adduced as supporting the fact of evolution,
but only a particular theory of evolution.

Other evidence for the fact of evolution

Teilhard's further piece of evidence for the fact of evolution comes
from field of biochemistry.

> The latest advances in biochemistry are beginning to establish the re-
> ality of molecular aggregates which really do appear to reduce to
> measurable proportions the gaping void hitherto supposed to exist be-
> tween protoplasm and mineral matter. ....Thanks to the discovery of
> these giant corpuscles [viruses] the foreseen existence of *intermediate
> states* between the microscopic living world [cell] and the ultra-
> microscopic 'inanimate' one has now passed into the field of direct ex-
> perimentation.[30]

One might question the significance of 'foreseen existence' of
intermediate states between the animate and the 'inanimate' worlds.

For he admits that 'foreseen' is no more than 'the intellectual need of continuity'. The intellectual need for continuity would seem to assume that evolution is a fact, for why otherwise would one feel the need for continuity in natural forms. But a more serious objection arises. The argument suggests that, because of their intermediate position as regards their size and their nature between the inanimate and animate worlds, viruses existed prior to the cell in the evolutionary process. But viruses are parasitic and require the existence of higher cell organisms to act as hosts. Hence it is likely that they arose later in evolution than the cell. Consequently Teilhard's argument does not support evolutionary continuity.

For Teilhard continuity in the forms of matter from the inanimate to the cell and to living organisms is most important as it points to the fact of evolution. He advances reasons for considering that the process of the formation of mega molecules in contrast to the proliferation of life was 'one of the utmost slowness ....perhaps longer than the whole of geological time from the Cambrian period to the present day' (p.85–86). Teilhard sees the formation of viruses and other mega molecules as a necessary basis for the emergence of life. One might ask why these transitional forms such as the viruses between inanimate matter and the cell did not disappear once they had set the stage for the emergence of life. While he does not take up this question directly he does allude to the fact that viruses may be modified by association with 'living tissue' and presumably persist because of this association. Teilhard's lengthy discussion of viruses is important because he considered that it meets 'our need of continuity'.

The absolutely unique character of the genesis of life is a crucial axiom for him as it supports his concept of continuity in the emergence of life from inanimate matter, although he does not draw this conclusion. Teilhard finds 'nothing inherently impossible about the continued birth to-day of living substance on the infinitesimal scale'[31]; he does not adopt it because of 'the fundamental similarity of all organic beings'.[32]

> Even if there is only one solution to the main physical and physiological problem of life on earth, that general solution would necessarily leave undecided a host of accidental and particular questions, and it does not seem thinkable that they would have been decided *twice in the same way.* ...naturalists are becoming more and more convinced that

the genesis of life on earth belongs to the category of absolutely *unique* events that, once happened, are never repeated[33].

If life continues to emerge from inanimate matter then the likelihood of it emerging in the same manner on different occasions is infinitesimally small. It follows that a unique and unrepeatable genesis of life gives rise to a fundamental similarity of all organic beings. This similarity argues against the multiple emergence of life on earth. But in the scientific essay 'The Singularities of the Human Species' (1954) shortly before his death, in a discussion of extraterrestrial intelligences, Teilhard changes his mind and now sees the genesis of life as inevitable:

> If at any point in sidereal space a star should chance to appear, in which temperature, pressure, gravity, etc., would allow the gradual formation of very large molecules, this would be enough for life immediately to hook on at this point ...and for life, once hooked on, to concentrate and intensify to the point of reflecting on itself.[34]

It is not clear whether this concession to the inevitability of life on other planets allows for the multiple emergence of life on earth.

A further piece of evidence for the fact of evolution advanced by Teilhard comes from the manner in which scientists practice their profession.

> Biologists and palaeontologists are still arguing to-day about the way things happen, and above all about the mechanism of life's transformations ...But on the general and fundamental fact that organic evolution exists, ...all scientists are today in agreement for the very good reason that they could not practice science if they thought otherwise.[35]

This appears to be an appeal to what Thomas Kuhn[36] would describe as the current paradigm of the biological establishment, that is, scientists must have a framework of accepted beliefs in order to function and develop research programs. In the case of biologists that framework is the fact of evolution. Consequently, the evidence advanced by Teilhard is no more than the belief that the theory of evolution best explains the current classification of organisms and offers the most fruitful framework for a study of biological nature. In short, until a better theory turns up a scientist remains within the current framework of evolution.

In an earlier essay 'The Basis and Foundations of the Idea of Evolution' (1926)[37] he discusses 'the group of facts, views and attitudes which constitute the basis and foundations of the evolutionary idea' and points to evolution as an 'inevitable form of human thought'. 'The most general proof (one might say the one and inexhaustible proof)', he writes, 'of an evolution of organic matter must be sought in the undeniable traces of structure which the world of life considered as a whole manifests on analysis'. This argument is an additional one to those presented above and is the central argument advanced in the essay. Teilhard sees life not simply present on earth as 'a sort of adhesion' but as 'bound to the very architecture of the earth', and he sees as a general characteristic of life over time, a general ascent towards greater consciousness. The initial purpose of the science of systematics, he observes, was a 'logical classification of beings', but 'under the pressure of facts' this science has become a 'veritable anatomy or histology of the layer of life on earth'. Teilhard draws the conclusion that the classification of beings is a sure sign of the fact of evolution:

> *Everything is classified; therefore everything holds together* ....One conclusion is inevitable; that it [the biosphere] took shape progressively. Alter things and words as we may, so far we have only found one way of explaining the structure of the world of life discovered by systematics; we can see it only as the result of a development, of an 'evolution'. Let us set down the truth; it would be easier to persuade a botanist or histologist that the vessels of a stem or the fibres of a muscle have been knit and soldered by a clever faker than to convince a naturalist, alive to the realities he is handling, of the genetic independence of living groups[38].

As mentioned previously, Teilhard insists that the fact of evolution is in no way dependent on any theory of evolution. Classification is not simply the placement of beings into arbitrary categories but in a real sense the discovering of evolutionary relationships between beings.

The fact of evolution has moral consequences, he says, and for this reason the passion displayed in discussions on the subject 'has a deeper origin; it is of a moral and religious order'. Opponents of evolution are persuaded that by attacking it they are defending virtue and religion. 'Correctly understood', Teilhard writes, 'transformism is, on the contrary, a possible teacher of spiritual idealism and high morality'[39].

Human fossil types

Though Teilhard regards the fact of evolution as what matters, and the mechanism of evolution as of far less concern, he nonetheless regards his theory of evolution as of the utmost importance. He devotes the major part of his literary and scientific effort to 'discussions of the scientific 'hows' and the metaphysical 'whys'' of evolution. As mentioned in Chapter 2, Teilhard has a theory of evolution which appears to have emerged from his involvement with the discovery of the skull of Piltdown Man. He never departed from the view that human beings evolved as a bundle of lineages moving in parallel directions, which allowed for the simultaneous presence of pre-hominid forms like Neanderthal Man and true ancestors of homo sapiens like Piltdown Man. The theory can best be understood by reference to a diagram illustrating the temporal distribution and the natural connexions of Fossil Men, Fig.12 in 'Fossil Men' (1943)[40] (see below). As already noted, the version of this paper appearing in the Éditions du Seuil has been editorially pruned of all reference to Eoanthropus and is thus unreliable for ascertaining Teilhard's views.

The fossil human types', Teilhard writes , 'fall into three successive curvilinear nappes (or sheets), fitting into each other: a primitive nappe (A); an intermediate nappe (B); and a modern nappe (C) . As shown by the figure , each nappe contains human types belonging to different anatomical and geological stages'. In other words Teilhard's theory predicts that ancestral and primitive stages of homo sapiens can coexist. In accordance with this theory Piltdown Man, a true precursor of Homo sapiens, existed before Neanderthal Man.

Teilhard summarizes the fossil evidence as follows:

> Whenever we look (and the deeper we look) back across the past, living groups seem to *displace* each other, rather than to pass into each other directly. From this point of view, neither Peking Man, nor Solo Man, nor Neanderthal Man have any direct offspring left to-day in the living world: they have been swept away by *Homo sapiens*; just as the Tasmanians have been, and the Australian Bushmen will soon be, replaced by the stronger white or yellow races.[41]

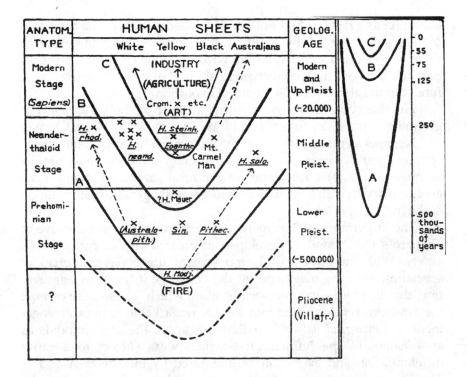

'This imbricated structure', Teilhard writes, 'will be questioned by some anthropologists, who claim that, between the *Sinanthropus* and the modern Mongoloids for instance, a continuous genealogic line can be traced; but I am convinced that the scheme here suggested much better fits in with the scientific evidence' (p.3933). These sheets of human evolution ultimately have a common trunk. Of the three 'human sheets the shortest is the Homo sapiens sheet, C, to which we belong. From the extreme shortness of this sheet Teilhard draws the conclusion that it is *just beginning to grow*' and it is the future of this sheet that is of prime importance to Teilhard. The imbricated structure of the human evolution provides for him the key to the past and the future. What is surprising is the lack of fossil evidence for Teilhard's theory. In fact, as noted in Chapter 2, Gould sees Piltdown Man (the skull alone) as the only available evidence of it, for its skull belonged to an advanced human which was older than primitive Neanderthal. Piltdown and Neanderthal man are thus confirmation of Teilhard's imbricated structure for human evolution which allows for the simultaneous presence of both ancestral and primitive forms of man. Before the discovery of Piltdown Man Teilhard had accepted evolution as a fact but had not yet developed a theory. The collection of his scientific papers by Schmitz-Moormann supports this view, as there is no evidence in any of his writings prior to 1920 of multiple parallel lineages and convergence within human evolution as a fundamental element in his theory of evolution.

His theory is consistent with his attitude to the various ethnic groupings. In a letter to a friend in 1927 he remarks on the Chinese and Negroes as possessing an 'anthropological substance ...inferior to our own' and considers that the' 'human stratum' may not be homogeneous'[42]. His acceptance of a central privileged stem on the evolutionary tree also inclines him to advocate genetic manipulation of the human species.

The importance of the emergence of Homo sapiens is decisive in Teilhard's theory and is developed at great length in many of his essays. With the advent of Homo sapiens the divergent forces of speciation are now overcome by the convergent forces of aggregation, that is, inbreeding and socialization, which 'continually compel the newborn types of men into a most remarkable ...super arrangement of a *biological nature*'[43]. Teilhard regarded the prehominoids as an offshoot of the human race, which were subject to a rapid differentiation and extinction as illustrated by the sheets A and B. The Homo sapiens type sheet C evolved independently of the prehominoids into the sole surviving species and ceased differentiation or divergence as Teilhard called it. Helmut de Terra, a distinguished German geologist and paleontologist who accompanied Teilhard on a number of expeditions in the Far East between 1935 and 1937, says of Teilhard's theory of human evolution that it 'neatly disposes of the necessity for a 'missing link' between man and ape'[44]. Typical of Teilhard's approach is the essay, 'The Australopithecines and the 'Missing Link'' (1950) in which he disposes of the claim that the Australopithecines represent a 'missing link' between ape and man. He relegates the Australopithecines to 'a particularly significant *intercalary group* (as an 'attempt at man, I dare to say) ...and subsequently 'disappearing without climbing higher or leaving any traces'[45]. This is in keeping with his theory shown in diagram above, where the various human fossil types fall into three sheets which '*displace* each other rather than pass into each other directly', and thus there is no 'missing link' to be found.

Convergence

With the appearance of Homo sapiens Teilhard held that a reversal took place, in that divergence, or division into separate groups, gave way to convergence. The convergent culmination of human evolution is represented in the following diagram taken from *The Phenomenon of Man*, in which Homo sapiens is shown as the sole surviving hominid.

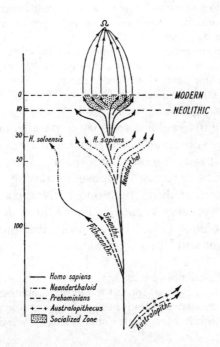

A new layer now emerges from the biosphere, the noosphere or layer of consciousness, concomitantly with the rapid spread of Homo sapiens. Noosphere, 'thinking layer' is a neologism coined by Teilhard. The noosphere arises from and covers earlier layers in the evolutionary process. 'Geologists', Teilhard writes,

> have long agreed in admitting the zonal composition of our planet ...the barysphere, central and metallic surrounded by the rocky litho-sphere that is in turn surrounded by the fluid layers of the hydrosphere and the atmosphere ...[then] the living membrane com-posed of fauna and flora of the globe, the biosphere.

> The recognition and isolation of a new era, the era of noogenesis, obliges us to distinguish correlatively a support proportionate to the

operation—that is to say, yet another membrane in the majestic assembly of telluric layers[46].

What evidence does Teilhard have for his theory of convergence? 'The concept of convergence of the human race was so essential to Teilhard's account of man's origin', de Terra's writes,

> that it is easy to understand why he was so greatly encouraged in that idea by his newfound knowledge of extinct types of primitive man in Java. With the disappearance of typal diversity within the Java and Peking Man group, modern man emerged as the sole surviving species and the one which dominated the entire world. What others regarded as a chance phenomenon of survival became, for Teilhard, a manifestation of some deeper meaning underlying the evolution of man. (p.120)

The evidence for Teilhard's theory of parallel lineages in human evolution and the subsequent convergence of Homo sapiens rests on extinct types of pre-hominoids and the Piltdown skull. After the appearance of Eoanthropus, supposedly dating from the Upper Pleistocene, no further differentiation or divergence took place and the period of convergence began. In 'Fossil Men—Recent Discoveries and Present Problems' (1943) He refers to this momentous change between the Lower and Upper Pleistocene:

> The Neanderthaloids have now entirely left the floor; and, replacing them, Men of the new type inhabit the Earth, fundamentally different and definitely modernized both in appearance and in their comportment, as the result of a triple (anatomical, psychical and social) transformation.[47]

When one looks at the accompanying figure 12, Eoanthropus (the skull) is recognized as the crucial piece of fossil evidence. Eoanthropus was human in appearance ('gone, and for ever, the low foreheads, the thick supra-orbital ridges') and was found accompanied by implements and animal fossils of the Upper Pleistocene period. For Teilhard, convergence was not simply the absence of further evolutionary differentiation and the birth of consciousness; it proclaimed a period of a 'universal biological process of socialisation'[48] which ultimately focuses on point Omega, the culmination of the evolutionary process.

It is on the matter of convergence in human evolution that Teilhard takes issue with Bergson. The writings of Henri Bergson, in particular *Creative Evolution*[49] and *The Two Sources of Morality and Religion*[50], had a profound influence on Teilhard's evolutionary views at an important time of his life. In his autobiographical essay 'The Heart of Matter' under the heading, The Discovery of Evolution, Teilhard mentions only one writer, Bergson, and in particular his *Creative Evolution*. But Teilhard seems reluctant to admit the strong effect that Bergson had on him, and he limits his influence to that of a catalyst for his own thought: 'the only effect that brilliant book had upon me was to provide fuel at just the right moment, and very briefly, for a fire that was already consuming my heart and mind'[51]. But it is difficult to accept Teilhard's statement that Bergson's ideas were no more than a catalyst for his own. Frequent references appear to Bergson in his letters during the First World War, and importantly in the essay, 'Creative Union'[52] (1917) whose title is a clear reference to Bergson's *Creative Evolution*. The eminent theologian Henri de Lubac remarks, 'if the essay is to be properly understood we must see it, as Père Teilhard himself did, in relation to Bergson's book'[53]. In this essay Teilhard clearly opposes his evolutionary mechanism to that of Bergson. It appears that Bergson's concept of a divergent evolutionary process was partly instrumental in Teilhard's formulating the opposite hypothesis, a convergent evolutionary process; for Teilhard only formulated it after reading Bergson. 'The fact that a pattern of convergence can be recognized', he writes,

> in the process of universal becoming is sufficient in itself to demolish the Bergsonian notion of a vital *impulse* without any final purpose, of a *vis a tergo*. Such a dynamism, indeed, cannot but introduce into its principle a centre of divergence. One cannot see how it could produce the confluence of the elements it drives before it.

> The force that creates the world can only be a *vis ab ante*, a force of attraction. (p.159)

Bergson's views on the nature of evolution are set out in Chapter 3 of *Creative Evolution*, entitled 'The Divergent Directions of the Evolution of Life'. 'The evolution movement would be a simple one', Bergson writes,

> and we should soon have been able to determine its direction, if life had described a single course, like a solid ball shot from a cannon. But it proceeds rather like a shell, which suddenly bursts into fragments destined to burst again, and so on for a time incommensurably long. (p.109)

> The unity [of life] is derived from a *vis a tergo*: it is given at the start as an impulsion, not placed at the end as an attraction. (p.115)

This could hardly be more different from Teilhard's view.

Teilhard, discussing the 'expansional power' of life in his essay, 'On the Biological Meaning of Human Socialization' (1952), agrees with Bergson that evolving matter betrays 'a sort of internal preference for growing consciousness: what Bergson used to call 'un élan vital''[54]. He accepts that the initial phase of evolution gives an illusion of being divergent and takes this to have led Bergson astray:

> As the elements of Spirit make their way together towards their common goal, they suffer a disintegration—what one might call an unravelling—of their fibres. That is why many phyla break away and give the illusion of a divergent evolution. This fragmentation is superficial and secondary. Basically, the whole of the world's psychism gravitates towards a single centre. (p.158)

The direction of evolution

In *The Phenomenon of Man* (1940) Teilhard remarks that although the majority of scientists now accept

> an evolution of one sort or another ...Whether or not that evolution is *directed* is another question. Asked whether life is *going anywhere* at the end of its transformations, nine out of ten will to day say no, even passionately.[55]

Dobzhansky[56] is correct in saying that the cardinal postulate of the 'Teilhardian synthesis' is articulated on p.142 of *The Phenomenon of Man*: 'men's minds are reluctant to recognise that evolution has a precise orientation and a privileged axis'. Weakened by doubt as to whether evolution has a direction, 'the forces of research are scattered', Teilhard writes,

> and there is no determination to build the earth ....Leaving aside all anthropocentrism and anthropomorphism, I believe I can see a direction and a line of progress for life, a line and a direction which are in fact so well marked that I am convinced their reality will be universally admitted by the science of tomorrow. And I want here to make the reader understand why.[57]

This issue, argues Dobzhansky, 'is *critical* [my emphasis] for the whole Teilhardian synthesis'[58]. But does Teilhard espouse 'orthogenesis' or 'finalism' in discussing the direction of evolution? In the essay, 'The Teilhardian Synthesis', Dobzhansky defines finalism as the belief that 'evolution occurred for the express purpose of producing man, and that evolutionary changes at all times were guided by some supernatural power or powers'. Orthogenesis, on the other hand, is the view that, at least in biological evolution,

> changes that occur are sequences of events determined by factors inside the organism, by the structure of its genetic endowment, and proceed straight toward a fixed objective, such as man. ....In contradistinction to finalism, orthogenesis does not necessarily assume supernatural forces guiding evolution ...an attractive analogy is that evolutionary development (phylogeny) is determined in the same way as is the development of an individual (ontogeny). Finalism and orthogenesis have this much in common: the evolutionary history of the living world was predestined at the beginning of life and even in primordial matter. (p.117–118).

In *The Phenomenon of Man* Teilhard appears to opt for orthogenesis: 'without orthogenesis life would only have spread; with it there is an ascent of life that is invincible' (p.109). 'There seems to be no lack of examples, in the course of biological evolution', Teilhard writes,

> of transformations acting horizontally by the pure crossing of characters. One example is the mutation we call Mendelian. But when we look deeper and more generally we see that the rejuvenations made possible by each reproduction achieve something more than mere restitution, They *add*, one to the other, and their sum increases *in a predetermined direction*. ...This law of controlled complication, the mature stage of the process in which we get the micro-molecule then the mega-molecule and finally the first cells, is known to biologists as *orthogenesis*. (p.108)

Teilhard gives two more definitions of the term orthogenesis. The second is given in a footnote to the passage quoted above, in response to some biologists who would like to suppress the word 'orthogenesis'. 'But my considered opinion', Teilhard writes, 'is that the word is essential and indispensable for singling out the manifest property of living matter to form a system in which 'terms succeed each other experimentally, following the constantly increasing values of centro-complexity" (p.108). Centro-complexity is a Teilhardian neologism to describe the supposed tendency of evolution to give rise to more advanced self-reflective units—man so far—with increasing biological organization. Teilhard sees this tendency as obeying the 'law of complexity-consciousness'. A third definition was given by Teilhard shortly before his death: '*directed* transformation (to whatever degree and under whatever influence 'the direction' may be manifested)'[59]. Simpson notes that this last definition of orthogenesis is broad enough to include the effects of Darwinian natural selection: 'but that was not intended, because Teilhard repeatedly contrasted selection with orthogenesis and indeed treated them as complete opposites'.

Teilhard sees the primates as a

> singular and privileged case, the particular orthogenesis of the phylum happened to coincide exactly with the principal orthogenesis of life it- self: ....in the well-marked region at the heart of the mammals, where the most powerful brains ever made by nature are to be found, they [the phyletic lines] become red hot. ....Thought is born ...Admittedly the animal knows. But it cannot know that it knows[60].

He maintains that if the evolutionary process were run over again from the beginning under the appropriate physical conditions, the same end result would be achieved, the emergence of intelligent life; for Teilhard accepts that thought has emerged on other planets. This seems to be a clear-cut case of orthogenesis, namely that matter, under the correct conditions, is programmed to give birth to thought.

Many scientists see Teilhard's claims as unjustified. Francisco Ayala rejects the view that evolutionary change necessarily proceeds along determined paths'[61], holding that theories like Teilhard's mistakenly take embryological development (ontogeny) as the model of evolutionary change and thus regard it as predestined. That Teilhard took embryology as a model for evolutionary change seems clear from his espousal of orthogenesis. The fact that evolution is not directionally consistent and occasionally is reversed is damaging to Teilhard's test of the orthogenetic nature of evolution. Even so, there is a discernible trend towards higher forms of life. 'To be sure', Dobzhansky writes,

> in some groups, such as various parasitic forms, evolution was often retrogressive (loss of organs, particularly degeneration of the nervous

system); in other groups evolution was seemingly given to the production of endless variations on the same theme. And yet, the net outcome
of evolution is that today the earth is no longer populated exclusively
by primordial viruses and amoebae. ...Most remarkably, evolution has
produced organisms with highly developed nervous systems[62]

But it does not necessarily follow from Dobzhansky's remarks that
the direction of the evolutionary process was determined in advance
as claimed by Teilhard. Ernst Mayr rejects Teilhard's insistence on a
'cosmic teleology'[63] and his view that evolution has some built-in
tendency or drive towards perfection.

Another prominent biologist, Stephen Jay Gould, remarks: 'Teilhard believed that evolution proceeds in a definite and irreversible
direction'[64]. Gould examines this claim in some detail and disagrees.
Teilhard held that as the spiritual component of matter increases, in
particular with the appearance of *Homo sapiens*, convergence begins
and the direction of a billion years of evolution are reversed as
mankind amalgamates at a single point, point Omega. Gould sees no
evidence in the fossil record of the domination of matter by spirit,
that is, increasing braininess in the history of life in general. But in
fairness to Teilhard, Gould's remarks seem to be at odds with his
own account of Teilhard's theory of multiple parallel, lineages in
human evolution of which only one gives rise to Homo sapiens. On
such a model one would not expect increasing braininess for life in
general but only for certain privileged lineages, in particular, for that
leading to Homo sapiens. 'In other mammals too, no doubt, the
nervous system and instinct gradually develop', Teilhard writes, 'But
in them the internal travail was distracted, limited and finally
arrested ...like the insect, to some extent prisoners of the instruments
of their swift-moving or predatory ways'[65].

Towers points to the 'central problem of randomness versus
purposiveness in evolution', and claims that Teilhard solved it with
his concept of 'groping'. 'Teilhard', he writes, 'speaks of

'groping' as the essential picture of the evolutionary process. The word
is a stoke of genius. Groping movements are bound to appear to be
random, may indeed be so when taken in isolation and without regard
to the eventual outcome. Perhaps one might gain some appreciation of
his concept by thinking in terms of a highly complex maze, made up of
a series of inter-connecting mazes each highly complex in itself and offering to the groping contestants unlimited opportunities for becoming
sidetracked into blind alleys. Correct solution of one maze allows the

group to proceed to the next. But the mere survival at the next stage may require that the earlier mazes be reasonably well explored and occupied.[66]

Towers considers that the exploration of interconnecting mazes, in some cases leading to blind alleys, explains the apparently faulty nature of evolution and yet its directional nature.

But Dobzhansky argues that 'in spite of himself, Teilhard was not an exponent of orthogenesis'[67], for he accepted the 'incredibly faulty' nature of evolution. How are these apparently contradictory comments to be reconciled? If we consider Towers comparison of evolution to the inter-connecting mazes, it is clear that there is only *one* correct solution to each maze which allows evolution to move onto the next maze. The series of correct solutions to each maze, therefore, is orthogenesis. Imperfections are the result of the blind alleys which are explored before a correct solution is found, and are, thus, in keeping with orthogenesis. Dobzhansky's objection, then, that 'in spite of himself, Teilhard was not an exponent of orthogenesis'[68] does not appear valid. Dobzhansky's claim that Teilhard rejects orthogenesis in *The Phenomenon of Man* also rests on the place Teilhard affords to freedom in biological evolution:

> The outcome of evolution is not predestined because, in Teilhard's words, 'There is a danger that the elements of the world should refuse to serve the world—because they think; or precisely that the world should refuse itself from perceiving itself through reflection'[69].

But a careful reading of the postscript, 'The Essence of the Phenomenon of Man', somewhat diminishes the force of Dobzhansky's claim that Teilhard did not espouse orthogenesis. Teilhard argues that evolution is

> intrinsically influenced in its effects by two uncertainties related to the double play—chance at the bottom and freedom at the top. Let me add, however, that in the case of very large numbers (such, for instance, as the human population) the process tends to 'unfallibilise' [misprint for infallibilise, s'infaillibiliser] itself, inasmuch as the likelihood of success grows on the lower side (chance) while rejection and error diminishes on the other side (freedom) with the multiplication of the elements engaged.[70]

Here is an acknowledgment that chance at the lower levels of evolution and freedom at the level of man could cause evolution to move along unpredictable paths. But Teilhard wants it both ways, an acceptance of the possibility of failure in the evolutionary process, because it involves chance in its biological workings, and yet a statistical assurance that the outcome is all but infallibly assured. He comes down on the side of orthogenesis, as 'the process tends to 'infallibilise' itself'.

Simpson is another biologist who finds fault with Teilhard's use of the term orthogenesis: 'the term orthogenesis in Teilhard's work seems at first sight to have no explanatory meaning whatever but to be tautological or circular'. Simpson backed up this assessment at a Symposium, 'In Quest of the Perfection of Man ' (1971)[7] by quoting from a scientific paper by Teilhard on a group of Chinese rodents, published in 1950. At the end of the paper Teilhard concludes that, 'The phenomenon [of 'orthogenesis'] can no longer be denied. But the correct explanation of the phenomenon is still to be found' (p.98). This remark, says Simpson, is clear acknowledgement by Teilhard that the term orthogenesis is not an explanation but only points out something that needs to be explained.

There is also a theological problem for Teilhard. If evolution followed a path, says Dobzhansky, which is 'predestined (orthogenesis), or is propelled and guided toward some goal by divine interventions (finalism), then ...the design was incredibly faulty. ...Why so many false starts, extinctions, disasters, misery, anguish, and finally the greatest of evils—death?' ...'The God of love and mercy could not have planned all this. Any doctrine which regards evolution as predetermined or guided collides head-on with the ineluctable fact of the existence of evil'. On a scientific level the faulty nature of evolution could be answered with the maze analogy, but how does Teilhard tackle the problem on a theological level? This problem will be discussed in detail in Chapter 8. Teilhard also opts for finalism in that he accepts evolution as guided by a supernatural force, point Omega. Evolution will reach its culmination at point Omega drawn by the cosmic Christ, and creation will transcend space and time. This aspect of his thought will be discussed later in the book. It is not necessary, however, to see orthogenesis and finalism as mutually exclusive, for God could have used orthogenesis to achieve his purpose (finalism). Simpson acknowledges, however, that when Teilhard says the direction is pre-determined and that there is 'only one direction—toward greater 'centro-complexity', toward Omega, ultimately God—then the statement may not be much more clearly explanatory, but it is no longer trivial'. In other words, Teilhard's argument has moved from the scientific to the theological plane, where theological explanations may not be scientifically testable.

Central to Teilhard's theory of evolution is the conviction that man must take control of the process, since he alone is aware of it: 'Man discovers that *he is nothing else than evolution become conscious of itself*, to borrow Julian Huxley's concise expression'[72]. Man's awareness of evolution is crucial for Teilhard's theory. One might have expected that Teilhard's acceptance of orthogenesis and finalism would not have favored a program of eugenics and genetic engineering, as both processes guarantee a predestined outcome for evolution. Teilhard thinks otherwise: man as the result of his freedom has the biological obligation to assist the progress of the human species. But as pointed out above, in Teilhard's opinion man's freedom does not endanger the direction of evolution in a large human population. In effect he accepts contradictory positions, on the one hand, orthogenesis and finalism, and on the other, human freedom. His effort to reconcile them rests on equating their effect in the light of a large human population, where the play of huge numbers orientates human freedom in a direction already predestined. This sounds like a statistical argument, and more in keeping with the application of statistics by physicists to large numbers of inanimate atoms or molecules to predict the behavior of matter. To use such an approach for human beings is unwarranted as it treats human freedom as if it were amenable to statistics.

Some writers, however, argue that Teilhard has no theory of evolution. For example, Dobzhansky writes: 'Rostand [a biologist] has shocked some admirers of Teilhard by saying that there is no such thing as Teilhard's theory of biological evolution. Now, Rostand is right'[73]. But it is clear from the discussion above that Teilhard espoused both orthogenesis and finalism to account for the direction of the evolutionary process.

NOTES

1 S. Gould, *Hen's Teeth and Horse's Toes*, (London and New York: W.W. Norton, 1983) pp.249–250.

2 Teilhard, *The Vision of the Past*, p.23.

3 Teilhard, *The Phenomenon of Man*, p.294.

4 Ibid., pp.218–9.

5 Teilhard, *Christianity and Evolution*, trans. R. Hague, (London: Collins, 1969) p.139.

6 Schmitz-Moormann, vol.1 p.71.

7 Ibid., p.72.

8 Ibid., p.406.

9 Teilhard, *The Vision of the Past*, p.116.

10 Ibid., p.123. and *La Vision du Passé*, (Paris: Éditions. du Seuil) p.173.

11 Ibid., p.123.

12 XV International Congress. of Zoology and the Linnean Society of London, *Evolution by Natural Selection*, (Cambridge: Cambridge University Press, 1958) p.268. Wallace wrote in his joint paper with Charles Darwin to the Linnean Society in 1858, announcing the theory of Natural Selection: 'It will be observed that this argument rests entirely on the assumption, that *varieties* occurring in a state of nature are in all respects analogous to or even identical with those of domestic animals, and are governed by the same laws as regards their permanence or further variation. But it is the object of the present paper to show that this assumption is altogether false, and that there is a general principle in nature which will cause many *varieties* to survive the parent species, and to give rise to successive variations departing further and further from the original type, and which also produces, in domesticated animals, the tendency of varieties to return to the parent form.'

13 Gould, *Hen's Teeth and Horse's Toes*, p.254.

14 Teilhard, *Christianity and Evolution*, p.139.

15 M. Ridley, *The Problems of Evolution*, (New York: Oxford University Press 1985) p.134.

16 T. Bethell, 'Deducing from Materialism', *National Review,* Aug 29, 1986, p.43.

17 K. Popper, *Unended Quest,* (Glasgow: Collins, 1976) p.168.

18 C. Patterson, *Evolution* (London: British Museum, Natural History) 1978) p.145–6.

19 K. Popper, *New Scientist,* 21 August 1980.

20 Popper, *Unended Quest,* p.167.

21 Gould, *Hen's Teeth and Horse's Toes,* p.255.

22 Teilhard, *The Phenomenon of Man,* p.82.

23 Ibid., pp.120–121.

24 Teilhard, *The Vision of the Past,* p.124.

25 Ibid., p.125.

26 Ibid., p.127.

27 Ibid., p.8.

28 Ibid., p.84.

29 C. Darwin, *Origin of Species,* 1859. See Chapter 6 "Difficulties of the Theory".

30 Teilhard, *The Phenomenon of Man,* pp.82–3.

31 Ibid., p.97.

32 Ibid., p.99.

33 Ibid., p.100.

34 Teilhard, *The Appearance of Man,* trans. J.M. Cohen, (London: Collins, 1965) p.229.

35 Teilhard, *The Phenomenon of Man,* p.140.

36 T. Kuhn, *The Structure of Scientific Revolutions,* 2nd Ed. (Chicago: University of Chicago) 1970.

37 Teilhard, *The Vision of the Past,* p.116.

38   Ibid., pp.121–2.

39   Ibid., p.133.

40   Schmitz-Moormann, Vol IX, p.3932.

41   Ibid., p.3933.

42   Teilhard, *Letters. to Two Friends. 1926–1952*, pp.67–8.

43   Schmitz-Moormann, Vol X, p.4483.

44   H. de Terra, *Memories of Teilhard de Chardin*, p.117.

45   Teilhard, *The Appearance of Man*, p.129.

46   Teilhard, *The Phenomenon of Man*, p.182 It is difficult to discern the precise meaning which Teilhard ascribes to this term. It will be discussed in Chapter 6.

47   Schmitz-Moormann, Vol IX, p.3930.

48   Teilhard, *The Appearance of Man*, p.237.

49   H. Bergson, *L'évolution créatrice*, (Paris. 1907) trans. A. Mitchell as *Creative Evolution*, (London and New York: Random House) 1911.

50   H. Bergson, Les. *deux sources. de la morale de la religion*, (Paris, 1932). Translated by R.A.Audra and C.Brereton, with the assistance of W.Horsfall–Carter, as *The Two Sources. of Morality and Religion*, (London and New York: Random House) 1935.

51   Teilhard, *The Heart Of Matter*, p.25.

52   Teilhard, *Writings. in Time of War*, trans. R. Hague, (London: Collins, 1968) p.151.

53   H. de Lubac, *The Religion of Teilhard de Chardin*, trans. R. Hague, (London: Collins, 1967) p.198.

54   Schmitz-Moormann, Vol X, p.4428.

55   Teilhard, *The Phenomenon of Man*, p.141.

56   T. Dobzhansky, *The Biology of Ultimate Concern*, (London: Rapp and Whiting, 1969) p.116.

57 Teilhard, *The Phenomenon of Man*, p.142.

58 Dobzhansky, *The Biology of Ultimate Concern*, p.120.

59 G.G. Simpson, "Review of the Phenomenon of Man" in *Scientific American*, April 1960, p.204.

60 Teilhard, *The Phenomenon of Man*, p.159–165.

61 T. Dobzhansky, F. Ayala, G. Stebbins, J. Valentine, *Evolution*, (San Francisco: Freeman, 1977) p.503.

62 Dobzhansky, *The Biology of Ultimate Concern*, p.119.

63 E. Mayr, Evolution, *Scientific American*, September 1978.

64 Gould, *Hen's Teeth and Horse's Toes*, p.245.

65 Teilhard, *The Phenomenon of Man*, p.159.

66 Towers, *Concerning Teilhard*, pp 51–52.

67 Dobzhansky, *The Biology of Ultimate Concern*, p.120.

68 Ibid., p.120.

69 Ibid., p.120.

70 Teilhard, *The Phenomenon of Man*, p.308 In a footnote Teilhard notes that 'cosmic involution is positively guaranteed by the 'redeeming virtue' of the God incarnate in his creation' (See Chapter 8 for comment.)

71 G.O. Browning, J.L. Alioto, S.M. Farber, *Teilhard De Chardin: In Quest of the Perfection of Man*, (Cranbury: Associated University Presses, 1973.

72 Teilhard, *The Phenomenon of Man*, p.221.

73 T. Dobzhansky, 'Pierre Teilhard de Chardin as a Scientist' in *Letters to Two Friends, 1929–1952*, p.226.

CHAPTER FOUR

THERMODYNAMICS AND EVOLUTION

> The fundamental pioneering achievement of Teilhard was to make sense out of the two most famous, but apparently contradictory, scientific ideas to come out of the nineteenth century: the theory of biological evolution on the one hand, and the second law of thermodynamics on the other.
>
> —Bernard Towers, *Concerning Teilhard*

Teilhard's mechanism of biological evolution involves radical reinterpretation of the science of thermodynamics. Towers points to the temporariness of the evolutionary process which is seemingly destined to give way before the inexorable second law of thermodynamics. Teilhard was not alone among biologists of his time in voicing concern over the apparent contradiction between the theory of evolution and the second law of thermodynamics. Shortly before his death, in 'The Reflection of Energy' (1953) he voices his life-long concern: 'What still makes contact between physics and biology impossible and in consequence delays the incorporation of the latter in the former inside a generalised physics is ultimately a problem of energy'[1].

At the very beginning of *The Phenomenon of Man* he grapples with the problem. He starts with a discussion of energy: 'Under this familiar name ...physics has introduced the precise formulation of a capacity for action or, more exactly for interaction' (p.42). He then denies the adequacy of physics to describe the course of the universe: 'Let us keep the proofs and indisputable measurements of physics. But let us not become bound and fettered to the perspective of final equilibrium that they seem to suggest' (p.43). Here, at the very beginning of his book, is a repudiation of the science of thermodynamics with its prediction of eventual 'heat death' of the universe, that is, the exhaustion of all energy capable of doing work. These comments are at the same time an indication that the science of thermodynamics is about to form an important part of Teilhard's mechanism and will undergo a substantial reinterpretation. Teilhard rejects the idea that the universe will 'find its stability and final unity *at the end of its decomposition*'.

Before considering the laws of thermodynamics Teilhard states that the universe must be considered as a whole, if a solution to the apparent contradiction between the science of thermodynamics and evolution is to be found: 'The stuff of the universe [is] woven in a single piece ...Structurally, it forms a whole' (p.45). This leads him to re-define energy with reference to space as a whole: 'If the natural unity of concrete space indeed coincides with the totality of space itself, we must try to re-define energy with reference to space as a whole'. From this premiss he draws a surprising conclusion. As 'a universal space is *the only space there is* —we are bound to admit that this immensity represents the sphere common to all atoms. The volume of each of them is the volume of the universe. The atom is no longer the microscopic, closed world we may have imagined to ourselves. It is the infinitesimal centre of the world itself'. This extraordinary statement is based on the laws governing how the attractive forces between atoms are attenuated with increasing distance between them. To use the law to claim that 'the volume of each of them is the volume of the universe' is arbitrarily stretching its applicability. These centers of action, Teilhard asserts, must express themselves 'in a global capacity for action' in duration (p.46). The capacity for action, for Teilhard, is no other than the capacity for the universe to evolve.

Teilhard now proceeds to explain how evolution can be reconciled with the science of thermodynamics. The laws of energy considered from a biological point of view, he says, may be reduced to two principles. The first principle is the first law of thermodynamics: 'During changes of a physico-chemical type we do not detect any measurable emergence of a new energy' (p.50). In other words, the total amount of energy in the universe is constant and no additional energy arises in the course of physico-chemical changes. So every synthesis can only achieved by utilizing the initial available energy in the universe, which means that the energy available for further synthesis, as in the evolutionary process, is depleted. 'The universe', Teilhard writes, is not 'capable of containing an ever greater reality within its embrace'. So Teilhard asks the question: 'Now whence does this increase [as in evolution] come?' (p.51)

The second principle, which is no other than the second law of thermodynamcs, is now discussed. This law adds further restriction, Teilhard remarks: not only is the total energy of the universe constant and unalterable, but the fraction of energy available for doing work decreases as spontaneous physico-chemical changes take place.

> In every physico-chemical change a fraction of the available energy is irrecoverably 'entropised', lost, that is to say, in the form of heat. Doubtless it is possible to retain this degraded fraction symbolically in equations, so as to express that in the operations of matter nothing is lost any more than anything is created, but that is merely a mathematical trick. As a matter of fact, from the real evolutionary standpoint, something is finally burned in the course of every synthesis in order to pay for the synthesis. p.51

Teilhard sees the second law of thermodynamics as predicting the relapse of improbable evolutionary structures into the primeval chaos from which they emerged. He rejects this prediction because it is based, so he thinks, on a preoccupation of science with the 'without' of the world:

> Within the scope of our experience, the material concrete universe seems to be unable to continue on its way indefinitely in a closed cycle, but traces out irreversibly a curve of obviously limited development ....Laboriously, step by step, the atomic and molecular structures become higher and more complex, but the upward force is lost on the way. ...Little by little, the *improbable* combinations that they represent become broken down again into simple components, which fall back and are disaggregated in the shapelessness of *probable* distributions. ....So says science: and I believe in science: but up to now has science ever troubled to look at the world other than from *without?*' pp.51–52.

In 'L'évolution' (1911) Teilhard foreshadowed the idea that science had neglected the 'within' of matter. Among the various theories of evolutionary mechanism Teilhard describes vitalist transformism. This school of transformism insists that life is an energy *sui generis* which science should acknowledge as such.[2] Although he does not opt for any particular theory in this paper, his inclination to Lamarckism and Vitalist Transformism is evident.

The theory of evolution postulates an ever increasing and irreversible biological organization of matter over time, in contrast to the second law of thermodynamics which points to the opposite conclusion, namely that the universe is on the road to heat death, the exhaustion of all available energy and the accompanying break down of ordered structures in the universe into simpler less ordered structures.

Did Teilhard succeed in making sense of the two seemingly adverse tendencies and achieve a pioneering scientific advance? Towers is alone among scientists in thinking so. Towers points to Teilhard's law of complexity-consciousness as running counter to the second law of thermodynamics. This supposedly important discovery of Teilhard will be discussed further in Chapter 6. Because of the law of complexity-consciousness, the 'physical death postulated by the second law of thermodynamics will be seen to have lost its sting' (p.98). But this is not quite the way Teilhard sees it. Teilhard *reinterprets* the science of thermodynamics, rather than opposing it to the law of complexity-consciousness, to avoid the conclusion that the heat death of the universe is inevitable.

Teilhard's anguish over Thermodynamics

It is important to look at the anguish Teilhard displayed over his perception of the science of thermodynamics. Scattered through his writings is concern that an established law of science threatened the theory of evolution. A few examples spanning most of Teilhard's lifetime illustrate Teilhard's worry. In the essay 'The Spirit of the Earth' (1931) Teilhard presents his perception of the problem in tones which do something to account for his influence:

> Once life has encroached so far, only one reality (in so far as it truly exists) remains to confront it, and can be compared to it in size and universality: this is entropy, that mysterious *involution* by which the world tends progressively to refurl on itself, in unorganized plurality and increasing probability, the layer of cosmic energy.[3]

Teilhard voices the same concern in 'The movements of Life' (1928):

> Everything around us seems to be descending towards the death of matter; everything except life. ....It will, we hope, be a future task for science to draw a general picture of things which will synthesize the two apparently opposed phases of entropy and life. Let us note that it has been the achievement of our century to discover once and for all that these are the two great currents identifiable by experience which between them divide the world.[4]

Teilhard made it his life's work to reconcile these great currents. On the way to China in 1929 he wrote:

> Entropy has been replaced for me by 'the highest consciousness' as the essential physical function of the universe.[5]

The mention of 'the highest consciousness' prepares us for the fully developed concept of 'radial energy' in *The Phenomenon of Man*. At the very beginning this work Teilhard sets out to lay the foundation for a reconciliation between thermodynamics and evolution.

Julian Huxley in the introduction to the English translation of *The Phenomenon of Man* describes the evolution of life as 'an anti-entropic process, running counter to the second law of thermodynamics with its degradation of energy and its tendency to uniformity'[6]. But he then adds that 'with the aid of the sun's energy, biological evolution marches uphill, producing increased variety and higher degrees of organization'. That is, he recognizes that the earth is an open system with energy coming into it from outside, from the sun, and thus nothing happens to contravene the second law.

Medawar devotes considerable space to Teilhard's discussion about the apparent conflict between evolution and thermodynamics, especially in the essay 'Herbert Spencer and the Law of General Evolution'[7]. He shows that Teilhard's concern arose from confusion regarding the second law. He begins with a clarification: 'If we confine ourselves to considerations of energetics, there is no problem; or at least no confusion'. By this comment he means that the second law applies to isolated systems and so 'the law in no wise excludes the existence of sub-domains in which entropy may be decreasing, though at the cost of a disproportionate increase of entropy elsewhere'; so that the overall entropy or loss of thermodynamic order of the isolated system increases. Teilhard was confused about the second law because he failed to appreciate the fact that the law applies only to isolated systems. But Medawar concedes that although the answer to the problem that living organisms are thermodynamically open systems has satisfied most physicists, a 'biologist might still protest that even if living systems obey the letter of the Second Law of Thermodynamics, they fail to observe it in spirit'.

Medawar argues that much of Teilhard's confusion arises from regarding biological order as a form of thermodynamic order and describing organisms in evolution as seats or centers of improbability or antichance. Medawar regards these equivalences as faulty, and consequently the 'the antithesis between evolution and entropy' disappears. But Medawar admits that, at least in Teilhard's time, physicists equated a loss of thermodynamic order or increase of entropy with a loss of biological order.

Creation Science and the Second Law

The 'creation scientists' make much use of the second law of thermodynamics to discredit the possibility of evolution, and their adversaries devote a considerable amount of their energy in elucidating what they see as the true nature of the science of thermodynamics. The current debate between evolutionists and 'creation scientists' is of significance with regard to Teilhard's view of thermodynamics. Teilhard accepts the position of the 'creation scientists' with regard to the second law of thermodynamics; namely that it seemed to exclude the possibility of evolution. Both fail to realize that living organisms are open systems, that is, energy pours into the earth from the sun. While evolutionists are quick to point out this fact to 'creation scientists', as seen from two representative examples below, they seem reluctant to do so in the case of Teilhard. 'The problem with 'creation 'scientists'', Ronald Strahan writes,

> is that the second law applies only to systems that are isolated, that is, systems that acquire no more energy than they started with. Life is not such a system. Energy constantly pours into the Earth in the form of radiation from the sun ....Life is, in this sense, a parasitic eddy adjacent to and dependent on the sun, whose energy state is degrading ...The net change in the whole isolated system is indeed increased entropy but along the way this same flow continually supports smaller flows in the opposite direction, that is towards decreased entropy. There is quite clearly nothing impossible about this and it in no way contradicts the second law.[8]

In view of this attack on 'creation scientists' it is surprising that Teilhard is praised by Ian Falconer later in the same book, *Confronting Creationism: Defending Darwin* (1987) (p.150), for his incorporation of evolution into theology when Teilhard fails just where the 'creation scientists' do: to grasp that living systems are not closed and thus do not infringe the second law.

There is also another similarity between the 'creation scientists' and Teilhard. In *Evolution versus Creationism* (1983),[9] a group of American academics engage in a debate with creation scientists on various aspects of evolution. Stanley Freske in the essay 'Creationist Misunderstanding, Misrepresentation, and Misuse of the Second Law of Thermodynamics', makes a statement which could in all fairness be applied to Teilhard:

We must take note of an elementary fact which is often missed in de-
bates on evolution and the second law: In spite of what they claim,
creationists are no longer talking about the second law. (p.288)

'Creation scientists' initially claimed that there was a contradiction between evolution and the second law of thermodynamics by
ignoring the fact that evolving systems are not isolated; now they
preclude entropy decrease in all systems, isolated or not. In doing so,
they assert, evolution is impossible in both open and isolated
systems, that is, impossible under any conditions. They prove this,
says Freske, by introducing their own version of the second law in
which four conditions must be fulfilled. For example, Duane Gish
one of the most articulate opponents of evolution, characterizes as
the answer given by evolutionists to 'creation scientists', that the
second law of thermodynamics applies only to isolated systems. 'An
open system and an adequate source of energy', Gish writes,

are necessary *but not sufficient* conditions, however, for order to be
generated and maintained, since raw undirected, uncontrolled energy
is destructive, not constructive ....a bull in a china shop performs work,
but he neither creates nor maintains organization. The work needed is
particular work; it must follow specifications; it requires information on
how to proceed'[10]

The four conditions advanced by Gish as necessary for biological
organization to be generated within a system are: (1) the system must
be open, (2) An adequate external energy source must be available,
(3) The system must possess energy conversion mechanisms, (4) A
control mechanism must exist within the system for directing,
maintaining, and replicating these energy conversion mechanisms.
The most important of these conditions for 'creation scientists' is that
the system must contain a directing program. Thus something
additional must be added to the system before an entropy decrease,
which Gish identifies with an increase in biological organization, is
produced.

Freske's criticism of the Gish proposal is that it replaces the second law of thermodynamics with something else which is still
referred to as the second law. But there is nothing in classical
thermodynamics to contradict a decrease in entropy being produced
in a system through which energy flows, that is an open system. So
the 'creation scientists' call for a directing program in an open system
before a decrease in entropy can be produced is unnecessary. The

assertion by 'creation scientists', then, that evolution is impossible in both open and isolated systems is not in accord with the second law. Of course the assumption is that evolution is associated with a decrease in entropy. Some recent views[11] on evolution and thermodynamics maintain that evolution is in fact an *entropic* process, that the system as a whole, organisms and surroundings, is accompanied by an increase in entropy and is driven by the entropic increase.

The 'creation scientists' assertion that a directing program is required before evolution can proceed, even in an open system into which energy is flowing, parallels the mechanism advanced by Teilhard. The energy in the universe, according to his view, consists of 'radial energy' and 'tangential energy'. One of these, 'radial energy', falls into the category of a directing program and, like that of the 'creation scientists' is a device to circumvent the second law. Radial energy draws on or responds to tangential energy to drive the evolutionary process, as Teilhard does not see energy in the physicist's sense—tangential energy—as being capable of doing this directly; it has first of all to be converted into or prompt radial energy. Teilhard toys with various ways in which physical energy can be used to set the all-important radial energy in action. The end result is the same as that of the creation scientists; namely that a directing program is necessary before an entropy decrease can occur in the system—in other words, before evolution can take place. Teilhard still wishes to retain the second law, but he is left with something which bears little resemblance to it.

But Teilhard goes much further than the 'creation scientists' in his reformulation of the science of thermodynamics. At no stage do they deny the validity of the first law of thermodynamics, the law of the conservation of matter/energy, namely, that energy/matter can neither be created nor destroyed. But, as will be shown later, Teilhard is prepared to transform this law to suit his evolutionary ideas.

Teilhard's Thermodynamics

In *The Phenomenon of Man* (1940) Teilhard sets out in the most developed form his understanding of the laws of thermodynamics. But these ideas are considerably modified in essays just prior to his death in 1955, particularly in 'Activation of Human Energy' (1953) and 'The Singularities of the Human Species' (1954). The most recent well-researched biography of Teilhard defends his attempt to reconcile the theory of evolution and the second law by suggesting that it opens up a most important field of investigation for science: 'Though Teilhard did not do any better than his colleagues', Lukas writes,

> in explaining *why* matter, whose natural state is one of complete disorganization, kept on associating into larger and more complex 'corpuscles' and progressing upwards to ever less probable states of being, his essay at least focussed attention on this point. To him 'radial energy' was itself the fundamental 'energy' of evolution and the most important field of investigation open to researchers of the future. Only when science had settled on a 'unified theory of energetics', he declared, would it be capable of presenting a comprehensible and 'livable' universe to man. And only when religion encouraged such investigation and integrated its conclusions into its doctrinal statements would it able to present to modern man articulations of the old dogmas of the Creation and Redemption awesome enough to bring him to his knees again.[12]

These comments illustrate the all-embracing nature of thermodynamics in Teilhard's theory of cosmic evolution. Teilhard's thermodynamical theory is of the utmost importance to his biological and theological conclusions.

The Phenomenon of Man begins in chapter one with 'The Stuff of the Universe' and proceeds to Teilhard's account of thermodynamics in chapter two, 'The Within of Things'. These two short chapters, in particular the section under the sub-heading 'The Problem of the Two Energies', are of the utmost importance in understanding the foundations upon which his evolutionary mechanism is built. 'Without doubt', Teilhard writes,

> *there is something* through which material and spiritual energy hold together and are complementary. In the last analysis, *somehow or other*, there must be a single energy operating in the world.[13]

Physical energy is the normal energy studied by the physicists. Spiritual energy Teilhard identifies with 'the objective reality of psychical effort and work'. No one doubts the reality of such energy, says Teilhard, 'yet there is none that is more opaque scientifically'. But his acceptance of the fact that there is only one energy in the universe, immediately raises the question of the relationship between material and spiritual energy. Although Teilhard does not pretend to offer 'a truly satisfactory solution of the old problem of spiritual energy', yet in his opinion his solution is the one science 'should adopt as its line of research and the kind of interpretation it should follow'.

The sub-section 'A Line of Solution' (p.64) must not be overlooked for an understanding Teilhard's reinterpretation of the science of thermodynamics. In it Teilhard proposes 'a basis for all that is to emerge later'.

To begin with, Teilhard points to two fundamental energies in the universe, physical and spiritual, and maintains that to avoid 'a fundamental dualism, at once impossible and anti-scientific' there must be a single energy operating in the world.' Furthermore 'they are constantly associated and in some way pass into each other (Elles sont constamment associées et passent en quelque façon l'une dans l'autre)'[14]. Teilhard's basic assumption about these two energies is that 'all energy is psychic in nature': the original English translation in 1959 erroneously has 'physical in nature'. No explanation is given of how physical energy can be psychic in nature. The points to note in the discussion in *The Phenomenon of Man* are the acceptance of only one energy in the universe, psychic, consisting of two components, material and spiritual, which are constantly associated and pass into each other. 'We shall assume', Teilhard writes,

> that, essentially, all energy is psychic in nature; but add that in each particular element this fundamental energy is divided into two distinct components [cette énergie fondamentale se divise en deux composantes distinctes]: a *tangential energy* ...and a *radial energy*.[15] (p.64–5)

Although there is only one energy, its two components have different functions. Tangential energy is the energy with which physicists concern themselves, 'as generally understood by science'. It is subject to the normal laws of thermodynamics; namely its ability to do useful work in a closed system decreases with time, overall the total amount of energy remaining constant. Radial energy, on the other hand, escapes the laws of thermodynamics and is the driving force of evolution, drawing matter 'towards ever greater complexity and centricity—in other words forwards'. Radial energy in someway utilizes physical tangential energy.

Teilhard is entranced by the idea that,

On the one hand, only a minute fraction of 'physical' energy is used up in the highest exercise of spiritual energy; on the other, this minute fraction, once absorbed, results on the internal scale in the most extraordinary oscillations. (p.64).

'The loftiest speculation, the most burning love', Teilhard writes, in *The Phenomenon of Man,*

are, as we know only too well, accompanied and paid for by an expenditure of physical energy ....Yet, seductive though it may be, the idea of the *direct* transformation of one of these two energies into the other is no sooner glimpsed than it has to be abandoned. (p.63–64)

Although Teilhard accepts that in some way tangential and radial energy 'pass into each other', and toys with the idea that the 'soul' is 'the focal point of transformation', he is not prepared to accept a *direct* transformation of the two components of energy. What is the reason for his rejection? "Only a minute fraction of 'physical' energy", Teilhard writes,

is used up in the highest exercise of spiritual energy ....a quantitative disproportion of this kind is enough to make us reject the naïve notion of 'a change of form' (or direct transformation) ...Between the *within* and the *without* of things, the interdependence of energy is incontestable'. (p.64)

So the reader is left with a confused explanation. The two energies 'in some way pass into each other', but there is no direct transformation. Subsequently in 'The Activation of Energy' (1953) and 'The Singularities of the Human Species' (1954) Teilhard rejects even the possibility of the two energies being able to pass into each other. The reasons for his change of mind will be discussed later.

Since in *The Phenomenon of Man* (1940) Teilhard accepts that radial and tangential energy 'in some way pass into each other', it comes as a surprise that he exempts radial energy from the laws of thermodynamics that govern the actions of physical or tangential energy. Explaining the relationship between the two postulated forms of energy, Teilhard says:

First of all, since the variation of radial energy in terms of tangential energy is effected, according to our hypothesis, by the intervention of an arrangement, it follows that as much as you like of the first may be linked with as little as you like of the second—for a highly perfected arrangement may only require an extremely small amount of work. This fits in with the facts noted in Section A above. (p.65)

According to Section A, under the heading, 'The Problem Of the Two Energies', 'only a minute fraction of 'physical' energy is used up in the highest exercise of spiritual energy'. The type of spiritual energy to which Teilhard is referring is thought or emotion. But what relationship is there between these particular spiritual energies and the energy required to effect an evolutionary arrangement of matter? Thought and love may not require much physical energy, but it does not follow that evolution requires little energy for its progress. Even if it were to be shown that evolution required only the minutest amount of energy, as Teilhard suggests, ultimately the available energy in the universe must be exhausted even though the time span might be enormous. But Teilhard insists that 'the entire edifice of the universe is constantly supported at every phase of its progressive "centration' ...by a certain primordial quantum of free tangential energy, which will gradually exhaust itself, following the principle of entropy' (p.66). As we shall see, however, in Chapter 6 the question arises as to why the second law is held in abeyance until point Omega.

Teilhard now moves on to discuss a much more serious problem, the apparent clash of the first law of thermodynamics with his proposed evolutionary mechanism. Referring to the energy in the universe Teilhard states that: 'In each particular element'—by element Teilhard means natural units, such as atoms, molecules, cells, organisms and ultimately human beings—'this fundamental energy is divided into two distinct components: *'tangential energy* which links the element with others of the same order (that is to say, of the same complexity and the same centricity) as itself in the universe; and a *radial energy* which draws it towards greater complexity and centricity'. Centricity is a measure of the consciousness of a particular natural element. 'Moreover, in the system here proposed'. Teilhard writes:

> we are paradoxically led to admit that the cosmic energy is constantly increasing, not only in its radial form, but—which is much more serious—in its tangential form (for the tension between elements increases with their centricity itself). This would seem to be in direct contradiction with the law of the conservation of energy. (p.65)

While Teilhard is well aware of the problem, the solution he offers is far from satisfactory. In fact he offers two solutions. Firstly in a footnote he remarks that the feebler the radial energy of an element "the more will its tangential energy reveal itself in powerful mechanical effects. Between strongly 'centered ' particles (i.e. of high radial energy) the tangential seems to become 'interiorised' and to disappear from the physicist's view. Probably we have here an auxiliary principle which could help to explain the apparent conservation of the energy in the universe" (p.65). Here Teilhard makes the very strange claim that as evolution progresses, physical or tangential energy disappears from the physicist's view so as to maintain 'the apparent conservation of energy'. How the disappearance of physical energy is compatible with the law of conservation of energy is not explained. It should be noted that Teilhard refers to the law of the conservation of energy as 'apparent'. He avoids the incompatibility of his mechanism with the law of the conservation of energy in the case of highly centered elements (high radial energy) by introducing the unwarranted hypothesis that excess tangential energy simply disappears, or as Teilhard describes it, the tangential becomes 'interiorised' and disappears from view.

Strangely, he does not develop this escape route in his proposed mechanism for explaining the apparent conformity of nature to the first law of thermodynamics; instead he opts for limiting the applicability of the first law of thermodynamics to elements of complexity below man, and without a gesture towards any evidence states that this is all that science requires. 'It must be noted', Teilhard writes,

> that this increase of the tangential of the second kind (the only one troublesome for physics) only becomes appreciable with very high radial values (as in man, for instance, and social tensions). Below this level, and for an approximately constant number of initial particles in the universe, the sum of the cosmic energies remains practically and statistically invariable in the course of transformations. And this is all that science requires. (p.66)

But the whole of *The Phenomenon of Man* is about this very situation, the emergence of Man. The reader is left with the conclusion that the emergence of Man is exempt from the laws of thermodynamics, a conclusion which would not be shared with any other scientist. A further difficulty arises: the gradual depletion of tangential energy, 'which will gradually exhaust itself, following the principle of entropy' (p.66). Since radial energy somehow draws from the pool of tangential energy there must be a limit to the ever-increasing organization of matter. In *The Phenomenon of Man* no answer is given to this difficulty, other than an appeal to the existence of point Omega which is supposed somehow to solve the problem. This aspect of his thought will be addressed in Chapter 6. We are told, however, that, 'In no case does the energy required for synthesis appear to be provided by an influx of fresh capital, but by expenditure. ...Nothing is constructed except at the price of an equivalent destruction' (p.51). Hence the conclusion must be drawn that point Omega does not provide fresh energy to sustain the evolutionary process. How, then, can point Omega meet the problems raised by Teilhard?

In summary, the whole section devoted to a discussion of the laws of thermodynamics and evolution is far from offering any solution to the apparent contradiction between the two scientific ideas. Instead, Teilhard shows deep confusion in his efforts to reformulate thermodynamics in support of his evolutionary mechanism.

Entropy in Teilhard's Thermodynamics

There are several definitions of entropy in *The Phenomenon of Man* which Teilhard regards as equivalent. He begins with the accepted thermodynamic account: 'In every physico-chemical change, adds thermodynamics, a fraction of the available energy is irrecoverably 'entropised', lost, that is to say in the form of heat'. He then considers evolutionary change as a particular case of physico-chemical change and sees it as being accomplished at the cost of energy degradation. 'Laboriously, step by step, the atomic and molecular structures become higher and more complex, but the upward force is lost on the way' (p.52). Teilhard then moves from considerations of energy to those of probability: 'Little by little, the *improbable* combinations that they represent become broken down again into more simple components, which fall back and are disaggregated in the shapelessness of *probable* distributions'.

In the essay 'The Movements of Life'[16] (1928). Teilhard accepts that 'everything around us seems to be descending towards this death of matter; except life. Opposing the leveling play of entropy, is life, a methodical construction, ceaselessly enlarged, of a building that grows continually more improbable'. These are constant themes of Teilhard's: evolution runs contrary to entropy and evolution is a movement towards improbability. But, according to Teilhard, there is a form of energy which *increases* with the progress of evolution, radial energy. This energy is a postulate of Teilhard's and it is associated with the growth of consciousness or 'noogenesis', to use his terminology.

In 'Some Reflections on Progress' (1941) he reflects on the preoccupation of the science of physics with the dissipation of energy predicted by thermodynamics:

> For a century and a half the science of physics, preoccupied with analytical researches, was dominated by the idea of the dissipation of energy and the disintegration of matter. Being now called upon by biology to consider the effects of synthesis, it is beginning to perceive that, parallel with the phenomenon of corpuscular disintegration, the Universe historically displays a second process as generalised and fundamental as the first: I mean that of the gradual concentration of its physico-chemical elements in nuclei of increasing complexity, each succeeding stage of material concentration and differentiation being accompanied by a more advanced form of spontaneity and spiritual energy. The outflowing flood of Entropy is equalled and offset by the rising tide of Noogenesis'[17]

Spiritual energy or radial energy is the counter to increasing entropy. The driving force of Teilhard's mechanism is a new form of energy, radial energy. In 'The Grand Option'[18] (1945) Teilhard asserts that although 'the fraction of unusable energy (entropy) is constantly increasing....the ascent of the universe [is] towards increasing improbability and personality'. Consciousness and personality now take their place alongside improbability as the end of evolution rather than the heat death predicted by the physicists.

Teilhard's later views on tangential and radial energies

In *The Phenomenon of Man*, Teilhard writes: 'In sum, all the rest of this essay will be nothing but the story of the struggle in the universe between the unified *multiple* and the unorganised *multitude*' (p.61). It is radial energy which accomplishes the great task of forming higher organisms from simpler structures. As noted earlier, this movement of matter at once brings him up against the problem of the relationship between the components of energy, tangential and radial. But the solution to the problem adopted in *The Phenomenon of Man* is rejected in later essays, 'Activation of Energy' (1953) and 'The Singularities of the Human Species' (1954). In a footnote to the latter essay Teilhard writes:

> Briefly, the 'trick' consists in distinguishing *two* types of energy (deux espèces d'Énergie): the first primary (*psychical or radial energy*) escaping from entropy; and the other secondary (*physical or tangential energy*) obeying the laws of thermodynamics: these two energies *not* being directly *transformable* into one another, but interdependent on one another in their functioning and evolution (the radial increasing with the arrangement of the tangential, and the tangential only arranging itself when prompted by the radial).[19]

The change in emphasis is noticeable; here the reference is to two types of energy (deux espèces d'Énergie) rather than to two components (deux composantes distinctes). Furthermore, both energies are now unable to pass into each other and are merely interdependent. In *The Phenomenon of Man* there is only one energy which is psychic, and this energy has two components, tangential and radial. In the quotation above the tangential and radial energies are merely interdependent on one another and their interconversion is expressly denied. The same position is taken in 'Activation of Human Energy' (1953)[20].

If physical energy is no longer transformable into radial energy, the driving force of evolution, whence is radial energy replenished? In his later essays there is no clear answer as to how radial energy continues to perform its evolutionary function without a source upon which to draw. Later in life Teilhard considered this question as misplaced, as can be seen from 'The Singularities of the Human Species' (1954). No longer is tangential energy postulated as a source of radial energy. Instead, radial energy is the primitive energy and physical energy is a minor product of the interactions between elementary centers of consciousness:

> We [the scientific] community have adopted the habit of reserving for 'tangential' effects (the proper domain of statistics and entropy) *both* the name of energy and the privilege of constituting the primal matter of things; the 'radial' being then regarded as only a subsidiary effect

...But, turning the perspective upside down, why not decide on the contrary that, of the couple under examination, it is the radial that is primitive and consistent, and the tangential being only a minor product statistically engendered by the interactions of the elementary 'centres' of consciousness, imperceptible in the pre-living' but clearly discernible to our experience once matter has reached a sufficiently advanced degree of arrangement? From this point of view, if one accepts it, the edifice of physical laws would remain absolutely intact and valid in the domain of pre-life, where the radial does not yet exist for our eyes ...all would continue to happen as if entropy were in command.[21]

These comments, far from clarifying the problem of energy muddy the stream even further. Tangential energy is now engendered (engendré) by radial energy, and not vice versa as postulated in *The Phenomenon of Man*, where spiritual energy arises from an expenditure of physical energy. Also the two energies merely respond to each other, without being able to pass into each other. But how can tangential energy continue to obey the laws of thermodynamics, as Teilhard says, if it is simply engendered by centers of consciousness? Tangential energy would then increase with evolutionary progress, infringing the First law of thermodynamics, the law of the conservation of energy. As noted earlier in *The Phenomenon of Man*, Teilhard accepts that tangential energy does increase as evolution proceeds.

Teilhard always regarded physical energy as of secondary importance. This is clear from his recasting of the laws of thermodynamics and confining them to the domain of pre-life. Secondly his earlier insistence on the existence of only one energy in the universe led him to conclude that tangential and radial energies must be capable of interconversion. Later he retreated from this position. The reason for the change of heart may have been the insuperable difficulties that the interconversion of tangential and radial energies presented for the laws of thermodynamics. But does the later position of two energies operating at different levels with no interconversion conform any better with the laws of thermodynamics?

Teilhard accuses the scientists in his day of failing to face this fundamental contradiction between the laws of thermodynamics and the theory of evolution. 'In our own day' Teilhard complains that, the two few scientists who have the courage to face the problem squarely seem to be looking for a way out of the difficulties ...by emphasizing the fact that life ...is seen experientially to obey the laws of thermodynamics. (*Activation of Energy*, p329)

The fact that the emergence of life is merely compatible with the second law of thermodynamics, he says, 'avoids the very basis of the problem'. The real problem is how life is 'born and develops in the very heart of the flood of entropy' (p.330). As we have seen, Teilhard's answer involves us in greater difficulties than the position he is criticizing, namely that the emergence of life is compatible with the laws of thermodynamics. Teilhard never departed from the position that the increase of radial energy is irreversible. This must be so, according to Teilhard, because evolution, which is a manifestation of increasing radial energy, is itself irreversible. The grounds upon which Teilhard asserts that the irreversibility of evolution are supposedly scientific will be discussed in Chapter 6.

It is interesting that Teilhard accepts that upon the death of an animal its stored radial energy is transformed into tangential energy (See Chapter 6). He seems unaware that this remark is at variance with his rejection of the direct transformation of the two energies. As Teilhard said nothing more on the subject it is impossible to see how he would have found a way out of the impasse.

The upshot of the discussion above is that Teilhard only gave lip service to the science of thermodynamics in *The Phenomenon of Man*. For he cast doubt on its validity, evidenced by his reformulation of the second law, and more importantly he accepted, contrary to the first law, that physical energy goes on increasing as evolution progresses. His solution of this problem was to confine the application of the first law to pre-life without any good reason. In his later essays he went further and relegated physical energy to being a minor product of the interactions between elementary centers of consciousness. Far from reconciling biological evolution and thermodynamics, as Towers claimed, Teilhard repudiates the whole of the science of thermodynamics.

In view of Teilhard's confusion and unsubstantiated assertions, one cannot accept the attitude of some commentators that Teilhard's work 'distinguishing two kinds of energy may well have a fruitful future'[22].

Radial energy as the driving force of evolution

As Teilhard came to the conclusion that all energy is psychic, it is not surprising to find that he identifies part of energy, radial energy, with the growth of consciousness. The idea of matter possessing a primitive consciousness which becomes more developed as evolution progressed is supposedly one of Teilhard's seminal contributions, but as Teilhard concedes, it was also a Bergsonian notion. The idea can be traced back to the Roman poet Lucretius and behind him to the Greek philosopher Epicurus. In the poem, *De Rerum Natura* of Lucretius, the philosophical disciple of Epicurus, we have several descriptions of the most primitive act of freedom, the 'parenklisis' or the 'swerve' of the falling atoms, which results in fruitful collisions between them, and the subsequent growth in complexity until the primeval 'swerve' manifests itself at the level of the human mind in a radically different form, 'free will'[23]. Teilhard sees the ideas of Epicurus and Lucretius as primitive attempts to explain the coming together of atoms to form more complex structures[24]. The existence of consciousness in matter at all levels of biological organization is a scientific fact for Teilhard. 'Consciousness', he writes,

> transcends by far the ridiculously narrow limits within which our eyes can directly perceive it ....we are logically forced to assume the existence in rudimentary form of some sort of psyche in every corpuscle, even in those (the mega-molecules and below) whose complexity is of such a low or modest order as to render it (the psyche) imperceptible.[25]

Referring to Teilhard's claim, Rideau concurs: 'If spirit exists in man, why should it not be found also deep in the heart of things?'[26]. To which an obvious answer is: Why should it be?

Teilhard's acceptance of radial energy as the internal driving force of evolution had the effect of his attaching little importance to the influence of external factors. For example, one is struck by the absence of any reference by Teilhard to the influence of great climatic changes on evolution. As a consequence it is not surprising that Darwinian natural selection plays little part in Teilhard's mechanism. In fact the term 'natural selection' does not even appear in the index of *The Phenomenon of Man*. This lacuna in Teilhard's thinking struck the paleontologist, Helmut de Terra. Referring to Teilhard's emphasis on the internal driving force of evolution, De Terra writes:

This determinist interpretation of the origin of man also explains why Teilhard bestowed such scant attention on environmental factors. How could an internally governed evolution have been influenced by climatic changes? ...Not to have given sufficient weight to such factors must be regarded as one of the weakest points in Teilhard's magnificent edifice of ideas.

In the case of the last glacial period, it is conceivable that changes in solar radiation had a bearing on the accelerated development of the primates' brain. It is strange that Teilhard makes no mention of such relationships between the Ice Age and anthropogenesis.[27]

In the previous chapter, under the heading 'The Direction of Evolution', it was concluded that Teilhard espoused orthogenesis, that is, he accepted that there is an in-built program in matter which causes it to evolve in a particular direction. It is difficult to see how Teilhard could accept orthogenesis and at the same time ascribe a role to natural selection. Gaylord Simpson makes a similar point: 'Teilhard repeatedly contrasted [natural] selection with orthogenesis and indeed usually treated them as opposites'[28] Teilhard does concede in a footnote in *The Phenomenon of Man* that he has been accused 'of showing too Lamarckian a bent in the explanations which follow, of giving an exaggerated influence to the Within in the organic arrangement of bodies' (p.149). These issues will be examined in the following chapter together with Teilhard's attitude to the Darwinian and Lamarckian mechanisms. Particular attention will be given to the perception that he effected a reconciliation of the two approaches.

NOTES

1 Teilhard, *Activation of Energy*, trans. R.Hague, London: Collins, 1970. p.329.

2 Schmitz-Moormann, Vol.1, p.71.

3 Teilhard, *Human Energy*, trans. J.M. Cohen, London: Collins, 1969, p.22.

4 Teilhard, *The Vision of the Past*, trans. J.M. Cohen, London: Collins, 1966, pp.149–150.

5 Teilhard, *Letters from a Traveller*, trans. R. Hague et al., London: Collins, 1962, p.151.

6 Teilhard, *The Phenomenon of Man*, p.27.

7 P. Medawar, *The Art of the Soluble*, Harmondsworth: Pelican, 1969, p.45.

8 D.R. Selkirk and F.J. Burrows (eds.), *Confronting Creationism: Defending Darwin*, Sydney: New South Wales University Press, 1987, p.106.

9 J.P. Zetterberg, *Evolution versus Creationism*, Phoenix: Oryx Press, 1983.

10 Ibid., p.185.

11 D.R. Brooks and E.O. Wiley, *Evolution as Entropy: Toward a Unified Theory of Biology*, Chicago and London: University of Chicago Press, 1988.

12 M. and E. Lukas, *Teilhard*, Glasgow: Collins, 1977, pp.308–9.

13 Teilhard, *The Phenomenon of Man*, p.63.

14 Ibid., p.64. and *Le Phénomène humain*, Paris: Éditions du Seuil, 1955, p.61.

15 Ibid., p.64–5. and ibid., p.62.

16 Teilhard, *The Vision of the Past*, p.143.

17 Teilhard, *The Future of Man*, trans. N. Denny, London: Collins, 1964, p.78.

18 Ibid., p.48.

19 Teilhard, *The Appearance of Man*, p.265. / *L'Apparition de l'homme*, Paris: Éditions du Seuil, 1956, p.363.

20 Teilhard, *Activation of Energy*, p.393.

21 Teilhard, *The Appearance of Man*, p.265.

22 Le Morvan (ed), *The Human Search*, p.61.

23 C. Bailey, *The Greek Atomists and Epicurus*, New York: Russell and Russell, 1928.

24 Teilhard, *Activation of Energy*, p.234.

25 Teilhard, *The Phenomenon of Man*, pp.301–302.

26 Rideau, *Teilhard de Chardin—A Guide to his Thought*, trans. R.Hague, London: Collins, 1967, p.99.

27 H. De Terra, *Memories of Teilhard de Chardin*, trans. J.M. Brownjohn, London: Collins. 1964, pp.46–48.

28 G. Simpson, *Scientific American*, April 1960, p.204.

CHAPTER FIVE

LAMARCK, DARWIN AND WALLACE

> We have heard a great deal in the last few years about transformism being in decline. This fall from favour actually affects only certain particular forms of transformism, in which the essentially evolutionary idea is associated either with particular explanations or certain philosophical views, such as Darwinism (natural selection), Lamarckism (adaptation under the influence of surroundings), and more generally all the naive theories that try to reduce the development of life to a few lines of simple evolution followed by a uniform movement under the influence of purely mechanical factors. True enough, none of these different individual theories is any longer considered satisfactory, for life appears more and more complicated every day.
> —Teilhard de Chardin, *The Vision of the Past*

Teilhard's insistence on radial energy as the internal driving force of evolution naturally raises the question of his attitude to the Darwinian and Lamarckian theories. Turk claims that Teilhard effected a reconciliation between the Darwinian and Lamarckian theories and writes:

> This is where Teilhard helps us considerably ...If the views of Darwin and Lamarck can be reconciled in this way and found operative in the interpretation of the patterns which we see in the evolution of organisms, very much will have been achieved. This seems to me an example of the germinal nature that can inhere in much of Teilhard's work and an indication of the role it may yet be seen to play in the history of science.[1]

But Teilhard dismisses both Darwinism and Lamarckism as 'naive'. The reason he gives for this opinion is that he sees both theories as postulating a mechanism which involves purely 'mechanical factors'. His referring to Darwinism as 'natural selection' emphasizes what he considers to be the external mechanism of the Darwinism: the survival of the fittest by factors extrinsic to the organism. And characterizing Lamarckism as adaptation under the influence of surroundings likewise focuses on what Teilhard regards as the purely mechanical response of organisms to external conditions. Whether this is a fair description of the two theories remains to be seen. He is preparing his readers for his own theory of mechanism. 'To be a transformist', he writes, as I have often said is not to be a Darwinian or a Lamarckian or the disciple of any particular school. It is simply to admit that the appearance of living creatures on earth obeys an ascertainable law, whatever that law may be.[2]

His reference to an ascertainable law governing evolution is a clear indication that his intention is to present such a law, ruling out Dobzhansky's opinion that Teilhard did not present or intend to present a theory of evolutionary mechanism.

Teilhard and Darwin

Darwin's theory was based on four fundamentals, two of which were also consistent with the theory of Lamarck. The first is that the world is not static but evolving. Species change continually, new ones originate and others become extinct. The second was that the process of evolution is gradual and continuous, it does not consist of discontinuous saltations or sudden changes. Darwin's other two fundamentals were essentially new. One was common descent, in contrast to Lamarck's view that each organism or group of organisms represented an independent evolutionary line, which began in spontaneous generation and constantly strove for perfection. Instead, Darwin held that similar organisms were related and descended from a common ancestor. He implied that all living organisms might be traced back to a single origin of life. The fourth and major fundamental of Darwin's theory was natural selection. Evolutionary change is not the result of any mysterious drive nor is it a simple matter of chance. It is the result of a two-step process of selection. The first step is the production of variation. In every generation, according to Darwin, an enormous amount of variation is produced. The second step is selection through survival in the struggle for existence. In most species of animals and plants a set of parents produces thousands if not millions of offspring. The ideas of Thomas Malthus suggested to Darwin that very few of the offspring could survive. The survivors would be those with the most appropriate combination of characters for coping with the environment, including climate, competitors and enemies. Their characteristics would be transmitted to the next cycle of selection.

Ernst Mayr in *One Long Argument: Charles Darwin and the Genesis of Modern Evolutionary Thought*[3] (1991) observes that is a mistake to see Darwin's theory of evolution as a unitary entity. The reason for seeing this as a mistake is 'that organic evolution consists of two essentially independent processes: transformation in time and diversification in ecological and geographical space. The two processes require a minimum of two entirely independent and very different theories' (p.35). Mayr lists five theories as part and parcel of what is known as Darwinism. The first four theories are what most modern evolutionists would see as the 'fact' of evolution; the fifth is its theory of mechanism, natural selection.

Natural Selection

Charles Darwin and Alfred Russel Wallace in separate papers made the first public statement of their theory of evolution by natural selection on the 1 July 1858 before the Linnean Society of London[4]. Darwin in his paper, 'On the variation of organic beings in a state of nature; on the natural means of selection; on the comparison of domestic races and true species', reflects how he first became aware of the enormous disparity between the approximately constant amount of food available and the geometrical increase of organisms, from reading the Robert Thomas Malthus' *The Essay on the Principle of Population* (1798). Darwin deduced that more organisms are produced than can survive. Those 'individuals are preserved, whether in the egg, or larval, or mature state, which are best adapted to the place they fill in nature' (p.263) and he named this process 'Natural Selection' (p.265). He also saw a secondary selection pressure 'at work in most unisexual animals, tending to produce the same effect, namely the struggle of the males for the females'.

Wallace in his contribution, 'On the tendency of varieties to depart indefinitely from the original type', refuted 'one of the strongest arguments which has been adduced to prove the original and permanent distinctness of species'. This argument was 'that *varieties* produced in a state of domesticity are more or less unstable, and often have a tendency, if left to themselves, to return to the normal form of the parent species; and this instability, even of those occurring among wild animals in a state of nature, ...constitute[s] a provision for preserving unchanged the originally created distinct species' (p.268). Wallace argues that:

The essential difference in the condition of wild and domestic animals is this, that among the former, their well-being and very existence depend upon the full exercise and healthy condition of all their senses and physical powers, whereas, among the latter, these are partially exercised, and in some cases are absolutely unused. ...The domestic animal has food provided for it. ....Again, in the domesticated animal all variations have an equal chance of continuance; and those which decidedly render a wild animal unable to compete with its fellows and continue its existence are no disadvantage whatever in a state of domesticity.' (pp.275–276).

Darwin, in a letter to Wallace dated 25 January 1859, conceded that Wallace's paper was the more impressive contribution: 'Everyone whom I have seen has thought your paper very well written and interesting. It puts my extracts (written in 1839, now just twenty years ago!), which I must say in apology were never for an instant intended for publication, in the shade'[5].

Wallace, however, in 'The Development of Human Races under the Law of Natural Selection'[6] (1870, an altered version of his 1864 essay 'The Origin of Human Races) came to differ from Darwin in maintaining that Man did not emerge by the unaided operation of natural selection. But it is in 'The Limits of Natural Selection Applied to Man' (1870) that we find the clearest expression of this view: 'the great laws which govern the material universe were insufficient for his production, unless we consider (as we may fairly do) that the controlling action of such higher intelligences is a necessary part of those laws ...some more general and fundamental law underlies that of 'natural selection''[7]. Although Wallace conceded in *Darwinism*[8] (1889) that his earlier objections to the inadequacy of natural selection to account for Man's unique bodily features were unfounded, he still exempted his moral and intellectual qualities.

But Wallace was not happy with the term 'natural selection' which he and Darwin had used. Of particular importance is Wallace's letter to Darwin, 2 July 1866. To avoid misunderstandings he urges Darwin in the next edition of *The Origin of Species* to replace the term 'natural selection' with 'the survival of the fittest' (an expression favored by Hebert Spencer). The reasons he gives for the change reveal Wallace's perspicacity. 'The theory of natural selection', Wallace writes in reporting a common objection, 'requires the constant watching of an intelligent "chooser", like man's selection to which you so often compare it'. Wallace tells Darwin that the problem arises from his choice of the term Natural Selection by which he frequently gives the impression of personifying nature. Whereas by adopting Spencer's term 'Survival of the Fittest' the plain expression of the *fact* is made evident; "Natural Selection' is a metaphorical expression of it, and to a certain degree *indirect* and *incorrect*, since, even personifying Nature, she does not so much select special variations as exterminate the most unfavourable ones"[9]. Wallace also expressed his concern that Darwin uses the term Natural Selection in two senses. In the first sense Darwin refers to the simple preservation of favorable and the rejection of unfavorable variations, in which it is equivalent to 'survival of the fittest'; and in the second sense he uses the term for the *effect* or *change* produced by the preservation, "as when you say 'to sum up the circumstances favourable or unfavourable to natural selection', and again, 'isolation, also, is an important element in the process of natural selection'". In the second sense it is not merely 'survival of the fittest', but *change* produced by survival of the fittest, that is meant.

As early as 1911 in 'L'évolution' Teilhard sees natural selection as achieving no more than the adaptation of a species to its surroundings by eliminating unfit individuals. He dismisses Darwinian natural selection, as incapable, by itself, of producing new characters in a species ['elle parâit incapable de faire croître, à elle seule, un caractère'[10]]. Neo-Darwinism, which combines the theory of natural selection with Mendelian genetics, is dismissed because it is in large part artificial, and does not take sufficient account of the environment ['Mais elle est en grande partie artificielle, et tient pas assez compte du 'milieu''[11]]. He never departed form this view.

It is noteworthy that the Darwinian term 'natural selection' is not mentioned in Teilhard's major scientific work, *The Phenomenon of Man* (1940), even though Darwin is referred to often. Oddly, Teilhard equates Darwinism with evolution by chance. In 'The Transformation and Continuation in Man of the Mechanism of Evolution' (1951) he writes:

> However little one may, by conviction or temperament, be 'Darwinist', it is impossible to deny the immense part (at least in the first stages of the phenomenon) played by chance effects in the appearance and intensification of life within our universe.[12]

The 'appearance and intensification of life' are ascribed to chance effects. By chance effects Teilhard appears to mean those which are unplanned, unintended or unexpected. How these chance effects arise is not discussed.

Again in *Man's Place in Nature* (1949) he ponders on three possible driving forces of evolution. The first is Darwinian natural selection. 'Should we first (this is the materialist line)', Teilhard writes,

> ascribe the enigmatic power of corpusculation to an automatic force of natural selection, *sui generis*, which drives matter (when it has succeeded, by the statistical operation of chance, in escaping from disorder and simple crystallisation) first to plunge over, and then, snow-balling, to roll with increasing momentum down the slope of a continually increasing complexification?'[13]

This quotation is very important as it comes from a period late in his life and thus represents his mature understanding of Darwinian natural selection. Consider the phrase 'when it has succeeded': to what does 'it' refer? Of course 'it' is matter. And how does matter escape from disorder? The answer is 'by the statistical operation of chance'. So natural selection, as understood by Teilhard, only comes into play when matter has escaped from disorder by the statistical operation of chance. In other words Teilhard sees Darwinism primarily as the operation of chance.

Again in a letter to Julian Huxley in 1953 he equates Darwinism with the statistical operations of chance. 'I am completely with you', Teilhard writes,

> in admitting that the prolonged effect, statistically, of large numbers is capable of starting a drift of some part of the universe towards the impossible. But how are we to explain the property we find in natural selection of persistently causing to increase in the world that particular form of the Improbable that leads to the most organically centered (and hence most conscious) arrangements?[14]

Here he goes even further than in the previous quotation and appears to *equate* natural selection with the statistical outcome of chance effects. He questions how a statistical outcome of chance effects can give rise to consciousness. Darwinism, as he understood it, offers no explanation.

In 'The Transformation and Continuation in Man of the Mechanism of Evolution' (1951) he shows the same tendency to ascribe the Darwinian driving force of evolution to chance. 'In other words', he writes, 'supposing we admit that, under the tentative play of chance, the *Weltstoff* behaves, by nature, as though by preference it fell into those forms of arrangement which are at the same time the richest, the most closely associated, and the most fully centered'.[15]

Simpson in 'The Divine Non Sequitur'[16] (1973) has rightly criticized Teilhard's identification of Darwinian natural selection with a statistically chance occurrence (According to the Darwinian theory, evolution, of course, comes about by chance, if chance is contrasted with intention). 'Teilhard', Simpson writes, 'spoke of Darwinism or Neo-Darwinism as evolution by chance. He did not deny that a process so labeled occurs, but he considered it unimportant. He betrayed a complete failure to grasp the theory that he called ' Neo-Darwinism" (p.92). Simpson says that he 'searched in vain for any clear statement on that subject [natural selection] by Teilhard'. It is unfortunate that he missed the quotations above, as they show that Teilhard did see Darwinism as evolution by chance. Interestingly, Simpson agrees with a French scientist, Georges Pasteur, who declared in 1971 that the French mentality in general is incapable of understanding natural selection (p.96). The absence of any mention of natural selection in *The Phenomenon of Man* is all the more puzzling in view of the large amount of space devoted to 'orthogenesis'. As orthogenesis was espoused by Teilhard one would have expected some discussion by him of Darwinian natural selection. 'Far from envisioning evolution by chance alone', Simpson writes, the Darwinian theory 'is the only theory of evolution that gives a role to a nonchance, directional process ...that process, the basic Darwinian factor, is natural selection' (p.92). Simpson is of course wrong, or at any rate misleading, in saying that (because natural selection is not a statistically chance process) it is a directional process.

In a footnote to *The Phenomenon of Man*, that will be referred to again, Teilhard mentions the Darwinian play of external forces and chance. 'I shall be accused', he writes,

> of showing too Lamarckian a bent in the explanations which follow, of giving an exaggerated influence to the *Within* in the organic arrangement of bodies. But be pleased to remember that, in the 'morphogenetic' action of instinct as here understood, an essential part is left to the Darwinian play of external forces and to chance. It is only really through strokes of chance that life proceeds, but strokes that are recognized and grasped—that is to say, psychically selected. (p.149)

But as we have seen earlier the phrase, 'the Darwinian play of external forces and ...chance', appears to mean no more than 'the statistical operation of chance'. In Teilhard's theory of evolutionary mechanism another selective mechanism is introduced, 'psychic selection'. Strokes of chance are recognized and selected by the organism itself. In spite of his protestations to the contrary his description is clearly Lamarckian. Selection is achieved by a psychic 'désir' of the organism. This will be discussed later.

But what is to be made of the following remark?

> Despite all the waste and ferocity, all the mystery and scandal it involves, there is, as we must be fair and admit, a great deal of biological efficiency in the *struggle for life*. In the course of this implacable contest between masses of living substance in irresistible expansion, the individual unit is undeniably tried to the limits of its strength and resources. 'Survival of the fittest by natural selection' is not a meaningless expression, provided it is not taken to imply either a final ideal or a final explanation.

> But it is not the individual unit that seems to count for the most in the phenomenon. What we find within the struggle to live is something deeper than a series of duels; it is a conflict of chances. By reckless self-reproduction life takes its precautions against mishap. It increases its chance of survival and at the same time multiplies its chance of progress.[17]

The first point to note is the peculiar phrase, 'Survival of the fittest *by* [my emphasis] natural selection', a combination of the Darwin's 'natural selection' and Spencer's 'survival of the fittest'. The expression is tautological, as we have seen from Wallace's remarks mentioned earlier. But Teilhard seems to think that natural selection is the mechanism by which the fittest survive. Whereas the phrase simply says that the fittest survive because the fittest survive. Also the first part of this comment appears to support Darwin's view of the struggle for existence. But he adds that there is 'something deeper than a series of duels; it is the conflict of chances'. It is difficult to see how the conflict of chances can be reconciled with Darwinian natural selection.

Later in life in the essay 'The Transformation and Continuation in Man of the Mechanism of Evolution' (1951) Teilhard gives a clear indication of his failure to understand natural selection or the 'survival of the fittest. 'We have just spoken of "specially favoured arrangements"'. What precisely should we understand by this expression', Teilhard asks, *'on which everything depends?'*

> In the classic formulations of 'Darwinian transformism', this nice point is generally expressed as 'the survival of the fittest'. To my mind, however, the phrase is unfortunate and unsatisfactory, and for two reasons.
>
> In the first place, because it is too vague and lends itself to no precise standard of measurement. And secondly, because by expressing a purely *relative* superiority among 'arrangements', it does not bring out that factor in the rise of life which, going beyond the effects of competition, gives unmistakable evidence of an exuberant tendency to expand and a sense of absolute advance.[18]

Teilhard finds the notion of the survival of the fittest 'quite useless', and suggests that it be replaced by 'the survival of the most complex', as it offers an explanation for the direction of evolution. 'Supposing, on the other hand we substitute *'most complex'* in our formula, for *'fittest'*, Teilhard writes,

> as an explanation (and, still more as a standard of measurement) of this so clearly oriented (or polarized) trend, to speak of 'the greatest capacity for survival in the organisms' is *quite useless* [my emphasis]. On the other hand, the situation is clarified and can be seen with accuracy if we envisage, as the basis of cosmic physics, the existence of a sort of second entropy (or anti-entropy) which, as an effect of the chances that are seized, draws a portion of matter in the direction of continually higher forms of structurization and centration.[19]

It is true that the fittest do survive and that the expression is not merely a tautology. But do the complex organisms have a survival advantage? Gould has answered this question earlier: 'Most animal species are insects, mites, copepods, nematodes, mollusks, and their cousins'[20]. They all have a remarkable rate of survival even though they are not complex in Teilhard's understanding of the term. Survival of the most complex does not appear to offer a better measure of survival than the survival of the fittest or a reason for the present distribution of organisms. But Teilhard does not address this issue. He is looking for a term which encapsulates a better explanation of the direction of evolution. It should be noted that chance effects are still an important aspect of the evolutionary process—'under the tentative play of chance'—but in Teilhard's mechanism of evolution certain 'chances are seized' by the organism rather than sifted by Darwinian natural selection.

Teilhard does refer to the term natural selection in some of his writings but always without a clear indication of what he means by the term. In the essay 'The Human Bound of Evolution'[21] (1948) he briefly considers the theories of Darwin and Lamarck. 'From the early beginnings of biological evolutionary theory, in the nineteenth century', he writes, 'two trends of thought have prevailed in scientific circles, developing side by side without mingling to any appreciable extent' (p.199). He is in no doubt that the world of living forms is the outcome of increasingly complex association of the material corpuscles of which the universe is composed. The important question is 'the generative mechanism of this "complexification"'. Teilhard begins by stating that matter is involved in a process 'which causes it to *arrange itself*'. He then considers the mechanisms which might bring about this association. Is it from within or from without? 'Does it proceed from within', he asks,

> being conceived and ensued *by psychic forces analogous to our human power of invention* [my emphasis]? Or does it simply come from outside, through the *automatic* selection of the more stable (or progressive) groupings among an immense number of combinations fortuitously and incessantly produced in Nature? It is curious to note how since the time of Lamarck and Darwin these two theories, while deepening in their respective ways, have become more sharply opposed. And with varying fortunes. Neo-Darwinism at present holds the ascendancy in the eyes of biologists, partly owing to a clearer and statistically sub-stantiated definition of the 'fittest', but principally because of the immense part, now recognised by modern genetics, played by the 'ac-tion of large numbers' in the formation of species. (p.199)

These comments are unexpected in view of his rejection of the term 'the survival of the fittest' as 'quite useless' as an explanation. For now he sees the notion as holding the ascendancy among biologists owing to 'a clearer and statistically substantiated definition of the 'fittest''. But reading on we see that Teilhard refers to Darwinism as the play of chance selection: 'It then appears that if the neo-Darwinians are right (as they possibly and indeed probably are) in claiming that in the pre-human zones of Life there is nothing but the play of chance selection to be detected in the advance of the organised world, from the time of Man, on the contrary, it is the neo-Lamarckians who have the better of the argument, since at this level the forces of arrangement begin to be clearly manifest in the process of evolution' (p.200). Once again he describes Darwinian natural selection as chance selection. The expression is unfortunate as natural selection is not chance selection but the selection of variations which are best adapted to survive.

Teilhard was at pains to contrast his theory of mechanism with Darwin's as a movement from within the organism rather than imposed from outside. While conceding a role to chance at the lower levels of evolution, Teilhard maintained that the driving force is interiorized as the process continues. 'By its very nature', he writes,

> as the cosmic stuff's power of self-arrangement is realized more fully, so there tends to be a gradual *interiorization* of its driving force and the methods it uses. As a universal experience of things teaches us, the increasing complexification of matter, while in its origins principally the effect of chance, is gradually shot through and loaded with 'choice'.[22]

Again Teilhard sees evolution as proceeding by chance, at the lower levels of biological organization. As evolution proceeds 'choice' becomes the important factor. In monocellular beings the power of self-arrangement is 'forcibly imposed or automatic; but among highly cerebralised beings it tends to become one of *active choice*'[23]. This statement is a development of the footnote in *The Phenomenon of Man* (p.149), which has been alluded too already, in which Teilhard sees the organism itself utilizing 'Darwinian chance' through its 'desire' for a particular arrangement.

Teilhard had reasons other than scientific reasons for rejecting Darwinism. At the very outset of *The Phenomenon of Man* a clue is given: 'Has science ever troubled to look at the world other than from *without?'*(p.52). And for him the Darwinian theory of mechanism was the theory which gave emphasis to extrinsic factors in directing evolution. Extrinsic factors he sees as incapable of guiding creation to the climax of the evolutionary process, point Omega.

Gradualism

An important feature of Darwinism is the gradualness of evolutionary change. In the face of difficulties Darwin insisted that evolution took place through infinitesimally small changes over vast periods of time. 'Natural selection', Darwin writes, can act only by the preservation and accumulation of infinitesimally small inherited modifications, each profitable to the preserved being; and as modern geology has almost banished such views as the excavation of a great valley by a single diluvial wave, so will natural selection, if it be a true principle, banish the belief of the continued creation of new organic beings, or any great and sudden modification in their structure'[24]

So important was the hypothesis of gradualness to Darwin's theory of evolutionary mechanism that in Chapter 6 of *The Origin of Species* he goes as far as saying: 'If it could be demonstrated that any complex organ existed [he has just discussed the evolution of the eye], which could not possibly have formed by numerous, successive, slight modifications, my theory would absolutely break down'. As noted earlier Popper makes the comment that 'Gradualness is from a logical point of view, the central prediction of the theory [Darwinism]. (It seems to me that it is its only prediction.)'.

What part does gradualism play in Teilhard's theory of mechanism? Teilhard is not clear on this matter. On the one hand he appears to accept Darwinian gradualism. 'Only a few years ago', Teilhard remarks, writing in 1938,

> what I have just said concerning the gradual conversion of the 'granule' of matter into the 'granule' of life might have been thought of as being suggestive, but at the same time as unfounded, as the first dissertations of Darwin or Lamarck on evolution.[25]

On the other hand he sees the birth of intelligence as a macromutation:

> We are happy to admit that the birth of intelligence corresponds to a turning in upon itself, not only of the nervous system, but of the whole being. What at first sight disconcerts us, on the other hand, is the need to accept that this step could only be achieved *at one single stoke* ....it is impossible to imagine an intermediary individual at this precise level. (p.171)

The concept of macromutation is the belief that evolution sometimes, if rarely, takes place, not only by the 'addition' of small variants moulded by natural selection, but also by large-scale changes occurring as it were instantaneously. There are other allusions to macromutations. He describes the appearance of the cell in the evolutionary process as sudden:

From an external point of view, which is the ordinary biological one, the essential originality seems to have been the discovery of a new method of agglomerating a still larger amount of matter in a single unit. This discovery was doubtless prepared over a long period by the tentative gropings in the course of which the mega-molecules gradually emerged; but for all that it was sufficiently *sudden* [my emphasis] and revolutionary to have immediately enjoyed prodigious success in the natural world.[26]

Even in the opening pages of *The Phenomenon of Man* Teilhard refers to evolution in saltational terms: 'in every domain, when anything exceeds a certain measurement, it suddenly changes its aspect, condition or nature ...[there are] jumps of all sorts *in the course* of development' (p.78). Although Teilhard shows some change of mind, his strong opinion is against Darwinian gradualism.

Teilhard and Lamarck

Lamarck's theory is based on four fundamentals. Initially Lamarck formulated only two fundamentals[27]: that the development and effectiveness of organs are proportional to the use of those organs, and secondly that everything acquired or changed during an individual's lifetime is preserved by heredity and transferred to that individual's progeny. In 1815, however, in his textbook of invertebrate zoology[28], he based his evolutionary theory on four fundamentals, and the initial two fundamentals became three and four in his new work. The first is that life by its own force tends continuously to increase the volume of every living body and to extend the dimensions of its parts, up to a limit which the living body imparts. This obscure statement seems to have been ignored by scientists and no one seems to have contradicted it. The second forms the central part of Lamarck's hypothesis, and states:

The production of a new organ in an animal body results from the need which continues to make itself felt, and from a new movement that this need brings about and maintains.

It is this second fundamental which has been principally associated with Lamarck's name. And it has often been referred to as his hypothesis of the evolution of organs by longing or desire; although Lamarck does not teach that the animal's desires affect its conformation directly, but that altered wants lead to altered habits, which result in the formation of new organs as well as in modification of those existing previously. Lamarck uses the word need ('besoin') to indicate the source of this movement. Many, however, take Lamarck's fourth fundamental, which implies belief in the inheritance of acquired characters, as representing the whole of Lamarckism.

As will be seen shortly, Teilhard explains an organism's ability to evolve as a desire ('désir') on the part of the organism rather than a felt need ('besoin').

How does Teilhard stand in relation to Lamarck? He summarizes Lamarckism in 'L'évolution' (1911) as follows: Species take shape and are transformed by the successive addition of characters—acquired mechanically, one after another, by usage and by the action of the environment—and transmitted by heredity (Les espèces se forment et se transforment par addition sucessive de caractères,—acquis mécaniquement, l'un après l'autre, par usage et l'action du milieu,—et transmis par hérédité'[29]). The weak aspect of Lamarckism, he writes, is acceptance of the hereditary transmission of acquired characteristics; he labels the problem 'troublesome' (péniblement).

Teilhard links Lamarckism with vitalistist transformism which proposes that species are transformed by virtue of an internal impulse. This internal impulse, which is not reducible to physico-chemical forces, perfects the species and adapts it to the circumstances. He makes two important points. Vitalistic transformism does not exclude but completes other theories of transformism, and it harmonizes particularly well with Lamarckism. Secondly, vitalistic transformism claims that life is an energy *sui generis* which science should accept as such. This remark anticipates those in Teilhard's autobiographical essay, 'The Heart of Matter' (1950)—'Deep down, there is in the substance of the cosmos a primordial disposition, *sui generis*, for self-arrangement and self involution'[30]. By 1911 Teilhard's inclination to accept Lamarckism complemented by vitalism is already evident.

In the 'Singularities of the Human Species'[31] (1954), just prior to his death, he gives clear evidence of his espousal of the Lamarckian acceptance of the transmission of acquired characteristics. 'Whatever the assurance of our modern neo-Darwinians', he comments,

> when they come to refute anything that looks like Lamarckism, one cannot quite see how in the case of animals (notably insects), a number of instincts, surely hereditary today, can possibly have been established without chromosomic fixation of certain *acquired habits* (methods

of making nests, hunting, etc) which have gradually become germinal
by force of repeated education (with or without social pressure) on a
sufficiently great number of generations. (p.240)

Earlier it was noted that Teilhard did not use Lamarck's word
'need' (besoin), but 'desire' (désir), a prelude to an act of the will, to
explain an organism's ability to evolve. 'What goes on in a phylum at
the moment of its birth', he writes in 'The Transformist Paradox'
(1925),

> is—in my opinion—to think of an invention. An instinctive invention,
> of course, neither analysed nor calculated by its authors. But an inven-
> tion all the same, or, what comes to the same thing, the awakening and
> translation into an organism of a desire and a potentiality [d'un désir
> et d'une puissance] ...Is it not, one would ask, a sort of attraction or an-
> ticipation of a capacity that launched terrestrial animals into the waters
> or the air, that sharpened claws or lightened hoofs. When we see to our
> astonishment, teeth becoming reduced and sharper along the phylum
> of the carnivores (that is to say, alterations in the organs best con-
> structed by their rigidity to escape the modifications resulting from
> usage), how can we avoid thinking of the accentuation of a tempera-
> ment or a passion, that is to say of the development of a moral
> character [un caractère moral: a mental character] rather than the evo-
> lution of an anatomical one? If we do so, immediately the perfect
> correlation of the various organic modifications at the moment of a
> mutation no longer seems in the least extraordinary. If it is no longer
> an isolated morphological element that is changing, but the very centre
> of co-ordination of all the organs that is shifting, the creature can only
> transform itself harmoniously and as a whole.[32]

No excuse is made for this long quotation as it exhibits the dis-
tinctly Lamarckian color of Teilhard's thinking. The difference from
Lamarck is Teilhard's use of 'desir' instead of 'besoin'. Teilhard sees
the desire of an organism to evolve as an 'instinctive invention,
neither analyzed nor calculated'. At a pinch this description ap-
proximates to Lamarck's idea, but it goes further, as the word desire
indicates.

Simpson maintains that Teilhard shared the general but not
completely accurate conception of Lamarckism as the inheritance of
acquired characters and notes that he uses the word 'invention' to
describe it, but he does not expand on the meaning Teilhard attaches
to the term. What is surprising is that he was aware that hardly any
evolutionist considers the Lamarckian factor as real let alone

dominant in evolution—'even if the Lamarckian view of the heritability of acquired characteristics is biologically *vieux jeu*, and decisively refuted'[33], nonetheless 'Up to the level of thought', he writes,

> a question could be asked of the science of nature—the question about the evolutionary value and transmission of acquired characters. As we know the biologist, when asked, tended, and still tends, to be sceptical and evasive; and perhaps he is right, as regards the fixed zones of the body he likes to confine himself to. But what happens if we give the psyche its legitimate place in the integrity of living organisms?...From reflection onwards, the reality of this mechanism [transmission of acquired characters] becomes not only manifest but preponderant.[34]

In these passages he vacillates between accepting and rejecting the inheritability of acquired characteristics.

Gould and Eldredge in propounding their theory of punctuated equilibrium as against Darwinian gradualism maintained that:

> gradualism is a metaphysical stance embedded in the modern history of Western cultures: it is not a high-order empirical observation, induced from the objective study of nature. The famous statement attributed to Linnaeus—natura non facit saltum (nature does not make leaps)—may reflect some biological knowledge, but it also represents the translation into biology of the order, harmony and continuity that European rulers hoped to maintain in a society already assaulted by calls for fundamental social change.[35]

And Colin Patterson, a well-known zoologist, has noted that the Darwinian-Mendelian theory of evolution appealed to capitalist societies and Lamarckian to Marxist societies. In the former case the primacy of the genes and the very gradual rate of change suited capitalism with its emphasis on our heritage from the past and the status quo, whereas rapid change and the possibility of betterment was more in keeping with the ideas of Lamarck. The Lamarckian doctrine, of directly inherited environmental effects, persisted in Russia until the 1960's. 'The reasons', Patterson says, 'were that the Lamarckian doctrine offered a shortcut to the perfectibility of man, his crops and domestic animals, that matched the Marxist programme'[36]. Teilhard was ideologically sympathetic to Lamarckism.

Psychic Selection

'Groping', according to Teilhard, is directed chance and the direction originates from inside the organism, it is not imposed from outside as in the case of natural selection. 'It would be a mistake to see it as mere chance', Teilhard writes,

> groping is *directed chance*. It means pervading everything so as to try everything. Surely in the last resort it is precisely to develop this procedure that nature has had recourse to profusion.[37]

If this comment is taken along with the footnote in *The Phenomenon of Man* (p.149) to which reference has been made above—'It is only really through strokes of chance that life proceeds, but strokes of chance which are recognized and grasped—that is to say, psychically selected'—it is clear that 'groping' is an activity of the organism and is thus appropriately designated 'psychic selection'. It is important to investigate this notion further, for it is Teilhard's substitute for natural selection.

Towers seems to miss the significance of the term 'groping' as used by Teilhard. 'Teilhard speaks of groping', Towers writes,

> as the essential picture of the evolutionary process. The word itself is a stroke of genius. Groping movements are bound to appear random, may indeed be so when taken in isolation and without regard to the eventual outcome.[38]

The point of 'groping' is that it is an acceptance of orthogenesis, in that the eventual outcome is determined in advance (see Chapter 3). It is thus incompatible with Darwinian natural selection. As a consequence it is wrong to see Teilhard's views, as Turk[39] does, as a reconciliation of Darwinism and Lamarckism.

Interestingly, Teilhard believes that the process of groping has not exhausted all the possibilities of evolution: 'Immense and prolonged as the universal groping has been since the beginning, many possible combinations have been able to slip through the fingers of chance and have had to await man's calculated measures in order to appear'[40]. Man, it seems, is to continue the primitive groping of the lower psyches. What this passage emphasizes is the operation of psyche in the profusion of life. Teilhard salutes those who have such a dream as continuing the primitive gropings of the lower psyches.—'they are the pinnacle of mankind' (p.250). The dream includes 'the development of our bodies and even our brains', control of 'the mechanism of organic heredity', the production of 'a new wave of organisms, an artificially provoked neo-life', (p.250). Also included in Teilhard's dream is eugenics and genetic manipulation of the human species to produce a better type of human being. Teilhard's dream of 'grasping the very mainspring of evolution, [and thus] seizing the tiller of the world', will be discussed more fully in Chapter 7.

He sees the process of groping as extending beyond the realm of biology and manifesting itself right up to the evil of disorder and failure in human society:

> Right up to its reflective zones we have seen the world proceeding by means of groping and chance. Under this heading alone—even up to the human level on which chance is most controlled—how many failures have there been for one success, how many days of misery for one hour's joy, how many sins for one solitary saint? To begin with we find physical lack-of-arrangement or derangement on the material level; then suffering, ...then, on a still higher level, wickedness and the torture of the spirit as it analyses itself and makes choices. Statistically, at every degree of evolution, we find evil always and everywhere, forming implacably in us and around us. ...This is relentlessly imposed by the play of large numbers at the heart of a multitude undergoing organisation.'[41]

True to his mechanism Teilhard sees evolution at all stages, from the assembling of primeval particles to moral choices in man, as due to groping and chance (unintended or unexpected events), with the outcome statistically 'imposed by the play of large numbers'. Why evil—and this includes moral evil—should be a statistical necessity is attributed to the manner God chose to create. Teilhard's attitude to physical and moral evil in the light of his evolutionary mechanism will be discussed in Chapter 8.

Divergence and Convergence

In the first edition of *The Origin of Species by Means of Natural Selection or the Preservation of Favoured Races in the Struggle for Life* (1859), Darwin writes under the heading, Divergence of Character: 'The principle, which I have designated by this term, is of high importance on my theory, and explains, as I believe, several important facts'[42].

According to this principle varieties are species in the process of formation. The important question for Darwin was: 'How, then, does the lesser difference between varieties become augmented into the greater difference between species?' McKinney[43] maintains that Darwin, by his own admission, had not worked out satisfactorily the problem of divergence in his earlier sketch of 1842 and his essay of 1844. And there is evidence that Darwin owed the solution of the problem to his reading of Wallace's paper of 1858, 'On the tendency of varieties to depart indefinitely from the original type'[44], even though Darwin's letter[45] to Professor Asa Gray of 5 September 1857 alludes to the principle of divergence. At any rate there is no doubt that Wallace gives the clearer account of the problem and its solution.

Teilhard, however, attributed divergence to the phenomenon of groping. Groping, unlike natural selection, is a process wholly internal to the organism, a conscious selection of choices offered to it. The process of groping leads, so Teilhard asserts, to increasing complexity and associated with it an increase in consciousness. Initially the evolutionary process is divergent but eventually becomes convergent with the appearance of *Homo sapiens*.

Convergence is a notion peculiar to Teilhard and central to his evolutionary mechanism. Convergence is a cessation of branching in the evolutionary tree after the appearance of man. 'The differentiation of groups in the course of human phylogenesis', he writes,

> is maintained up to a certain point, that is to say so far as—by gropingly creating new types—it is a biological condition of discovery and enrichment. After that (or at the same time)—as it happens on a sphere where the meridians separate off at the pole only to come together at the other—this divergence gives place to, and becomes subordinate to, a movement of convergence in which races, peoples and nations consolidate one another and complete one another by mutual fecundation.[46]

Biological evolution continues in man but it is no longer divergent, that is, it is no longer 'gropingly creating new types'. Neither Darwinism nor Lamarckism contemplates the cessation of the formation of new species in the evolutionary process. Teilhard finds the reason for the convergence of the cosmos in the law of complexity-consciousness. This law, he holds, predicts that evolving organisms will become more complex and, associated with this increased complexity, will become more conscious. With the advent of *Homo sapiens* reflective consciousness appears. Why reflective consciousness should give rise to convergence is not clear, but Teilhard claims to have paleontological evidence for it, which is discussed later in this chapter. While the convergence to which Teilhard refers is psychic convergence, he makes it clear that it is biological in nature: 'in as much as it is productive of consciousness [it] is *ipso facto* to be classed as biological in nature and value'[47]. Psychic convergence goes hand in hand with the biological convergence of complexification. One is left with the clear impression that the two are not just complementary aspects of a single process, but one and the same thing.

In 'The Energy of Evolution' (1953) Teilhard speaks of the old and new evolution. It is clear that the old evolution is Darwinism, 'improved by genetics, but nonetheless still essentially the transformism of the nineteenth century'. The old evolution 'is essentially phyletic and divergent—based on chromosomic heredity—and maintained by the combined play of chance and selection'[48]. There are several remarks to be made about this passage. Firstly, he sees Darwinian evolution as 'divergent', that is, as giving rise to an ever-increasing number of species. Secondly, the new variety of evolution, which he refers to as 'a perfected form of evolution', overlays and incorporates the 'old' zoological evolution. Teilhard ascribes three properties to the new evolution. It is self-directing through the process of groping or 'invention'. Secondly, it is characterised by the transmission of acquired characteristics (education); and finally the new evolution is convergent (by socialization) in contrast to the 'old' (p.364).

In the quotation above Teilhard gives what appears to be a non-biological interpretation of the three properties of the new evolution; but this is not his primary understanding of them. We have seen that for him acquired characteristics are transmitted primarily biologically, and not simply by education. Likewise convergence for Teilhard is a biological term as he shows clearly, later in the same essay. He describes convergence as 'a biological concentration of mankind upon itself' (p.371). And in the same passage he illustrates what the term convergence means in relation to the human phylum; for only in Man is this phenomenon manifested. 'Man represents', he writes,

> the single magnificent example to be found of a phylum which, instead
> of branching out, folds back its branches ever more closely—and of

this the most immediately evident consequence is the rise in us of the phenomena of co-invention and co-consciousness. (p.371)

In the 'Singularities of the Human Species' (1954) Teilhard returns to the idea of the 'New Evolution' and refers to its ability to account for the transmission of acquired characteristics:

> This New Evolution' has become capable of utilising for its own ends an equally new form of heredity, much more flexible and richer, without being any less 'biological' on that account. It is no longer a matter only of combinations of chromosomes transmitted by fertilisation, but educative transmission of a complex continuously modified and augmented by conduct and thought.[49]

But it is clear from the same essay that he accepts that repeated education leads to biological transmission of acquired characteristics.

Although Teilhard espouses a Lamarckian view he nonetheless maintains that both Darwinism and Lamarckism are powerless to produce biological convergence. The clue to convergence is the appearance of Man. 'With and since the coming of Man', he writes,

> a new law of Nature has come into force—that of convergence. The convergence of the phyla both ensues from, and itself leads to, the coming together of individuals within the peculiarly 'attaching' atmosphere created by the phenomenon of Reflexion.[50]

So biological convergence leads to psychic convergence. But does this suggested reconciliation between the two theories explain why evolution should be convergent?

It will become clearer in Chapter 6 what great importance Teilhard attached to the idea that evolution is convergent. But it is very difficult to see what experimental evidence he had for the notion of convergence. Helmut de Terra, a paleontological colleague of Teilhard, does not hesitate to say that Teilhard's claim that biological convergence is a scientific fact, and supported by paleontological evidence, is unfounded. 'Teilhard's scientific work', de Terra writes,

> gave the impression that he had already formulated his ideas and was only waiting for external observation to prove them well-founded. Although it is the distinguishing characteristic of all inspiration to hurry on ahead of the scientific evidence ...His vision of the common destiny of mankind had become so much of a mission with him that the new scientific data had to take second place.[51]

De Terra makes a perceptive observation with regard to Teilhard's first visit to the sites of fossil man's discovery in Java. Teilhard
described the visit as 'providential ...I am sometimes disturbed when
I think of the uninterrupted succession of such strokes of luck that
runs through my life. What does it mean, and what is God expecting
of me?'[52]. But 'What was so fateful about this trip?' De Terra asks:

> The concept of convergence was so essential to Teilhard's account of
> man's origin that it is easy to understand why he was so greatly en-
> couraged in that idea by the new-found knowledge of extinct types of
> primitive man in Java. With the disappearance of typal diversity
> within the Java and Peking Man group, modern man emerged as the
> sole surviving species and the one that dominated the entire world.
> What others regarded as a chance phenomenon of survival became, for
> Teilhard, a manifestation of some deeper meaning underlying the
> evolution of man.[53]

Teilhard's theory that *Homo sapiens* was not a descendant of
contemporaneous types, like Java and Peking Man, has the advantage, so De Terra states, of disposing 'of the necessity of a 'missing
link' between man and ape' (p.117). It is of the utmost importance
that Teilhard saw the discovery as confirmation of his theory of
human origins based on the discovery of the Piltdown skull. The
words of his 1920 article on Piltdown Man quoted in Chapter 1 merit
repeating. 'Above all', Teilhard writes,

> it is henceforth proved that even at this time [of Piltdown] a race of
> men existed, already included in our present line and very different
> from those that would become Neanderthal, and also probably very
> different from those that were to become Mauer Man. Thanks to the
> discovery of Mr. Dawson, the human race appears to us even more
> distinctly, in those ancient times, as formed of strongly differentiated
> bundles, already quite far from their point of *divergence* [my empha-
> sis].[54]

He puts the beginning of biological convergence within Man
shortly before the appearance of Piltdown Man in the Pleistocene
age.

There is nothing in Darwinism or Lamarckism or in Teilhard's
concept of groping to suggest that evolution is convergent. One can
only conclude that as early as 1920 he had other reasons for making
such a suggestion. Cultural convergence was obvious but why would
he insist on biological convergence? A clearer understanding of the

importance of biological convergence for Teilhard will emerge in Chapter 6 where his views on noogenesis and point Omega will be discussed.

NOTES

1   A. Hanson (ed.), *Teilhard Reassessed*, Darton, Longman and Todd, London: 1970, p.20.

2   Teilhard, *The Vision of the Past*, p.98.

3   E. Mayr, *One Long Argument: Charles Darwin and the Genesis of Modern Evolutionary Thought*, Cambridge, Massachusetts: Harvard University Press, 1991.

4   XV International Congress of Zoology and the Linnean Society of London: *Evolution by Natural Selection*, Cambridge: Cambridge University Press, 1958, pp.259–279.

5   J. Marchant, *Alfred Russel Wallace*, London: Cassell, 1916, Vol.1, p.135.

6   A.R. Wallace, *Contributions to the Theory of Natural Selection*, London and New York: Macmillan, 1870, p.303.

7   Ibid., p.360.

8   A.R. Wallace, *Darwinism: An Exposition of the Theory of Natural Selection with Some of Its Applications*, London: Macmillan, 1889, p.455.

9   J. Marchant, *Alfred Russel Wallace*, Vol.1, p.170–171.

10   Schmitz-Moormann, Vol.1, p.70.

11   Ibid., p.70.

12   Teilhard, *Activation of Energy*, trans. R. Hague, London: Collins, 1970, p.301.

13   Teilhard, *Man's Place in Nature*, R. Hague, London: Collins, 1966), p.34.

14   C. Cuénot, *Teilhard de Chardin*, trans. V.Colimore, London: Burns and Oates, 1965, p.304.

15   Teilhard, *Activation of Energy*, p.302.

16 G.O. Browning, J.L. Alioto and S.M. Farber (eds.), *Teilhard de Chardin: In Quest of the Perfection of Man*, Cranbury: Associated University Presses, 1973, p.88.

17 Teilhard, *The Phenomenon of Man*, p.109.

18 Teilhard, *Activation of Energy*, p. 302.

19 Ibid., pp.302–3.

20 Gould, *Hen's Teeth and Horse's Toes*, p.249.

21 Teilhard, *The Future of Man*, p.196.

22 Teilhard, *Activation of Energy*, p.303.

23 Ibid., p.303.

24 C. Darwin, *The Origin of Species by Means of Natural Selection*, First edition, London: John Murray, 1859, Chapter 4.

25 Teilhard, *The Phenomenon of Man*, p.82.

26 Ibid., p.86.

27 Lamarck (1809), Philosophie *Zoologique*, 2nd edition, edited by Charles Martins, 2 vols., Paris: Savy, 1873.

28 Lamarck (1815–22), *Histoire naturelle des Animaux sans Vertebres*, 1st edition, 7 vols., Paris: Verdiere, 1815.

29 Schmitz-Moormann, Vol.1, p.70.

30 Teilhard, *The Heart of Matter*, p.33.

31 Teilhard, *The Appearance of Man*, p.208.

32 Teilhard, *The Vision of the Past*, pp. 96–7. /*La Vision du passé*, Paris: Éditions du Seuil, 1957, p.135.

33   Teilhard, *The Phenomenon of Man*, p.179.

34   Ibid., p.178.

35   S. J. Gould, and N. Eldridge, 'Punctuated Equilibria: The Tempo and Mode of Evolution Reconsidered', *Palaeobiology*, 1977, 3, p.145.

36   C. Patterson, *Evolution*, London: British Museum, 1978, pp.177–178.

37   Teilhard, *The Phenomenon of Man*, p.110.

38   Towers, *Concerning Teilhard*, p.51.

39   Hanson (ed.), *Teilhard Reassessed*, p.20.

40   Teilhard, *The Phenomenon of Man*, p.250.

41   Ibid., p. 312.

42   C. Darwin, *The Origin of Species by Means of Natural Selection or the Preservation of Favoured Races in the Struggle for Life*, London: John Murray, 1859, Chapter 4.

43   H. Lewis McKinney, *Wallace and Natural Selection*, New Haven and London: Yale, 1972, p.141.

44   The Linnean Society of London: *Evolution by Natural Selection*, Cambridge: University Press, 1958, p.268.

45   The Linnean Society of London: *Evolution by Natural Selection*, p.264.

46   Teilhard, *The Phenomenon of Man*, p.242.

47   Teilhard, *Man's Place in Nature*, p.102.

48   Teilhard, *Activation of Energy*, p.362.

49   Teilhard, *The Appearance of Man*, p.242.

50   Teilhard, *The Future of Man*, p.165.

51 H. de Terra, *Memories of Teilhard de Chardin*, trans. J.M. Brownjohn, London: Collins, 1964, p.121.

52 Teilhard, *Letters from a Traveller*, trans. B. Wall et al., London: Collins, 1962, p.221.

53 H. De Terra, *Memories of Teilhard de Chardin*, p.120.

54 Schmitz-Moormann, Vol.1, p.214.

CHAPTER SIX

THE LAW OF COMPLEXITY-CONSCIOUSNESS, THE NOOSPHERE AND POINT OMEGA

> When the great war broke out which at one blow brought crashing down the whole structure of a decrepit civilisation—the short-sighted or the ungenerous-minded, those with no faith in the World, knew a bitter triumph. Like the Pharisees, they jeered at the bankruptcy of Progress and the exposed vanity of all social betterment.
> —Teilhard de Chardin, *The Heart of Matter*

> Among the very few things which we are able to predict with certainty in the domain of Life this is one of the surest: nothing, absolutely nothing can prevent mankind, under the *combined influence* of *planetary structure* and *biological properties of human substance*, from becoming (in a [sic] way or in the other) arranged into a single whole.
> —Teilhard de Chardin, *On the Trend/Significance of Human Socialisation*

The Law of Complexity-Consciousness

Towers greets Teilhard's law of complexity-consciousness as 'a really great pioneering concept ...that has a generality about it that makes it applicable to matter anywhere in the universe'[1]. He goes even further: 'This [law] will in due course become known, as is customary in science, as 'Teilhard's Law''[2]. What exactly is the law of complexity-consciousness? 'It is the nature of Matter', Teilhard writes, 'when raised corpuscularly to a very high degree of complexity, to become centred and interiorized—that is to endow itself with consciousness'[3]. This raises several questions. What is meant by complexity? On what grounds does Teilhard base his law of complexity-consciousness? It is of great importance to realize that Teilhard's notion of complexity-consciousness arose from his study of Man, the subject of his seminal work, *The Phenomenon of Man*. On the basis of that critical point in the evolutionary process, the emergence of *Homo sapiens* and consciousness, he hypothesized an attenuated form of consciousness in matter at all levels of complexity below Man. Furthermore he moves forward from Man, by means of the same hypothesis, to map out how evolution will continue right up to its culmination at point Omega.

Teilhard takes up the definition of complexity in some detail in *Man's Place in Nature* (1949). 'Life', he writes, as I shall continue to insist throughout what follows, appears experimentally to science as a *material effect of complexity*. What then, in this particular case, is the exact, technical meaning of 'complexity'?[4]

He begins by dismissing several misunderstandings of the term complexity. It is not simple aggregation, such as a heap of sand which contains many particles, or even the stars and the planets (apart from certain zonal groupings of complexity). Likewise he does not apply the term to 'connote simple, undefined, geometric *repetition* of units (however varied they may be, and however numerous their axes of arrangement), such as we find in the astonishing and universal phenomenon of crystallisation'. He then goes on to give a definition of complexity. 'I shall strictly confine my use of the word', he writes,

> to the meaning of *combination*, i.e. that particular higher form of grouping whose property it is to knit together upon themselves a certain fixed number ...of elements ...within a closed whole of determined radius: such as the atom, the molecule, the cell, the metazoon, etc. (p.20)

The essence of complexity is that it gives rise to 'a certain 'centricity'—not of symmetry, but of action. 'The essence of complexity is not the possession of geometrical symmetry but of a centre of control and action. To put it more briefly and exactly, we might call it "centro-complexity"' (p.21). But what is centricity? 'Radial energy', he writes, 'draws it [an element in the universe] towards even greater complexity and centricity', that is to higher states of consciousness. Centricity is a measure of 'psychic centering'[5]. This association of complexity with consciousness is Teilhard's Law of complexity-consciousness. Natural units, such as the atom, the molecule and the cell, possess a rudimentary psyche as a result of their 'complexity'. Increasing consciousness extends to the 'highest and greatest complexity achieved (so far as we know) in the universe, what I shall later call planetised humanity—the noosphere'.

It is his aim to show that the 'still hardly coherent universe of the physicists and biologists' can be arranged from top to bottom in the light of this concept of centro-complexity. As a very rough approximation, as a measure of complexity for the smallest natural units, Teilhard selects the number of atoms grouped in the corpuscle.

However, he points out that beyond the proteins the number of atoms 'ceases to be measurable or to have any precise meaning'. But this is not the reason for his changing his measure of complexity for corpuscles beyond the proteins. In fact he offers no parameter of complexity beyond the proteins, certainly not until he comes to discuss organisms which possess a nervous system. So there is a vast gap between the proteins and organisms with a nervous system for which there is no reliable measure of complexity. But it is the nervous system as a measure of complexity which is of chief interest to him. He produces what he calls the universe's *curve of corpusculisation*, 'a grouping of the *natural* corpuscles we know according to their two coefficients of length and complexity [number of atoms]'. The natural corpuscles are the 'key-objects identified so far by science in nature, from the smallest to the largest', and include such objects as electron, virus, cell and Man. For Teilhard this curve is of fundamental importance to understanding the universe—'if we know how to interpret it' (p.23).

Two points are drawn from the curve of corpusculisation. Firstly, a third infinity must be added to the usual infinities, the infinitesimal and the immense: the immensely complicated. Teilhard then looks to physics to draw a still more important conclusion. 'Every infinite, physics teaches us', he writes,

> is characterised by certain 'special' effects proper to that infinite ...Once we admit this, we have to ask what can be the specific effect proper to the vast complexes we have just recognised as constituting a third infinite in the universe. If we consider that question carefully, surely we must answer that the specific effect is in fact precisely what we call life—life, with its two series of unique properties: one, a series of external properties (assimilation, reproduction etc.) the other internal (interiorisation).

> If my conclusion is correct, we reach here, in fact, the emancipating prospect on which depends for us the meaning and future of the world. (p.23)

The final startling sentence aside, let us examine the logic of this statement. Teilhard is in no doubt that material complexity produces life and ultimately reflective thought. But can consciousness be the 'specific effect' of complexification? Such a view is at odds with the traditional dualism of matter and spirit. Indeed, Teilhard in his autobiographical essay 'The Heart Of Matter' (1950) states in the clearest terms that Matter and Spirit are 'no longer two things, but two *states* or aspects of the one and the same cosmic Stuff'[6]. On what evidence is Teilhard's the Law of complexity-consciousness based? It is based on his curve of corpusculisation, which he believes gives a *natural classification* of the principal key-objects identified so far by science in universe. From this premiss he argues that 'we are justified, therefore, in adding that it gives an *order of birth*' (p.25).

More importantly, he saw the appearance of Man as the clue to the law of complexity-consciousness. The appearance of the nervous system and the increasing cerebralisation in the case of mammals provide a more suitable standard than the number of atoms by which to ascertain the complexity of higher organisms.

As noted already, Teilhard insists that a rudimentary form of psyche exists in every corpuscle, even in the mega-molecules and below—'just as the physicist assumes and can calculate those changes of mass (utterly imperceptible to observation) occasioned by slow movement'[7]. In a footnote, much earlier in the book, he quotes an almost identical remark by J.B.S. Haldane. What is the logic which forces him to assume a rudimentary form of psyche in the simplest particle? It is no more than a hypothesis that consciousness is 'a specific effect' of complexity. He seems to have taken up and elevated into a law Haldane's remark that, 'We do not find obvious evidence of life or mind in so-called inert-matter, and we naturally study them most easily where they are most completely manifested; but if the scientific point of view is correct, we shall ultimately find them, at least in rudimentary forms, all through the universe' (p.57). Teilhard's comparison with the physics of movement in which the mass of a body increases with increasing velocity is inappropriate. In the case of the mass of a moving body the mass increase may be imperceptible, but it is in principle measurable, whereas in the case of consciousness there is no scientific evidence for the existence of consciousness at the level of pre-life.

Towers, after describing the law of complexity-consciousness as Teilhard's greatest contribution to science, gives as his sole reason for thinking so that it is 'open to verification. If it is tested and found to be valid, and if its implications are accepted'. So Teilhard's law is really no more than a hypothesis, as Towers admits: 'of all the original hypotheses invented by Teilhard, the central one is that which he stated as the 'law of increasing complexity-consciousness''[8]. But Towers is certain that the hypothesis, once tested, will become established as a law. Towers eulogizes Teilhard's radial energy 'largely ignored by scientists ...which leads to a build up of "stored complexity"', from the building blocks of hydrogen (or rather its component sub-particles) to the staggering organisation that is self-reflective man (or, even Christ, who was a man and made of matter)'[9].

An interesting question arises for Teilhard as a result of his law. What is the fate of consciousness upon the death of an organism? 'By death in the animal, the radial is reabsorbed into the tangential, while in man it escapes and is liberated from it'[10]. So the animal's radial energy or consciousness reverts to physical energy, whereas in the case of man it no longer is subject to this reversion and escapes. These comments are not in accord with his own law of complexity-consciousness. Why should the nexus between complexity and consciousness be broken with death, as the law maintains a necessary connection between complexity and consciousness? And why should there be such a distinction between the animal and man? He explains the difference as follows: below the level of self-reflection in Man 'lay the relapse into multiplicity: above it, the plunge into growing and irreversible unification'[11].

Teilhard does not seem aware that this difference between humans and animals is not in accord with his law. One would conclude that the law of complexity-consciousness, stressing the intimate link between complexity and consciousness, would predict that upon death with associated disintegration and loss of complexity, consciousness would cease. Death should mean the end of life, consciousness and reflective thought; instead Teilhard sees death as giving rise to a new and higher form of life for Man. Man escapes the fate of animals. But both humans and animals infringe the law of complexity-consciousness. In the case of animals radial energy or consciousness does not disappear with the breakdown of complexity but is converted into tangential or physical energy. If radial energy is converted into tangential energy upon the death of animals Teilhard is faced with the problem of the interconversion of radial and tangential energies. Teilhard rejected 'the idea of the *direct* transformation of one of these energies into the other'[12]. It is clear that death presents a very serious problem for Teilhard's law.

Why does Teilhard insist in ignoring his own law when it comes to the death of the organism? The answer appears to be that without the survival of consciousness in the case of man his cherished ideas of the noosphere and point Omega would have no support. Another important question arises. Do the surviving consciousnesses of dead humanity form part of the noosphere, or is the noosphere limited to the living? He appears to limit the noosphere to living and evolving humanity as will be come clear later from his discussion of the end of the world. In brief, Teilhard sees the end of the world, point Omega, as the Noosphere reflecting on itself. But he also sees another possibility, a 'split of the noosphere', and only a part of it laboriously 'synthesising itself to the very end'[13]. These remarks indicate that Teilhard confined the noosphere to living and evolving humanity.

The driving force of evolution

For Teilhard radial energy, unlike tangential or physical energy, is not subject to the laws of thermodynamics. Unlike physical energy it is not depleted as it does its work of arranging matter into ever increasingly complex forms. Not only that, it actually increases in magnitude with the increasing complexity it generates, as predicted by the law of complexity-consciousness: 'Moreover, in the system here proposed, we are paradoxically led to admit that cosmic energy is constantly increasing, not only in its radial form, but much more serious—in its tangential one'[14].

In handling these two separate problems of increasing radial energy and increasing tangential energy, Teilhard tackles that of increasing tangential or physical energy, in an effort to save the apparent transgression of the law of conservation of energy. He makes no effort to cope with the problem of increasing radial energy, and in failing to do so, accepts that it is a property of radial energy to increase in magnitude without any apparent source. Point Omega as a solution to the difficulty[15]—'these questions must await a much later chapter, when the study of man will have led us to the concept of a superior pole to the world—the *Omega point* ' (p.68)—shifts the source of evolution's driving energy from something within matter, radial energy, to something outside matter, point Omega.

In his autobiographical essay 'The Heart of Matter' (1950), he switches his focus from radial energy as the driving force of evolution—'Deep down, there is in the substance of the cosmos a primordial disposition, *sui generis*, for self-arrangement and self-involution'[16] to a *new* power for evolutionary progress. He draws a parallel between this new power and gravitation:

> Was it by mere chance that the place of this mysterious energy [gravi-tation], whose study was technically beyond my powers, was taken by another entity, as wide in its embrace and as powerful in its attraction, which gradually became apparent to me in a field that was easier for me to work in and closer to the very axis of Cosmogenesis? This was no longer universal 'attraction' gradually drawing around itself the cosmic Mass—but that as yet undiscovered and unnamed power which forces Matter (as it concentrates under pressure) to arrange itself in ever larger molecules, differentiated and organic in structure. (p.33)

What can be made of these remarks? It is now this unnamed power, not radial energy which 'forces matter to arrange itself in ever larger molecules'. What relation do these two energies bear to each other, and how can radial energy and this unnamed power be reconciled as they both perform the same function? Or are they one and the same energy seen from different aspects. These questions will be considered later in the chapter.

Another point needs to be made. The arrangement of matter into more complex forms by radial energy and/or the unnamed power is irreversible: 'The great biological principle of 'maximum arrange-ment' in Matter...explained the persistent and irreversible rise of Cerebration and Consciousness over the face of the earth that runs through the geological eras' (p.34–5). Teilhard is sure that the science of paleontology points to the progressive spiritualisation of matter and as a consequence guarantees the irreversible nature of the process. 'I never really paused for a moment', he writes, 'to question that the progressive Spiritualisation of Matter—so clearly demon-strated to me by Palaeontology—could be anything other, or anything less, than an *irreversible process*'[17]. On the one hand he attributes the irreversibility of the evolutionary process to the law of complexity-consciousness: 'it was this', the great biological principle of maximum arrangement, 'that explained the persistent and irreversible rise of Cerebration and Consciousness' (p.35). On the other hand he attributes the irreversibility of evolution to a pole of attraction at the apex of the evolutionary process which is 'not simply of attraction, but of *consolidation*—and that means a Pole which imparts the quality of *irreversibility*' (p.28).

The acceptance of irreversibility is of course crucial for Teilhard's evolutionary theory: without it he is forced to accept the second law of thermodynamics with its prediction of heat death and the ultimate state of the universe as one of uniform multiplicity. It is an interesting fact that irreversibility of natural processes is also the key prediction of the second law of thermodynamics. Commenting on the second law, Denbigh and Denbigh state that 'the concept of *irreversibility* is more fundamental than the concept of entropy, and is also more widely applicable'[18]. The important difference, of course, is that goal of irreversibility in the case of the second law lies in the opposite direction to that posited by the law of complexity-consciousness. However unconvincing the evidence offered for the irreversibility suggested by "Teilhard's Law", this irreversibility is essential for an understanding of his Noosphere and point Omega.

The Noosphere

As a consequence of the law of complexity-consciousness Teilhard was led to postulate the existence of the noosphere, 'the highest and greatest complexity achieved (so far as we know) in the universe'[19]. But what is the noosphere? With the appearance of Man and reflective thought, 'Man has gradually been raised to the position of constituting a specifically new envelope to the earth. He is more than a branch, more even than a kingdom; he is nothing less than a 'sphere'—the noosphere (or thinking sphere) superimposed upon, and coextensive with (but in many ways more close-knit and homogeneous) [than] the biosphere'[20].

He appears to equate the noosphere with 'Socialisation...nothing more nor less than a higher effect of corpuscularisation...the final and supreme product in Man of the forces of social ties'. But the subsequent sentence makes us pause. The noosphere can 'take on full and final significance only if one condition be satisfied. That condition is that we look on the noosphere, taken in its global totality as constituting one vast corpuscle in which ...the biospheric effort towards cerebralisation attains its objective'.

Surprisingly it was his deep-seated need for durability and permanence, emanating from his earliest childhood[21] that led him to postulate the existence of the noosphere. 'My attention and my interest' he writes,

> (still guided by the *same fundamental need for Solidity and Incorruptibility* [my emphasis]) were gradually and almost imperceptibility climbing

from the extremely simple core of the Planet to its ridiculously thin,
but dauntingly active and complex, peripheral layers [the noosphere].[22]

What is so durable about 'the ridiculously thin' noosphere? Teilhard
gives the answer in his autobiographical essay: 'I found myself
inevitably, and paradoxically, obliged to identify the extreme Solidity
of things with *an extreme organic complexity*'[23]. Because the noosphere
is the most complex, consciousness and irreversible entity in the
evolutionary scheme, it satisfied all the requirements of permanence
sought by Teilhard.

How did the noosphere arise from the biosphere of *Homo
sapiens*? In his long essay *Man's Place in Nature* (1949) Teilhard gives
the fullest account of the Noosphere. With the advent of self-
reflective human beings the law of complexity-consciousness
predicts that a new sphere, the thinking sphere, becomes superimposed on the biosphere. 'The Formation', he writes,

of tribes, nations, empires, and finally of the modern state, is simply a
prolongation (with the assistance of a number of supplementary factors) of the mechanism which produced the animal species.[24]

And what is the mechanism that produced animal species? According to Teilhard the mechanism is groping or directed chance.
But does human history proceed by the same mechanism or an
analogous mechanism as that which controls biological evolution?
The phrase 'the mechanism which produced the animal species'
makes it clear that Teilhard sees history as subject to the same
mechanism as biological evolution.

In his autobiographical essay, 'The Heart of Matter' Teilhard
gives what appears at first sight to be, an unexpected account of his
discovery of the noosphere, the 'Earth's thinking envelope'[25],
surrounding the biosphere. He explains how he became aware of the
noosphere 'through prolonged contact with the huge masses of
mankind that were facing each one another in the trenches of France,
from Yser to Verdun'[26]. 'The 'Human-million'', he writes,

with its psychic temperature and its internal energy, became for me a
magnitude as evolutively, and therefore as biologically, real as a giant
molecule of protein.[27]

Teilhard was 'astonished' that few agreed with him.

Some writers try to minimize Teilhard's view of the noosphere as a biological reality. For example, de Lubac dismisses any biological interpretation of the noosphere. 'If therefore he refuses to separate "biological" and "spiritual", and before that "biological" and "social"', de Lubac writes,

> it is not by any means because he wishes to reduce the spiritual or even the social to the biological, ...There is no reason to take exception to Teilhard's language when he speaks, for example, of the 'psychic temperature' that would be produced by the Noosphere 'at the planetary scale', or of the 'Mega-man' who would represent a certain magnitude 'as biological as a gigantic molecule of protein', 'as real in the evolutionary process', or again, 'of human mega-molecules'...All the reader may do, according to his mood, is to smile at the language that sometimes verges on the comic, or to appreciate its ingenuity.[28]

If Teilhard's language 'sometimes appears to us too extreme', de Lubac writes, 'we should not take exception to it until we are sure that it is only because of what we have been used to'. He adds a just remark: 'those who have no experience to describe, no new seed of thought to bring to fruition, know nothing of the difficulties, the hesitancies, the approximations, the awkwardnesses, that accompany the attempt to express one's ideas adequately. They have little to contribute to mankind:'[29].

There is ample evidence, however, to show that Teilhard blurred, if not obliterated, the distinction between the social, the spiritual and the biological. Discussing his initial awareness of the noosphere from his contact with 'the front' in the first World War, Teilhard says that the experience led him to cease 'to notice any break (if no difference) between "physical" and "moral", between "natural" and "artificial". The "Human-million", with its psychic temperature and its internal energy, became for me as biologically, real as a giant molecule of protein'[30]. Teilhard also sees 'no difference' between Matter and Spirit: 'Spirit is the higher state of Matter' (p.35).

But why did it take the experience of war to convince him of the reality of the noosphere? What was unique about the war? Certainly there was a mass of humanity assembled at certain place with one purpose in mind—the destruction of the opposing force. A clue is his reference to the discovery of the 'reality and organicity of collective magnitudes', in this case, the 'huge masses of mankind that were facing one another in the trenches'. 'Because the individual human being represents a *corpuscular magnitude*', Teilhard writes, 'he must be subject to the same development as every other species of corpuscles in the World: that means that he *must* coalesce into physical relationships and groupings that belong to a higher order than his'. Then follows the strange remark that 'it is quite impossible for him [human being] to apprehend these groupings directly'. Nonetheless there are unique human beings, of which Teilhard is one thanks to the experience of the war, who have the gift of *'perceiving* the reality and organicity of collective magnitudes'. The real discovery for him was the discovery of the 'complete and final incorruptibility, which permeates the very marrow of the Noosphere'[31]. This discovery was a revelation for Teilhard, since it satisfied his longing from boyhood for the 'fundamental need for Solidity and Incorruptibility'.

De Lubac denied that Teilhard's description of the noosphere 'as real as a giant molecule of protein' is any more than a figure of speech, but later acknowledged that Teilhard's acceptance of a second critical point of reflection, the reflection of the noosphere upon itself, poses serious problems. 'We may wonder', de Lubac writes,

> whether, to express the envisaged 'planetization of man' or 'second hominisation', if taken in the literal sense that Père Teilhard sometimes seems to give them, are not too strong, or whether they are not even self-contradictory.[32]

Surely, then, de Lubac criticism of Teilhard's hypothesis of the reflection of the noosphere on itself indicates that Teilhard saw the noosphere as a biological reality and not as a figure of speech.

De Lubac also dismissed, as no more than a forceful analogy, Teilhard's reference to the noosphere as a "super organism' ...made up of all human individuals just as the biological individual is made up of cells'[33]. But this dismissal is also at odds with de Lubac's difficulty with Teilhard's idea of the noosphere's evolution towards a second critical point of reflection. 'Here, however, we meet a question', de Lubac writes,

> that cannot be evaded: is it possible to conceive a 'critical point' of collective reflection, which possesses so extraordinary a property and nevertheless allows the whole effect of the first 'critical point' to remain operative?[34]

De Lubac is correct in drawing attention to this problem since Teilhard refers to the second critical point of reflection as being of a 'higher order' than the first which gave rise to *Homo sapiens*.

It comes as no surprise, then, that Teilhard assigns a personality to this evolving noosphere which has passed through the second critical point of reflection. 'There is a 'creative tide'', he writes,

> which is carrying the human 'mega-molecules' towards an almost un-believable quasi 'mono-molecular' state; and in that state, as the bio-logical laws of Union demand, each *ego* is destined to be forced con-vulsively beyond itself into some mysterious *super ego* [chaque *ego* est destiné à atteindre son paroxysme dans quelque mystérieux *super-ego*].[35]

Although he rejected any idea of a single soul for the super-ego—'It is not a single soul, but a soul that animates all the assem-bled souls'—Teilhard regarded the noosphere as a 'super organism' as real as Man himself, who arose as the result of the first point of reflection. 'The human group', he writes, 'is in fact turning, by arrangement and planetary convergence of all elemental terrestrial reflections, towards a second pole of reflection of a collective and higher order'[36].

The Noosphere is clearly much more than a simple unity of cul-ture. Teilhard admits that the idea of a super-human organism seems fantastic and crazy. 'The very first time we meet it,' Teilhard writes,

> the idea of a super-human organism seems fantastic [semble fan-tastique], We are so thoroughly used to refusing to admit that any-thing could exist in nature higher than ourselves! Nevertheless, if, in-stead of rejecting *a priori* what upsets the accustomed routine of our thinking (and in particular the dimensional limits within which we think), we are willing to entertain it, and then begin to examine it more deeply, it is surprising what order and clarity is introduced into our outlook on the universe by the hypothesis that at first seemed crazy [qui paraissait folle].[37]

The 'order and clarity' refers to his hypothesis that the super organism, formed by the noosphere reflecting on itself, is in accord with his law of increasing complexity-consciousness.

A problem different from sheer unbelievability also arises: what happens to those who have died before the second critical point is reached? Do they pass through the second critical point or do they remain in a state of arrested development? And if they do remain in an arrested state what is their ultimate fate?

The formation of the Noosphere

Love is the power which will forge the super-organism with its own consciousness, the noosphere. For Teilhard love 'in its most general form and from the point of view of physics...is the internal, affectively apprehended, aspect of the affinity which links and draws together the elements of the world, *centre to centre.*'[38]. This is odd because we were told that radial energy was responsible for the arrangement of matter into to ever more complex forms and was associated with this complexity and ever increasing consciousness. We were also told that there is an elementary psyche in the simplest particle of matter. Now it seems that there is also love, however rudimentary. 'Love is the power', Teilhard writes, 'of producing inter-centric relationship. It is present, therefore (at least in a rudimentary state), in all natural centres, living and pre-living, which make up the world'[39]. Love and radial energy appear to perform the same function. Are they two aspects of the same power?

Again, it has to asked: what is the noosphere and how did it come into existence? It is extremely difficult to get a clear picture of what Teilhard means by the noosphere. He notes in 'The Formation of the Noosphere' (1947) that 'until the coming of Man the pattern of the Tree of Life was always that of a fan of morphological radiations diverging more and more, each radiation culminating in a new 'knot' and breaking into a fan of its own'[40]. He saw the Piltdown skull as that 'coming of man' with the birth of Reflection: 'the animal knows; but only man knows that he knows'[41]. But how does Reflection give rise to the noosphere? 'In Man', Teilhard writes,

> heredity, hitherto primarily chromosomic (that is, carried by the genes) becomes primarily 'Noospheric'—transmitted , that is to say, by the surrounding environment. In this new form, and having lost nothing of its physical reality (indeed, as much superior to its first state as the Noosphere is superior to the simple, isolated phylum) it acquires, by becoming exterior to the individual, an incomparable substance and capacity.[42]

What does Teilhard mean by this description of the Noosphere? Is the Noosphere, 'by becoming exterior to itself', no more than the accumulated store of human knowledge which could be destroyed by a flood or conflagration, or is it something independent of the physical means of storage. It is not clear. He compares the chromosomic with the Noospheric storage of information: 'what system of chromosomes would be as capable as our immense educational system of indefinitely storing and infallibly preserving the huge array of truths and systematised technical knowledge which, steadily accumulating, represents the patrimony of mankind?'[43].

What Teilhard is driving at is the acceptance of a universal consciousness for humanity. He draws on similarities between the individual human brain 'with its milliards of interconnected nerve cells, and the apparatus of social thought, with its hundreds of millions of individuals thinking collectively'[44]. Teilhard notes 'a major difference' between the human brain and 'the apparatus of social thought: 'in the case of the individual brain thought emerges from a system of non-thinking nervous fibres: in the case of the collective brain each separate unit is in itself an autonomous centre of reflection'[45]. But surely the major difference is that the brain is a biological organ whereas humanity is a social organization. What he is maintaining is a coming into being of 'a sort of universal consciousness'. Human socialization with its psychic convergence, a reflecting on itself, gives birth to a superorganism, replete with a psyche of its own, which is the noosphere. The noosphere is the brain of collective humanity. 'Is it not possible', he writes, 'that by the direct converging of its members it [humanity] will be able release psychic powers whose existence is unsuspected?' Consequently it is not surprising that Noosphere will make 'the phenomenon of telepathy, still sporadic and haphazard, both general and normal'[46].

And where is this process of increasing consciousness taking humanity? Teilhard discusses the evolution of the noosphere. 'We are still refusing', he laments, 'to accept the possibility of continuing improvement, passed on from one generation to another, in the actual *organ* of vision'[47]. By the organ of vision he means the Noosphere. When the second point of reflection is reached and the noosphere reflects on itself, the 'ultra-human' will emerge, the superego to which reference has been made. Teilhard distinguishes two points of convergence, the convergence of the human phylum at the time of Piltdown man and the emergence of self-consciousness, followed by the convergence of the noosphere upon itself, the second point of reflection. After the final convergence has taken place 'the great *Law of complexity-consciousness:* a law that itself implies a psychically convergent structure and curvature of the world', can offer no further predictions for the future. The apex of the evolutionary process has been reached, which Teilhard refers to as point Omega.

The World Wars and the growth of the Noosphere

Little attention has been paid to the influence of war on the development of Teilhard's concept of the noosphere. It strikes readers how little the horrors of war struck Teilhard. He saw the World Wars as particularly crucial steps in Man's evolutionary progress and the growth of consciousness. As already observed, the First World War was instrumental in formulating his concept of the Noosphere. In that terrible struggle he was a medical orderly, acting as a stretcher-bearer. In the Second World War he was in China, well away from the battle zones. But we have his essay, 'The Rise of the Other' (1942) on the nature of the conflict, and also his reaction to the Atom bomb in the essay 'Some Reflections on the Spiritual repercussions of the Atom Bomb' (1946). Again there is Gabriel Marcel's stunned reaction on hearing Teilhard brush aside the extermination of millions in Soviet slave camps as a mere episode in a march towards a glorious future[48]. What is one to make of these incidents?

In 'The Nostalgia for the Front' (1917), written in the heat of the First World War, Teilhard shows unrestrained enthusiasm for 'the front' in words that dismayed his contemporaries, forgotten when he became famous in the sixties. 'Those more than human hours', Teilhard writes, 'impregnate life with a clinging, ineradicable flavour of exaltation and initiation, as though they had been transferred into the absolute. When I look, all the magic of the East, all the spiritual warmth of Paris are not worth the mud of Douaumont'[49]. Teilhard's essay, 'The Promised Land' written in February, 1919, at the conclusion of the First World War was an effort 'to determine just what *remains to us* of all the effort we put into the war'[50]. As for its publication—'I've no illusions about that'[51]. And he was correct, the editor of Études and a confrère of Teilhard, L. de Grandmaison, refused to publish this essay when it was submitted.

The essay, 'The Great Monad' (1918), is particularly disturbing. In it he sums up his attitude to the First World War as follows: 'When the great war broke out which at one blow brought crashing down the whole structure of a decrepit civilisation—the short-sighted or the ungenerous-minded, those with no faith in the World, knew a bitter triumph. Like Pharisees, they jeered at the bankruptcy of Progress and the exposed vanity of all social betterment'[52]. Teilhard considered civilization decrepit, as will be indicated below, not because of any moral shortcomings but because of its failure to share his evolutionary vision of progress and social betterment. At this early stage of his thinking he expressed his belief in the Noosphere and the second critical point of reflection, the reflection of the Noosphere upon itself. 'When the thinking earth', he writes, 'has completed its closing in upon itself, then only shall we know the true nature of a Monad'. The 'Monad' was Teilhard's earliest name for the Noosphere.

Similar ideas on the creative aspect of the First World War are expressed in 'The Promised Land', (1919): 'This great tumult ...was a crisis of growth. The youthful envelope of a new humanity could be seen beneath the cracks of the old husk'[53]. The war was a test of humanity's response to 'the evolutionary reserves, the potential of our species'. In both 'The Great Monad' and 'the Promised Land' it is the evolutionary potential of the human species which fascinates him, the horrors of war are incidental: 'we must not grieve at the cruelty of war'[54].

From the period of the Second World War there are similar comments to those on the First. At the time Teilhard was in China. One interesting difference is that in the First World War, he saw the struggle as 'directed against evil'[55]; in the Second War (letter from China, August 1941) he describes 'his inability to take sides'[56], and 'Less and less I am able to make a clear internal choice between the conflicting forces'[57]. In the letter from which the former comment is taken, he views the true "enemies' [as] those who deny Progress' [These words are omitted by the French editors [58]].

Teilhard's attitude to the explosion of the atom bomb is also consistent with his view of war as a critical point in humanity's evolving consciousness, the noosphere. In 1946 Teilhard wrote an essay, 'Some Reflections on the Spiritual Repercussions of the Atom Bomb'. Among the issues he raises is the right of scientists to pursue knowledge to the end without hindrance: 'As though it were not every man's duty to pursue the creative forces of knowledge and action to the uttermost end'[59].

In reference to the bombing of the two Japanese cities, he asks, 'what did such things matter' as 'the quicker ending of the war', 'when the very worth of science itself was on trial? Perhaps even more important than the vindication of the worth of science was involved. This is that Man 'had discovered ...another secret pointing to his omnipotence''[60]. And what is the omnipotence which humanity had discovered? It is none other than that of the Noosphere; 'the largest number of brains were enabled to join together in a single organism, the most complex and centrated, for the purpose of research'. And this showed that 'nothing in the universe can resist the converging energies of a sufficient number of minds'[61].

In answer to the question: 'How is the use of this terrifying power to be organised and controlled?' Teilhard replies 'This is for the worldly technicians to answer'. Teilhard mentions that witnesses to the experiment in Arizona 'in the depths of their hearts were *praying*' for its military success.

It is, therefore, surprising to find there is little or no mention of his attitude to war among writers on Teilhard. Rideau[62] gives the impression that Teilhard had a solely negative attitude to war. In particular he quotes two passages from Teilhard to support his view. In the first Teilhard refers to war as 'the great open sore (could not one say?) which drains the overflow of energy engendered by anthropogenesis'[63]. Reading on, one discovers that Teilhard wants human energy directed from war and leisure to research.

The other reference given by Rideau is from a wartime essay, 'The Rise of the Other' (1942). He sees as an outright condemnation of war an essay which is particularly important for an understanding of Teilhard's view of war in human evolution. Teilhard begins with an analysis of the 'causes of the conflict'. Teilhard dismisses the attitude which regards war as 'no more than a crisis of disruption, of disintegration'. War is a necessary step in humanity's evolutionary march. 'The true cause of what is happening in the world today', he writes,

> is to be found ...in the eruption, within mankind, of a flood of new be-ing which, precisely because it is new, comes initially as something foreign to what we ourselves represent. What takes us by surprise in to-day's events, what so upsets and terrifies us—but what in fact we must look straight in the face so that we can analyze its mechanism

and its phases, and distinguish good effects it has side by side with what evil effects—is, in my view, the implacable cosmic tide: it is this that, having first raised each one of us up to its own level, is now at work, beating in a new rhythm, to expel us from our selves: it is the eternal 'rise of the other' within the human mass.[64]

And what is 'the rise of the other', the title of the essay? It is the convergence of mankind into a 'sort of super-organism ...trying to, establish itself beyond the individual'[65] with its own super-consciousness, the noosphere. Teilhard maintains that human collectivization is the same biological process as gave rise to the hive and the termitary, which emerged millions of years ago. This tendency to collectivization should not surprise us, he claims. 'What has attracted less attention', he writes,

> in this life of the species is the tendency they all display, once they have attained maturity, to group themselves in various ways in large socialized units: as though, in colonies of polyps or in the fantasticaly differentiated associations formed by insects, a sort of super-organism were trying to establish itself beyond the individual.[66]

The super organism towards which mankind is moving explains 'many things in this paradoxical war, in which the libertarian hostility of nations is so strangely combined with a totalisation'. Teilhard sees the war as contributing to human collectivization but marred by the hostility which gave rise to the war. Although the war was instrumental, indeed was a necessary step, in calling humanity's attention to the human 'super-organism' which lies in the evolutionary future, humanity still treats as 'fantastic and crazy' 'the idea of a super-organism'[67].

If Teilhard was merely referring to the tendency of humanity towards a shared common culture with the growth of population and increasing communication, he would not refer to the idea of a super-organism as 'fantastic and crazy'; for when he wrote there was general agreement that a common culture among mankind would eventuate. But Teilhard is referring to something, 'the other', which on the face of it is unbelievable, a super-organism, beyond the individual with its own consciousness.

Point Omega

Earlier in the chapter it was mentioned that Teilhard referred to an unnamed power which forces matter to arrange itself biologically. An analogy was drawn with the gravitational force which compresses the cosmic mass. Teilhard identified this unnamed power with point Omega. This pole of attraction, point Omega, is supposed to answer the three questions raised in the discussion of radial and tangential energies in *The Phenomenon of Man*. Two of the questions will be dealt with shortly: Is there a limit to the evolutionary process, and is the final form of radial energy subject to reversal?

It is the first question, however, which is puzzling: 'By virtue of what special energy does the universe propagate itself along its main axis in the less probable direction of higher forms of complexity and centricity?'[68] For on the previous page Teilhard has answered this very question: it is '*radial energy* which draws it [matter] towards ever greater complexity and centricity—in other words forwards'. The implication of Teilhard's again asking the question is that radial energy is not the ultimate driving force of evolution. Later in the book under the heading 'The Attributes of the Omega Point' Teilhard confirms that radial energy is somehow activated by point Omega. 'During the immense periods in the course of evolution', he writes, 'the radial [is] obscurely stirred up by the action of the *Prime mover ahead*'[69]. The Prime mover ahead is point Omega, and is also identified with Christ, the motor of evolution. But what does Teilhard mean by saying that the radial is 'obscurely stirred up'? Is radial energy no more than activated by Omega? This can not be so since he refers to Omega as 'the special energy' which propagates the universe towards 'higher forms of complexity'. There seems to be no satisfactory way in which to reconcile Omega with radial energy, as they both perform the same function.

We are also told that the super-ego into which each ego is forced, this 'mysterious focal point of Noogenesis...the final critical point of ultra-reflection' is point Omega'[70]. The term point Omega, the culmination of evolution, was used by Teilhard in contrast to primordial matter, point alpha. The terms also have a theological connotation: in the Apocalypse in the New Testament Christ is referred to as the Alpha and the Omega, the beginning and the end.

'Modern astronomers have no hesitation', he writes,

in envisaging the existence of a sort of primitive atom in which the entire mass of the sidereal world, if we took it back several thousands of
millions of years, would be found to be included. Matching, in a way,
this primordial physical unit, is it not odd that if biology is extrapo-
lated to its extreme point ...it leads us to an analogous hypothesis of a
universal focus (I have called it Omega), no longer one of physical expansion and exteriorisation, but of psychic interiorisation—and it is in
that direction the terrestrial noosphere in process of concentration
(through complexification) seems to be destined, in some millions of
years, to reach its term.[71]

But point Omega is not a scientifically observable point, according to what is said in 'The Formation of the Noosphere' (1947),
because it lies outside space and time. The reflection of the noosphere
upon itself will cause it to 'break through the material framework of
Time and Space to escape somewhere towards an ultra-centre of
unification and wholeness'[72]. Why does Teilhard consider that point
Omega is outside space and time? The sole reason is that once the
second critical point of reflection has been reached, that of the
noosphere upon itself, his law of complexity-consciousness has come
to the end of its predictions; 'the compass that guided us has run
amok'[73]. 'It was by the law of 'complexity and consciousness' that we
set our course:' he writes,

a consciousness becoming ever more centrated, emerging from the
heart of an increasingly vast system of more numerous and better organised elements. But now we are faced by an entirely new situation:
for the first time we have no multiple material under our hands'[74].

Teilhard remarks that once the reflection of the noosphere upon
itself has been reached, it seems that 'the cosmic impulse towards
consciousness has been exhausted, condemned to sink back into the
state of disintegration implacably imposed on it by the laws of stellar
physics'. It is not the possibility of the 'total extinction of the
individual' which concerns Teilhard; it is the thought of humanity's
extinction as a whole that 'revolts and sickens' him[75]. He maintains
that is psychologically impossible for the individual to work unless
'the best of his work is preserved from destruction'. This is even
more true for humanity as a whole. Only the certain glory of point
Omega can provide the impetus for action.

The Noosphere, once having arrived at the second critical point
of reflection, reflection upon itself, achieves a state of irreversibility.

There is no return to lower states of evolution for humanity at its peak of evolution. The cosmic consciousness is not lost. The noo-sphere, 'apparently incapable of any further synthesis ...will break through the material framework of Time and Space to escape somewhere towards an ultra-centre of unification and wholeness'[76]. Beyond this second critical point of reflection of the noosphere upon itself, 'We would be unable to distinguish anything as a phenomenon since, by the very fact that it forms a *threshold of irreversibility* , it *coincides* with an emergence from the structures and dimensions of evolution. .... [an] escape from the temporo-spatial envelope of things'[77].

The two essential features of point Omega are irreversibility and personality. 'If the pole of psychic convergence', he writes,

> towards which matter, as it arranges itself, gravitates, were nothing other than, or nothing more than the totalised, impersonal, and re-versible grouping of all the grains of cosmic thought reflected momen-tarily in one another—then the world's convolution upon itself would (in self-disgust) discontinue, in exact step with evolution's becoming more clearly aware, as it advanced, of the blind alley it was ending in.[78]

Human beings can only love something which is indestructible and personal. In a paroxysm of joy Teilhard exclaims, 'The 'piece of iron' of my first days has long been forgotten. In its place it is the Consis-tence of the Universe, in the form of Omega Point, that I now hold, concentrated into one single indestructible centre, WHICH I CAN LOVE'[79].

'Is it not conceivable', he writes, 'that Mankind ...may reach a critical level of maturity where, leaving the Earth and stars to lapse slowly back into the dwindling mass of primordial energy, it will detach itself from this planet and join the one true, irreversible essence of things, the Omega point?'[80]. For some unexplained reason Teilhard now allows the second law of thermodynamics, held at bay for the duration of evolution, to operate, and organized matter, other than humanity, to revert to its primordial state and heat death. He gives no reason for this state of affairs other than that humanity has attained its purpose, and apparently there is no reason now to forestall the operation of the second law.

But what is the fate of those who have died prior to the noo-sphere's reflection upon itself at point Omega? If they have survived, as Teilhard assures us, what point is there in conjecturing a point

Omega? Teilhard fails to address these important questions. In fact he compounds the problem by claiming that 'This hypothesis of a final maturing and ecstasy of Mankind, [is] the logical conclusion of the theory of complexity'[81]. But point Omega, far from being the logical conclusion of his law of complexity-consciousness, is in conflict with it, and also with the second law of thermodynamics. For one would expect, from the law of complexity-consciousness, that those who die prior to point Omega should cease to exist with the breakdown of complexity. Whereas Teilhard asserts that their consciousnesses survive. If they have reached a state of irreversibility and permanence, what need is there for point Omega, which alone was meant to guarantee their irreversibility and indestructibility.

Teilhard felt that he had found scientific evidence to support his theological position in which he identifies point Omega with the end of the world in which God will be all in all' (1 Corinthians xv. 26–28). 'Of all the theories which may evolve concerning the end of the Earth', Teilhard writes, the law of complexity-consciousness 'is the only one which affords a coherent prospect wherein, in the remote future, the deepest and most powerful currents of human consciousness may converge and culminate: intelligence and action, learning and religion'[82].

NOTES

1   Towers, *Concerning Teilhard*, p.97.

2   B. Towers, *Teilhard de Chardin*, London: Lutterworth Press, 1966, p.32.

3   Teilhard, *The Future of Man*, p.218.

4   Teilhard, *Man's Place in Nature*, trans. R. Hague, London: Collins, 1966, p. 19.

5   Teilhard, *The Phenomenon of Man*, p.60.

6   Teilhard, *The Heart of Matter*, trans. R. Hague, London: Collins, 1978,p.26.

7   Teilhard, *The Phenomenon of Man*, pp.301–302.

8   Towers, *Concerning Teilhard*, p.96.

9   Towers, *Teilhard de Chardin*, p.33.

10 Teilhard, *The Phenomenon of Man*, p.272.

11 Ibid., p.272.

12 Ibid., p.64.

13 Ibid., p.289.

14 Ibid., p.64.

15 Ibid., p.66.

16 Teilhard, *The Heart of Matter*, p.33.

17 Ibid., pp. 27–28.

18 K.G. Denbigh and J.S. Denbigh, *Entropy in Relation to Incomplete Knowledge*, Cambridge University Press, 1985, p.118.

19 Teilhard, *Man's Place in Nature*, p.22.

20 Ibid., p.80.

21 Discussed in Chapter 9.

22 Teilhard, *The Heart of Matter*, p.32.

23 Ibid., p.28.

24 Teilhard, *Man's Place in Nature*, p.87.

25 Teilhard, *The Heart of Matter*, p.31.

26 Ibid., p.31.

27 Ibid., p.31.

28 De Lubac, *The Religion of Teilhard de Chardin*, trans. R. Hague, London: Collins, 1967, pp. 191–192.

29 Ibid., p.194.

30 Teilhard, *The Heart of Matter*, p.31.

31 Ibid., p.33.

32 De Lubac, *The Religion of Teilhard de Chardin*, p.209.

33 Ibid., p.208.

34 Ibid., p.209.

35 Teilhard, *The Heart of Matter*, p.38. / *Le Coeur de la matière*, Paris: Éditions du Seuil, 1976, p.48.

36 Teilhard, *The Phenomenon of Man*, p.307.

37 Teilhard, *Activation of Energy*, p.68. / *L'Activation de l'énergie*, Paris: Éditions du Seuil, 1963.

38 Ibid., p. 70.

39 Ibid., p. 70.

40 Teilhard, *The Future of Man*, p.158.

41 Ibid., p.158.

42 Ibid., p.163.

43 Ibid., p.163.

44 Ibid., p.166.

45   Ibid., p.166.

46   Ibid., p.177.

47   Teilhard, *The Heart of Matter*, p.37.

48   B. Chobuda, *Of Time, Light and Hell: Essays in Interpretation of the Christian Message*, The Hague: Mouton, 1974, p.72.

49   Teilhard, *The Heart of Matter*, p.178 and p.180.

50   Teilhard, *The Making of a Mind*, trans. R. Hague, London: Collins, 1965, p283. Teilhard, *Writings in Time of War*, trans. R. Hague, London: Collins, 1968), p.277.

51   Ibid., p.285.

52   Teilhard, *The Heart of Matter*, p.184.

53   Teilhard, *Writings in Time of War*, p.281.

54   Ibid., p.287.

55   Ibid., p.284.

56   Teilhard, *Letters to Two Friends, 1926–1952*, p.99.

57   Ibid., p.160.

58   Teilhard, *Accomplir L'Homme, Lettres inédites (1926–1952)*, Paris: Éditions Bernard Grasset, 1968, p.121.

59   Teilhard, *The Future of Man*, p.140.

60   Ibid., p.143.

61   Ibid., p.144.

62   Rideau, *Teilhard de Chardin: A Guide to his Thought*, p.120.

63   Teilhard, *The Appearance of Man*, p.162.

64   Teilhard, *Activation of Energy*, pp.61–62.

65   Ibid., p.65.

66   Teilhard, *Activation of Energy*, p.64.

67   Ibid., p.68.

68   Teilhard, *The Phenomenon of Man*, p.66.

69   Ibid., p.271.

70   Teilhard, *Activation of Energy*, p.71.

71   Teilhard, *Man's Place in Nature*, p.116.

72   Teilhard, *The Future of Man*, p.180.

73   Ibid., p.179.

74   Ibid., p.179.

75   Ibid., p.180.

76   Ibid., p.181.

77   Teilhard, *The Appearance of Man*, p.171.

78   Teilhard, *Man's Place in Nature*, pp. 120–121.

79   Teilhard, *The Heart of Matter*, p.39.

80   Teilhard, *The Future of Man*, pp. 122–123.

81   Ibid., p. 123.

82   Ibid., p. 123.

CHAPTER SEVEN

THE REACH OF EVOLUTION

> The mass of humanity is profoundly inferior and repulsive. Don't you find it so?
>
> —Teilhard de Chardin, *How I Believe*

A host of philosophical systems have been spawned by the theory of biological evolution. Many of the more recent have been collected by Mary Midgley in her book, *Evolution as a Religion*[1]. She views them as myths and dramas in that they purport to meet the need for meaning in the lives of their adherents. All of them, she considers, have three features in common. Firstly, they center on the theme of evolution. Secondly, they use scientific language but they do not concur with currently accepted scientific theories. Thirdly, they are powerfully emotive and sustaining, providing their adherents with a lively faith to give meaning to their lives (p.132).

Midgley appears to exclude Teilhard from her strictures without clear evidence from his works. Teilhard is mentioned only twice in the book (pp. 68 and 72) and on both occasions Midgley presents a favorable picture of his views. Contrasting Nietzsche and Teilhard, she writes: 'The Jesuit biologist Teilhard de Chardin'—he was a paleontologist—'offers a different future, in which Nietzsche's twin abominations, physical science and Christianity, are both exalted and find their final synthesis'. And she sees 'traditional' Christianity as Teilhard's guiding light: 'Traditional Christianity, however difficult it may be to fit in with [Teilhard's] ambitious scheme, is certainly still conceived as the main guiding thread' (p.72).

Philosophical systems which draw their inspiration from the theory of evolution are liable to place great emphasis on genetic engineering. But surprisingly Midgley exonerates Teilhard from her condemnation of champions of genetic engineering.

> Faith in life and in the human race becomes less evident when we turn from those who rely on continued natural growth, like Teilhard and Dobzhansky, to the champions of genetic engineering. They want us to put faith in certain techniques, or at most in the intellectual skills and capacities which make these techniques possible. But these are means. What we need is to hear about are aims. (p.68)

Here again Midgley is mistaken. Teilhard is an enthusiastic champion of genetic engineering and sees it as essential for what he considers is the progress of humanity. Teilhard makes special mention of H.G. Wells and Aldous Huxley, two novelists in particular who have discussed intervention in unfettered human reproduction, for the benefit of society. He dismisses both of them for presenting a caricature of 'the idea which is right and grand'[2]. Teilhard shows some confusion here, as Aldous Huxley in *Brave New World* certainly caricatures the meddling with human reproduction, whereas Wells in *Anticipations*[3] (1901), in the section, 'Faith, Morals, and Public Policy of the New Republic', advocates the breeding of what is fine and efficient and beautiful in humanity and the checking of 'the procreation of base and servile types'. Indeed, as will be seen, some of Teilhard's comments with respect to racial and individual improvement are remarkably similar to those of Wells. Teilhard's friend and literary executor Julian Huxley[4], who had a profound influence on Teilhard's biological evolutionary view of society and religion, assigned evolutionary importance to eugenics.

The improvement of humanity

Mary Midgley dedicated her book, *Evolution as a Religion* (1985) 'to the memory of Charles Darwin who did not say these things': but there is evidence that Darwin wittingly or otherwise, provided a footing for racism of the sort Wallace would not[5], and furnished arguments for the most ardent eugenicist[6]. 'With savages, the weak in body or mind are soon eliminated;', Darwin writes in *The Descent of Man, and Selection in Relation to Sex* (second edition, 1874),

> and those that survive commonly exhibit a vigourous state of health. We civilised men, on the other hand, do our utmost to check the process of elimination; we build asylums for the imbecile, the maimed, and the sick; we institute poor-laws; and our medical men exert their utmost skill to save the life of every one to the last moment. There is reason to believe that vaccination has preserved thousands, who from a weak constitution would formerly have succumbed to small-pox. Thus weak members of civilised societies propagate their kind. No one who has attended to the breeding of domestic animals will doubt that this must be highly injurious to the race of man. It is surprising how soon a want of care, or care wrongly directed, leads to the degenera-

tion of a domestic race; but excepting in the case of man himself, hardly any one is so ignorant as to allow his worst animals to breed.[7]

Darwin's co-proposer of the theory of evolution by natural selection, Alfred Russel Wallace, also expressed sentiments which become commonplace among Social Darwinists in the latter decades of the nineteenth century. For example, in both his 1864 paper and the modified version of 1870 entitled 'The Development of Human races under the Law of Natural Selection' Wallace writes: 'It is the same great law of the 'preservation of favoured races in the struggle for life', which leads to the inevitable extinction of all those low and mentally undeveloped populations with which Europeans come in contact'[8]. Later in life he abandoned these sentiments[9] and in his everyday dealings with the native peoples he encountered on his travels Wallace showed no sign of this attitude[10]

It is surprising how few writers refer to the extreme importance Teilhard attaches to genetic engineering for the future of humankind; not only for the individual but more importantly for different ethnic types. One would have expected a great deal of comment on such a controversial subject from those who have written about Teilhard; instead there is almost complete silence. If the topic had been a minor part of Teilhard's evolutionary plan the silence would be understandable; but in fact without an appreciation of Teilhard's attitude to genetic manipulation of the human species an essential element in his evolutionary thought is missed.

The eminent Jesuit theologian Henri de Lubac[11] in his discussion of the religion of Teilhard makes no mention of eugenics even when the context calls for it; for example, in Chapter 18 of *The Religion of Teilhard de Chardin* dealing with Creation, Cosmogenesis, Christogenesis.

Emile Rideau[12] in his extensive guide to Teilhard's thought, which is acknowledged as one of the authoritative works in the interpretation of Teilhard, also fails to mention the topic. There are several entries under heredity and genetics in the index of the book, but the reader finds only a discussion of Lamarckism and Darwinism and 'social heredity'. One of the first books dealing with Teilhard, by Claude Cuénot[13], makes the briefest mention of the topic of the utmost importance to Teilhard. Cuénot does quote Teilhard's letter to Torrès-Bodet on UNESCO's attitude to racial problems:

Even if some minds, insufficiently 'humanized', found themselves
shocked by the fact that, in mankind's common advance, there are not
only 'better endowed' individuals but also 'better endowed' groups,
'leader groups'—need that disturb us?...In sociology, as in physics,
there are laws we cannot trifle with (301).

But the only explicit reference to eugenics by Cuénot is a reproduction of a memorandum from Teilhard to Julian Huxley who was
organizing a 'brains trust' to examine the human phenomenon. In
this memorandum the establishment of an 'Institute for Human
Studies' for the investigation and control of human self-evolution is
proposed, divided into two branches, one theoretical and one
applied. Under the applied branch appears a section on Eugenics.
(p.305)

Even those who do allude to Teilhard's attitude to eugenics do
not indicate the extreme importance that Teilhard attaches to it.
Delfgaauw, for example, does admit its importance. He sees Teilhard
as looking in the short term to 'individual and social psychology,
sociology and pedagogy as providing access to the higher reaches of
culture for many more people. In the longer term Teilhard looks to
the biological sciences to make a significant contribution in this
respect'[14]. That is all Delfgaauw says.

Another important writer on Teilhard's thought, Bernard Towers[15], then professor of anatomy at the University of Cambridge,
whose subject specialty would have indicated an interest in eugenics,
does not refer to the subject. Many writers actually give the impression that Teilhard was prepared to leave natural processes to achieve
evolution's goal.

A mature statement by Teilhard of his attitude to eugenics appears in 'The Directions and Conditions of the Future', written in
1948.

Above all, how are we to ensure that the maximum population, when
it is reached, shall be composed of elements harmonious in themselves
and blended as harmoniously as possible together? Individual eugenics (breeding and education designed to produce the best possible
individual types) and racial eugenics (the grouping or intermixing of
different ethnic types being not left to chance but effected as a controlled process in the proportions most beneficial to humanity as a
whole), both, as I well know, present apparently insuperable difficulties, administrative and psychological.[16]

Teilhard's comment that individual and racial eugenics must not be left to chance, points to the inadequacy of purely natural processes to carry evolution forward to its ultimate goal, the Omega point, the culmination of the evolutionary process. Teilhard is not prepared to leave biological evolution to proceed without human intervention. Indeed with the appearance of self-consciousness, Teilhard insists in his most famous book that Man must direct the evolutionary process.

> So far we have certainly allowed our race to develop at random, and we have given too little thought to the question of what medical and moral factors *must replace the crude forces of natural selection* should we repress them. In the course of the coming centuries it is indispensable that a nobly human form of eugenics, on a standard worthy of our personalities, should be discovered and developed.[17]

And again, in a less placid tone, he expresses the same idea:

> Concerning [Julian] Huxley's book, it is strange how close we come to each other. But I got 'angry' at the reviewer, when he criticized Huxley's warning that in the near future we' shall be able to control genetically the products of human generation; because, the reviewer says, it is impossible or dangerous to decide what should be the 'best' human type. A very stupid criticism (probably expressing some anti-communist feeling), underestimating the fact that, if Man really succeeds in controlling his own heredity, no force in the world will prevent him from using his power. I recognize that planning is dangerous. But the question is not there. The question is to decide whether Man can avoid being forced to plan, by the very process of cosmic evolution. And the answer is that he *cannot*: because planning is the essence of life.[18]

Being forced to engage in evolutionary planning 'by the very process of cosmic evolution' because 'planning is the essence of life', is a Teilhardism that a commentator can do nothing with. We shall look instead at reasons Teilhard gives to show that planning should be engaged in. Before the advent of human beings evolution was controlled by 'the crude forces of natural selection'. We are apt to look on these forces as infallible, he says, and in doing so 'we are up against the mirage of instinct, the so-called infallibility of nature'[19]. But with the appearance of self-consciousness, human beings are able to intervene in the evolutionary process. What motivates the need for this science is disclosed in the following passage:

I greatly admired the view of the castle you sent me. It seemed to me like a proud affirmation of the need for an elite, which is, I believe, one of the most decisive convictions I've acquired in recent years. None but a race of men, strong and conscious of having outstripped their fellows, could have conceived and built those towers, proudly poised on the rock, overlooking the torrent. The whole difficulty (and secret) of real democracy is to encourage the renewal and recruitment of the elite, and to make inclusion in it as universal as possible. But in itself, the mass of humanity is profoundly inferior and repulsive. Don't you find it so?[20]

In a similar vein Teilhard admits in a letter to a friend: 'Instinctively I'd much rather have an earth full of animals than one inhabited by men. Every man forms a little world on his own, and this pluralism is essentially distasteful to me'[21]. Even in his spiritual classic *Le Milieu Divin* Teilhard expresses similar sentiments. 'I find no difficulty in integrating into my inward life everything above and beneath me in the universe—matter, plants, animals; and then powers dominions and angels', he writes,

these I can accept without difficulty and delight to feel myself sustained within their hierarchy. But 'the other man', my God—by which I do not mean 'the poor, the halt, the lame and the sick', but 'the other' quite simply as the 'other', the one who seems to exist independently of me because his universe seems closed to mine, and who seems to shatter the unity and the silence of the world for me—would I be sincere if I did not confess that my instinctive reaction is to rebuff him? And that the mere thought of entering into spiritual communication with him disgusts me?[22]

A fellow Jesuit, Thomas Corbishley, while lauding Teilhard's spirituality is somewhat shocked by his attitude towards the rejects of the evolutionary process, 'the poor, the lame and the sick'. He discusses Teilhard's two images of the evolving universe in 'The Significance of the Positive Value of Suffering' (1933)[23]. Teilhard's first comparison is to a growing tree, where owing to the accidents of weather or other adverse conditions, there are liable to be bruised or broken twigs, branches and blossoms. His second comparison is to that of soldiers being thrown into battle in which victory is bought at the price of human suffering. These images are meant to give meaning to human suffering. 'Sufferers of whatever species', Teilhard writes, 'are the expression of this stern but noble condition. They are not useless and dwarfed. They are simply paying for the forward march and triumph of all. They are casualties, fallen on the field of Honour'[24]. Corbishley, however, confesses 'that there is something a little facile and almost heartless about this line of thought'[25]. As a prominent German theologian, Jürgen Moltmann, has rightly commented: 'Not even the best of all possible stages of evolution justifies acquiescence in evolution's victims, as the fertilizers of that future—not even the Omega Point, with its divine fulness'[26].

Criteria for the improvement of the human species

If there is to be intervention in the evolutionary process, what are to be its criteria? In 'The Phenomenon of Spirituality', (1937)[27] Teilhard distinguishes two types of morality, 'morality of movement' and 'morality of balance', of which only the former is conducive to the advancement of the evolutionary process. 'Morality has until now', he writes,

> been principally understood as a fixed system of rights and duties in-tended to establish a static equilibrium between individuals, and at pains to maintain it by a *limitation* of energies, that is to say of force ....The highest morality is henceforth that which will develop the phe-nomenon of nature to its upper limits. No longer to protect but to develop, by awakening and convergence, the individual riches of the earth.[28]

For Teilhard the value of human actions assumes new features, primarily those which advance the evolutionary process. Teilhard labels traditional morality, 'closed morality', and his new 'morality of movement', 'open morality'. Closed morality was meant to 'protect', but open morality will 'develop' human beings. Teilhard is indebted to Bergson's *The Two Sources of Morality and Religion* for these terms and their meaning. Just as Bergson unfavorably contrasts closed morality as 'system of *orders* dictated by *impersonal* social require-ments' with open morality, 'a series of *appeals* made to the conscience of each of us by *persons* who represent the best that there is in humanity '[29], so Teilhard lauds

> the boldest mariners of tomorrow who will sail out to explore and humanize the mysterious ocean of moral energies. To try everything and to force everything in the direction of the greatest consciousness;

this, in a universe recognized to be in a state of spiritual transformation, is the general and highest law of morality.[30]

Though to discern what Teilhard means by 'forcing everything
in the direction of the greatest consciousness' defeats elucidation, it is
clear that the criterion for the new morality justifies eugenics. At
what sort of ideal might the manipulation of the human species aim?
A picture of the ideal human being is presented in 'The Sense of
Man', (1929)[31]. He will 'recognize, love and serve with passion the
universe of which he forms a part'[32]. The airman who sacrifices his
life in establishing an airmail route is mentioned, the mountain
climber who risks his life in the conquest of Everest, and the doctor
who loses a limb by exposure to X-rays. Their greatness lies in their
'cooperation in a triumph which is greater than they'. All three have
one characteristic in common, a willingness to sacrifice their life. For
what are they willing to sacrifice their life? Teilhard offers no answer;
instead he dismisses those who fail to grasp the supposedly obvious
answer with the comment, 'anyone who does not understand loses
our esteem' (p.22). As Teilhard was a Jesuit priest it is understandable that he sees the sacrifice of one's life as the greatest act of love.
But in the Christian tradition the sacrifice of one's live is praised
when the giving of one's live is for someone else. However, in none
of his three ideal human beings is there a willingness to give one's
life to save another human being but for something much more
abstract, 'the growth of the world'.

In spite of his concern to improve the human stock, demanded
'by the process of cosmic evolution', Teilhard admits the dangers
inherent in such an endeavor. In 'Human Energy'[33](1937) he considers
'the improvement of the human particles' not only by the conquest of
disease and physical deterioration but also by the formation of 'a
higher human type' (p.127).

> Such an ambition has long appeared, and still appears to many, fantas-
> tic or even blasphemous. Some refuse to imagine any profound change
> in what seems 'to have always been'; others by a false religious fear of
> violating the Creator's irrevocable rights over His work both of
> thought and flesh. For a complex of obscure reasons, our generation
> still regards with distrust all efforts proposed by science for controlling
> the machinery of heredity, of sex determination and development of
> the nervous system. It is as if man had the right and power to interfere
> with all the channels in the world except those which make him him-
> self. And yet it is eminently on this ground that we must try *everything*,

to its conclusion. A delicate undertaking, if ever there was one; but precisely because of their delicacy, these undertakings require, if they are to be soundly, reverently and religiously pursued, the precautions and surveillance of methodically conducted research. No longer only man experimenting on his fellows; but humanity feeling out in order to give its members a higher quality of life. (p127–8)

In a long scientific essay, 'The Singularities of the Human Species'[34] (1954), which appeared in *Annales de Paléontologie*, a year before his death, Teilhard admits that laying one's hands on 'the mechanism of reproduction, embryogenesis and selection' gives rise to justifiable repulsion and disquiet'; and 'like everyone else', he says, 'I gauge the many mortal dangers involved in the possession of such power, but even more in the experiments leading to its acquisition' (p.255). Nevertheless in spite of 'all these objections of heart and head', he is prepared to proceed with the risky enterprise because it is going to happen anyway:

On the one hand (whether we like it or not) let us finally realise that nothing, absolutely nothing, will ever prevent man (driven to it as he is by an inner urge of cosmic nature) from going *in every direction*—and more especially in the biological field—*to the utmost extent* of his powers of research and invention. (p.255)

A second affirmation follows which 'may raise enough hopes to temper the too brutally evident aspects' of this one:

Let us not forget that the concomitant development of certain psychological characteristics is probably necessary, precisely in order that the structure of [human] self-evolution may be physically realisable. To leave this out of account would be to render the results of our prognostications improbable or monstrous.

In the first place Teilhard sees benign characteristics as only 'probably necessary'. But what are these psychological characteristics? And why are they necessary (even if only probably) to the development of human self-evolution? 'In the particularly confused field of so-called ethical values', Teilhard writes,

in which so many emotional and traditional factors are in danger of dulling the light of facts and the sense of words, I will try, once again, to find a high enough vantage point (or what comes to the same thing, to recognise a sufficiently general law of evolution) for the prognosti-

cations on which I think I can rely to be made with complete and se-
rene objectivity.

And, as always in such cases, I will revert to the process of complexity-
consciousness which, by transforming the energy released by the com-
pression of planetary humanity into *order* and *psyche*, supports the
progress of what I have called *co-reflexion*'[35]

Teilhard's appeal to his law of complexity-consciousness has as
the morally benign psychological characteristics required for self-
evolution those favoring the progress of 'co-reflexion'. 'Co-reflexion',
of which Teilhard sees the growth of society as one aspect, is a higher
form of consciousness, the crossing of a new reflective threshold for
man as the result of evolutionary convergence. But this higher state
of man is a hypothetical postulate of Teilhard's theory of the
evolutionary progress, which brings us no closer to identifying the
morally benign characteristics required to achieve it. He does,
however, refer to one human quality which is essential to the process
of co-reflexion—'the most humanising moral quality we know: the
team spirit' (p.259). And self-evolution is only possible through the
team effort of the whole human species: 'co-reflexion leads us to the
idea of a growing self-integration of the zoological group to which
we belong' (p.257).

Teilhard sees genetic manipulation as necessary not only on the
level of the individual but also on that of society. Current ideas of
genetic manipulation are usually discussed in terms of the individual, as correcting some individual genetic defect or other, but
Teilhard is interested primarily in the genetic improvement of the
human species 'by directed selection'. Reflections upon ethnic
differences come into the picture:

I see an increasing possibility of another hypothesis, namely that the
Chinese are arrested primitives, victims of retarded development
whose anthropological substance is inferior to ours. ....Neither the
Christian attitude of love for all mankind, nor the humane hopes for an
organized society must cause us to forget that the 'human stratum'
may not be homogenous. If it were not, it would be necessary to find
for the Chinese, as for the Negroes, their special function, which may
not (by *biological* impossibility) be that of the whites.[36]

In his essay 'Human Energy'[37], 1937, under the section entitled,
Organization of Total Human Energy, Teilhard enumerates the major

problems facing humanity in its use of human and material resources. He sees racially unprogressive groups and 'life's rejects in
hospitals' as impeding our progress and he calls for a redirection of
our energies:

> We are incredibly slow to achieve (or even conceive) the realization of
> a 'body of humanity. All sorts of related questions, scarcely yet raised
> despite their urgency, are attached to it. What fundamental attitude,
> for example, should the advancing wing of humanity take to fixed or
> definitely unprogressive ethnical groups? The earth is a close and lim-
> ited surface. To what extent should it tolerate, racially or nationally,
> areas of lesser activity? More generally still, how should we judge the
> efforts we lavish in all kinds of hospitals on saving what is so often no
> more than one of life's rejects? Something profoundly true and beauti-
> ful (I mean faith in the irreplaceable value and unpredictable resources
> contained in each personal unit) is evidently concealed in persistent
> sacrifice to save a human existence. But should not this solicitude of
> man for his individual neighbour be balanced by a higher passion,
> born of the faith in that other higher personality that is to be expected,
> as we shall see, from the world wide achievements of our evolution?
> To what extent should not the development of the strong (to the extent
> that we can define this quality) take precedence over the preservation
> of the weak? How can we reconcile, in the state of maximum effi-
> ciency, the care lavished on the wounded with the more urgent
> necessities of the battle? In what does true charity consist? (p.132–3)

The editor of Teilhard's essay, in a footnote to the extract above,
comments that 'Teilhard's constant efforts to encourage the weak and
inspire the strong prove that he knew how to make this reconciliation'. But Teilhard is not aiming at a reconciliation; he refers to a
higher passion than caring for the individual, born from the
achievements of evolution. Teilhard wants a different basis for
determining the allocation of human effort, evident from his
reference to the 'advancing wing of humanity' and the attitude 'to
fixed or unprogressive groups'. It is unclear on what basis the
distinction will be made. His constant reference to scientific research
as the highest form of human activity suggests that this will provide
the grounds for classifying the various ethnic groups as advancing or
unprogressive.

Teilhard's understanding of society

Teilhard's motivation for the genetic manipulation of the human species is also evident in his plan for the organization of human society. In his characteristic manner, he describes the 'welding of peoples and individuals one to another, for all their recalcitrance, in a more sublime intoxication'[38]. In *The Phenomenon of Man* he remarks: 'Monstrous as it is, is not modern totalitarianism really the distortion of something magnificent and thus quite near to the truth' (p.257); and in 'the Grand Option' (1939) he asserts: 'the modern totalitarian regimes, whatever their initial defects, are neither heresies nor biological regressions: they are in line with the essential trend of 'cosmic' movement'[39]. Teilhard praises 'Fascism [as] a fairly successful small-scale model of tomorrow's world' and as an educator of mankind in its human role:

> It may perhaps be a necessary stage in the course of which men have to learn, as though on a smaller training ground, their human role. But it will become what we are waiting for only if, when the time comes, it abandons the narrow nationalism that obliges it to exclude from its constructions all the elements that really come up to the scale of the earth.[40]

It is relevant that Fascism was concerned with racial purity and embarked on a eugenics program to achieve that end. One of the reasons for Teilhard's sympathy with totalitarian regimes may well be that only under such systems could his desire for genetic improvement of mankind be achieved.

In *The Phenomenon of Man* Teilhard asserts the possibility 'of foreseeing with certainty (*if all goes well*) certain precise directions of the future' (p.308). He introduces the qualification 'if all goes well' because he sees biological and social evolution as influenced by two uncertainties, chance at the molecular level of matter, and freedom in the human sphere. But he dismisses these sources of uncertainty as being of little influence in practice:

> Let me add, however, that in the case of very large numbers (such, for instance, as the human population) the process tends to 'infallibilise' itself, inasmuch as the likelihood of success tends grows on the lower side (chance) while that of rejection and error diminishes on the other side (freedom) with the multiplication of the elements engaged. (p.308)

And as a footnote he adds:

For a Christian believer it is interesting to note that the final success of hominisation (and thus cosmic involution) is positively guaranteed by the 'redeeming virtue' of the God incarnate in his creation. But this takes us beyond the plane of phenomenology.

There are a series of important claims here which need to be examined in some detail. Teilhard asserts that his account of evolution is able to predict its future and that of society. Karl Popper has criticized such claims in *The Poverty of Historicism*[41] as a failure to distinguish between trends and scientific laws. As evolution is a unique sequence series of events (like an historical process), there is no Law of Evolution although trends may be discernible in the process. 'The crucial point is this', Popper writes,

> although we may assume that any actual succession of phenomena proceeds according to the laws of nature, it is important to realize that practically *no sequence of, say, three or more causally connected concrete events proceeds according to any single law of nature.*[42]

But Teilhard is claiming much more than a trend, as will be seen later in this chapter. He affirms that the culmination of the biological evolutionary process, point Omega, is a scientific certainty. 'Indeed there is no longer any possible doubt'[43].

Briefly, Popper's argument proceeds as follows: the course of human history is strongly influenced by the growth of human knowledge (even those who see scientific ideas as merely the by-products of material developments admit this). Rational or scientific methods cannot predict the future growth of scientific knowledge: 'Attempts to do so can attain their result only after the event, when it is too late for a prediction; they can attain their result only after the prediction has turned into a retrodiction'[44].

It comes as somewhat of a surprise after his insistence that eugenics must 'replace the crude forces of natural selection' that he gives such emphasis to the purely unaided natural evolution in the formation of society and in the determination of its future direction. By insisting on intervention in evolution, Teilhard presents a future different from that resulting from the forces of natural selection, and one to be largely determined by our wishes. No attention seems to have been paid to this tension in his thought.

Teilhard sees biological evolution and the growth of human society as a continuum. He views association or social organization as a general evolutionary principle, present at the molecular level and at other critical stages in the emergence of humanity and culminating in the social organization of humankind[45] In the 'The Grand Option', 1945, he is adamant that what he has to say 'does not anywhere go beyond the field of scientific observation' (p.126). Few, if any scientists, accept that the formation of society and its institutions are in any real sense a biological process. And Teilhard himself gives no evidence to support his view. He sees social organization as the final stage of the general principle of association found in all crucial stages of the evolutionary process, beginning with the formation of molecules from atoms, then in the development of the cell through the organization of complex molecules, and so on through the various stages of evolution to the appearance of Man:

> Everything happens as though, in the course of its phyletic existence, every living form achieved (with more or less success) what may be called a period, or even a point of socialisation.[46]

Welcoming the attempt to wed biology and sociology, Teilhard writes:

> Only recently, and yet timidly, sociology has ventured to set up the first bridges between biology and itself. ...We see Nature combining molecules and cells in the living body to construct separate individuals, and the same Nature, stubbornly pursuing the same course but on a higher level, combining individuals in social organisms to obtain a higher order of psychic results. The process of chemistry and biology are continued without a break in the social sphere. This accounts for the tendency, which has been insufficiently noted, of every living phylum to group itself towards its latter end in socialised communities. Above all, in the case of Man it explains the rapid psychic rise accompanying socialisation.[47]

'The process of chemistry and biology' refers to the natural combination of atoms into molecules and the further association of complex molecules and cells into biological units. But is it valid to identify such associations with social groupings of the human species and the growth of human society? The two processes are analogous, but to claim that the growth of socialized communities is the continuation of the same process as that present at the level of chemistry and biology is an assertion that requires substantiation which there is nothing to indicate.

In his essay 'The Essence of the Democratic Idea—A Biological Approach'[48], Teilhard attempts to show that society is a purely biological phenomenon. He makes the claim 'that the growth of modern Democracy, and the impulses underlying it, will become more intelligible if, disregarding the political and juridical aspects, we approach the problem in biological terms' (p.238). 'The question asked', says Teilhard 'is, 'What is democracy?' Let me rephrase it.' What exactly is *hidden* behind the idea of democracy?''. Teilhard claims that the biological basis of democracy has been overlooked, and that people, who study or order society, attempt to mould 'social man' without realizing 'that the living substance they are manipulating is, by reason of its formation, characterised by certain narrowly defined lines of growth'. It becomes clear that the 'limits of growth' are those peculiar to Teilhard's own biological evolutionary mechanism.

Teilhard identifies the spirit of Democracy with the "evolutionary sense' or the 'sense of the species'—the last signifying, in the case of Man, not merely the instinct of permanence through propagation, but also a will to grow through the organised arrangement of the species upon itself' (p.240). This rests on a biological principle central to Teilhard's evolutionary mechanism, 'convergence', a term which expresses the turning of evolution upon itself (after the initial evolutionary 'divergence' at the lower level of evolution) as the result of the increasing 'within of things' or spiritualisation of matter. With the appearance of Man, convergence begins. But even at a lower stage of evolution Teilhard claims that there is a movement towards increasing consciousness:

> Whether insects or vertebrates, it is rare for a living group of any kind, provided one can follow it over a long enough space of time, not to show a notable advance in what we call indifferently cephalisation or cerebration. The global result of this has been to convince us that ....the mass of cerebralised matter has unceasingly increased within the biosphere. ('The Singularities of the Human Species', p.220)

Stephen Gould rejects this claim of Teilhard as having no scientific basis:

> Teilhard's florid and mystical writing is often more difficult to decipher than his role at Piltdown but I believe that the general line of his argument can be simply expressed. ....As the spirit gains the upper hand, convergence shall begin ...The direction of a billion years shall be

reversed, and the conscious lineages will begin to converge as spirit gains rapidly in its sway over matter ....What can one say to such a scheme? Would it be too literal and mean spirited to argue that it seems to fail at its only points of testable contact with the fossil record. Few paleontologists can discern any general, much less inevitable, trend to increasing braininess in the history of life. Most animal species are insects, mites, copepods, nematodes, mollusks, and their cousins, and I, at least, can see no pervasive trend among them toward the domination of matter by spirit.[49]

In 'The Essence of the Democratic Idea–A Biological Approach'[50] (1949), Teilhard discusses Democracy from the viewpoint of biology, in relation to 'the legendary attributes, Liberty, Equality, and Fraternity, which are indissolubly associated in our minds with the idea of government of the people by the people; and then to the conflict, now more acute than ever, which has divided Democracy into two factions, liberal and socialist'(p.240). Teilhard insists that 'their undeniable, if vague, attraction takes on a clearer aspect if we consider them from a biological standpoint', from what is in fact the standpoint of his evolutionary mechanism. Liberty is the opportunity to develop the individual's potential to the fullest extent. Equality is the right to participate in the common endeavor to promote the future of the individual and the species. And Fraternity is the sense of organic interrelation between members of the human species, 'based not merely on our more or less accidental coexistence on the surface of the earth, or even on our common origin, but on the fact that we represent, all of us together, *the front line*, the crest of an evolutionary wave still in full flood' (241). Liberty, Equality, Fraternity are 'no longer indeterminate, amorphous and inert, but directed, guided, dynamised by the growth of a fundamental impulse which underlies and sustains them'[51].

Directed evolution is central to his process and dynamised refers to the increasing radial energy or spiritualisation of matter. Teilhard lets fall no clues as to how the ideas of Liberty, Equality and Fraternity have been made determinate and active.

The type of human being Teilhard wants has been described already. The type of society he plans to produce becomes clearer from some of his writings, a society formed around a scientific elite:

Research has for long been considered by men as an accessory, an eccentricity or a danger. The moment is approaching when we shall perceive that it is the highest of human functions. [52]

> The Christian scientist seems to everyone the best situated and the best prepared to develop in himself and foster around him the new human type seemingly awaited at present for the further advancement of the earth: the seeker who devotes himself, ultimately through love, to the labours of discovery. No longer a worshipper of the world but of something greater than the world, through and beyond the world in progress.[53]

'The Christian scientist seems to everyone...'; but who is 'everyone'? It is important not to let the appellation 'Christian scientist' hide the fact that Teilhard regards a society governed by a scientific elite as the ideal and called for by the evolutionary process. In a report to a study week organized by the Society of Jesus in 1947[54] Teilhard lauds the religious value of research and compares its rank and dignity with 'nutrition and reproduction'. He asks the question: How should we interpret the modern rise of scientific research? His answer: man is part of a continuing biological evolutionary process, and he and he alone is 'capable of discovering and controlling the material sources of energy that will in all probability enable it (by direct action on the laws of reproduction, heredity and morphogenesis) to stimulate and influence at will—within limits we cannot yet foresee—the transformation of its own organism (including the brain)' (p.200). So not unexpectedly Teilhard ascribes the importance and dignity of scientists to their ability to forward evolution and hence the future direction of society: 'It is inevitable that under the influence of the almost magical powers that science gives him of controlling the progress of evolution, modern man should feel himself tied to the future, to the progress of the world, by a sort of religion which is often (wrongly, I believe) treated as neopaganism'[55].

A constant theme that appears in Teilhard's discussion of society is the threat of boredom, taedium vitae:

> Consider all around you the increasing number of those who are privately bored to tears and those who commit suicide in order to escape life. The time is close at hand when mankind will see that, precisely in virtue of its position in a cosmic evolution which it has become capable of discovering and criticising, it now stands biologically between the alternatives of suicide and worship.[56]

Teilhard's solution to this threat is to become part of this evolutionary movement, although he admits that there are some who will not want to be part of the society of the future based on his evolutionary principles.

In 'The Singularities of the Human Species' (1954), Teilhard sees those who refuse to accept 'the investigations and recontructions of science' for the furtherance of human society as abnormal: 'It is conceivable that certain abnormal individuals will exercise their liberty of refusal and break free (to their loss) from this aspiration of the 'evolutionary vortex'[57]. But the conclusions which he lists as deducible from the investigations of science are no more than his own view of how evolution proceeds, namely the appearance of man through the principle of complexity-consciousness, the biological movement of pan-human convergence of the human species, ultimately leading to a 'peak of hominisation', point Omega. In a letter to a friend December 3, 1948, however, Teilhard openly confesses that he will rely on *events* to guide him in foreseeing the direction of society.

> The study of the 'human social phenomenon' is just about the only thing I really care about. But it is hard to see how I might tackle the subject at my age without remaining in generalities. I count on events to guide and show me a solution.[58]

So in spite of confident claims in his published work to discern the direction of the human species, Teilhard in private correspondence reveals his true thought on the matter.

The final stage of socialization, Point Omega

In line with his public confidence, Teilhard dismisses attempts by other writers, such as Eddington, Julian Huxley and Charles Galton-Darwin, to foresee the future course of society as mere 'chance gropings into the future, rather than serious extrapolations'[59]. What surprises Teilhard about these various chance gropings 'is the absence of all firm principle as a basis for the conjectures put forward', whereas his extrapolation, he asserts, is based on 'the investigations and reconstructions of science'. It is strange that Teilhard should so belittle the predictions of Julian Huxley when he agrees with so much of Huxley's thought and feeling about evolution. On the other hand Huxley indicates his inability to understand

Teilhard's point Omega, in his Introduction to *The Phenomenon of Man*:

> Teilhard, extrapolating from the past into the future, envisaged the process of human convergence as tending to a final state, which he called 'point *Omega'*, as opposed to the *Alpha* of elementary material particles and their energies ...[At] point Omega the noosphere will be intensely unified and will have achieved a 'hyperpersonal' organisation. Here his thought is not fully clear to me.[60]

Point Omega, the culmination of the evolutionary process, is for Teilhard a scientific fact:

> Indeed there is no longer any possible doubt that the play of the planetary forces of complexity-consciousness, *normally extended*, summons us to and destines us for the peak of hominisation (or, as I have become accustomed to calling it the *point Omega*).[61]

Biologists almost universally reject Teilhard's views as mere speculation and in no way justified by the scientific evidence. An example is Stephen Jay Gould's referring to Teilhard's point Omega: 'All previous life existed for us and for what *we* could become. ...This is the anthropocentric vision with a vengeance'[62]: Another example is George Gaylord Simpson's rejecting as extra-scientific all the fundamental ideas in *The Phenomenon of Man*:

> Which are the premises and which are the conclusions?....Teilhard's major premises are in fact religious and, except for the conclusion that evolution has occurred, most of his conclusions about evolution derive from those and not from scientific premises ....That is evident, too, in the complex concept of Omega that is the key to Teilhard's personal religious system and to his purpose in writing the book.[63]

For Teilhard point Omega is *the* crucial aspect of what he sees as a scientific account of evolution; without it none of his mechanism for evolution has any significance.

He considers three objections that may be brought against the attainment of point Omega. Two of the objections do not cause him concern. The first is the likelihood that the earth will be subject to some catastrophic disaster thus annihilating the human species before it reaches its goal—unlikely in view of great age of the earth in comparison with the age of the human species and also because the human species differs from others in having attained the level of reflection and thus being better able to survive. The second objection, the exhaustion of the material resources necessary to sustain the human species on its evolutionary path, can be set aside in view of Man's discovery of ever different forms of energy. The serious objection for Teilhard lies in the question, 'shall we have enough *inner* genius and drive'? In this connection he remarks that he finds that most scientific essays on the future of Man accept that Man is unchangeable and imperfectible—an attitude also common among theologians. 'In the majority (if not all) of the scientific essays', Teilhard writes,

> lately devoted to the future of man, nothing is more disturbing than the authors' assurance in prefacing their evaluations of the future with the categorical postulate that human nature is definitely unchangeable and imperfectible. In his qualities (or failings) and in his social reactions, man will be tomorrow exactly as we see him to-day ....From the religious point of view, the prospects envisaged are no more rosy. According to Karl Barth, 'Men have never been good, they are not good, they never will be good'[64]

Teilhard dismisses such attitudes because they ignore the existence of biological convergence which he claims makes our descendants 'ultra hominised'. The claim becomes more extraordinary when the necessity of taking genetic control of the evolution of the human species is insisted upon—'self-evolution', Teilhard calls it. The genetic engineers are to decide what is moral and biological perfection. 'Who dares affirm today', Teilhard exclaims,

> (despite the brilliant caricature by Aldous Huxley in *Brave New World*) that ten thousand years hence this wild imagination of yesterday may not have become a reality?[65]

That yesterday's imagination might become tomorrow's reality is just what Aldous Huxley was afraid of.

In an originally unpublished appendix to his essay 'The Singularities of the Human Species' (1954) Teilhard rejects any accusation that he is leaving scientific enquiry—'having decided not to leave the ground of fact in these pages, I will not enter into metaphysical considerations'—and lists the attributes of point Omega. At point Omega perfected humanity is gathered into a 'hyperpersonality', somehow without a loss of individual personalities, and escapes from death and space-time to be joined to the Risen Christ.

Furthermore Teilhard in 'The Directions and Conditions of the Future'[66] (1948) assures us that Christianity guarantees the final biological success of Man. 'For a Christian', Teilhard writes,

> provided his Christology accepts the fact that the collective consummation of earthly Mankind is not a meaningless and still less a hostile event, but a pre-condition (necessary, but not sufficient in itself) of the final, 'parousiac' establishment of the Kingdom of God—for such a Christian the eventual biological success of Man on Earth is not merely a probability but a certainty: since Christ (and in Him virtually the World) is already risen. (p.237)

'The 'parousiac' establishment of the Kingdom of God' is a reference to Christ's second coming at the end of time. The statement above is, however, a tautology for the Christian whose Christology accepts 'the collective consummation of earthly Mankind'. For the Christology which Teilhard advocates identifies this consummation with the biological perfection of humanity. There is no denying that Teilhard is an originator in thinking that the parousiac establishment of the Kingdom of God involves the biological perfection of humanity. It has never before come within the orbit of Christian thinking.

Extra-terrestrial Intelligences

The existence of extraterrestrial intelligences is not just an after thought in Teilhard's evolutionary scheme but an essential element of it. In his 'Life and the Planets'[67] (1945) Teilhard makes a fleeting reference to the existence of life on other planets as an aside to the discussion of the formation of a hyperpersonality, at point Omega.

> This idea of the planetary totalisation of human consciousness (with its unavoidable corollary, that wherever there are life-bearing planets in the universe, they too will become encompassed like the Earth, with some form of planetised spirit) may at first sight seem fantastic: but does it not exactly correspond to the facts, and does it not logically extend the cosmic curve of molecularisation.[68]

In 1953 Teilhard writes that 'the idea of *single* hominised *planet* in the universe has become in fact almost as *inconceivable* as that of a man who appeared with no genetic relationship to the rest of the earth's animal population'[69]. And elsewhere he asserts the unquestionable existences of extra-terrestrial intelligences as a necessary consequence of his evolutionary ideas.[70] Matter of its very nature must evolve and produce intelligent life. 'If at any point in sidereal space', Teilhard writes,

> a star should chance to appear, in which temperature, pressure, gravity, etc., would allow the gradual formation of very large molecules, this would be enough for life immediately to hook on at this point ...and for life, once hooked on, to concentrate and intensify to the point of reflecting on itself—if all goes well. ....Planets with noosphere, so far from being a curiosity in nature, would simply be *the normal and ultimate product of matter carried to its completion.*[71]

Teilhard's preoccupation with Man's position on the evolutionary path towards point Omega led him beyond advocating the improvement of the human species and society to measuring the degree to which humankind has advanced along this evolutionary path. But how is such a measurement to be obtained? Teilhard finds an answer to this question in the certainty of living beings on other planets. He talks of cosmic contact with other Noospheres 'across space and time' and the more than probable discovery that will allow us to discover the presence and gauge the 'psychic temperature' of *living planets* by means of some radar or some emulsion sensible to the distant influences of organized matter. By use of this method, we might determine what point *our* own Noosphere has reached in its evolution'[72].

What does Teilhard hope to obtain from such a measurement? The answer can be gauged from hints he gives in the essay. "We are still hesitating not only about the conditions but about the reality (or even the possibility) of a drift capable of carrying us, by way of always increased reflexion, towards some form of 'Ultra-humanity'"[73]. Teilhard showed real irritation with those who refused to accept that biological evolution is still continuing. It appears that he saw a contact with intelligent beings on other planets as a sure way to silence critics of his view that biological evolution is continuing. Elsewhere he shows that he is talking specifically of biological evolution and not simply cultural evolution. It was at Columbia University's bicentenary symposium, devoted to the unity of human knowledge, a few months before his death, that Teilhard strongly attacked critics of his view that biological evolution is continuing:

It was a demonstration—only to be expected—of the deep 'cleavage plane' between 'scientists' and 'humanists' as they call themselves; the latter, unlike the former, being either unable or unwilling to entertain the idea of a biological ultra-evolution of the human.[74]

Teilhard appears, then, to have two reasons for insisting on the inevitability of other intelligent beings in the universe. Firstly, a discovery of such beings would point to the inevitable evolution of intelligence from inanimate matter and thus support his view of pre-ordained directed evolution. Secondly, it would allow Teilhard to show that Man is still evolving by measuring the difference between the evolutionary state of such beings and ourselves.

NOTES

1   M. Midgley, *Evolution as a Religion*, London: Methuen, 1985.

2   Teilhard, *Human Energy*, p.127 and *The Appearance of Man*, p.255.

3   H.G. Wells, *Anticipations*, London: Chapman and Hall, 1901.

4   J. Huxley, *Religion without Revelation*, London: C.A. Watts, 1967, p.150.

5   A.C. Brackman, *A Delicate Arrangement*, New York: Times Books, 1980, pp346–347.

6   The recently published *Dictionnaire du Darwinisme et de L'Evolution*, ed. P. Tort, Presses Universitaires de France, 1995, argues otherwise.

7   C. Darwin, *The Descent of Man, and Selection in Relation to Sex*, second edition, London: John Murray, Vol. 1, 1874, pp.205–6.

8   A.R. Wallace, *Contributions to the Theory of Natural Selection*, London and New York: Macmillan, 1870, p.318.

9   M. Fichman, *Alfred Russel Wallace*, Boston: Twayne Publishers, 1981, pp.107–109.

10 A.C. Brackman, *A Delicate Arrangement*, New York: Times Books, 1980, p.346.

11 H. De Lubac, *The Religion of Teilhard*, trans. R. Hague, London: Collins, 1967.

12 E. Rideau, *Teilhard—A Guide to his Thought*, trans. R. Hague, London: Collins, 1967.

13 C. Cuénot, *Teilhard*, trans. V. Colimore, London: Burns and Oats, 1965.

14 B. Delfgaauw, *Evolution—The Theory of Teilhard de Chardin*, trans. H. Hoskins, London: Collins, 1969, p.91.

15 B. Towers, *Concerning Teilhard*, London: Collins, 1969.

16 Teilhard, *The Future of Man*, p.234.

17 Teilhard, *The Phenomenon of Man*, p.282.

18 Teilhard, *Letters to Two Friends 1926–1952*, trans. H. Weaver, New York: Rapp and Whiting, 1968, p.186.

19 Teilhard, *The Phenomenon of Man*, p.283.

20 Teilhard, *The Making of a Mind*, trans. R. Hague, London: Collins, 1965, p.233.

21 Ibid., p.202.

22 Teilhard, *Le Milieu de Divin*, trans. B. Wall et al., London: Collins, 1960, p.145.

23 Teilhard, *Human Energy*, p.48.

24 Ibid., p.50.

25 T. Corbishley, *The Spirituality of Teilhard*, London: Collins, 1971, pp.115–116.

26 J. Moltmann, *The Way of Jesus Christ*, trans. M. Kohl, London: SCM Press, 1990, p.297.

27 Teilhard, *Human Energy*, p.93.

28 Ibid., p.106.

29 H. Bergson, *The Two Sources of Morality and Religion*, p.75.

30 Teilhard, *Human Energy*, p.108.

31 Teilhard, *Toward the Future*, p.13.

32 Ibid., p.24.

33 Teilhard, *Human Energy*, p.113.

34 Teilhard, *The Appearance of Man*, p.208.

35 Ibid., p.256.

36 Teilhard, Letter April 20 1927 in *Letters to Two Friends 1926–1952*, p.67–8.

37 Teilhard, *Human Energy*, p.113.

38 Teilhard, *Toward the Future*, p.20.

39 Teilhard, *The Future of Man*, p.46.

40 Teilhard, *Science and Christ*, trans. R. Hague, London: Collins, 1968, p.141.

41   K.R. Popper, *The Poverty of Historicism*, London: Routledge and Kegan Paul, 1961.

42   Ibid., p.117.

43   Teilhard, *The Appearance of Man*, p.246.

44   K.R. Popper, *The Poverty of Historicism*, p.vi–vii.

45   Teilhard, *The Future of Man*, pp.37 and 124

46   Ibid., p.38.

47   Ibid., p.131.

48   Ibid., p.238.

49   S.J. Gould, *Hen's Teeth and Horse's Toes*, pp.245–249.

50   Teilhard, *The Future of Man*, p.238.

51   Ibid., p.240.

52   Ibid., p.38.

53   Teilhard, *Human Energy*, p.180.

54   Teilhard, *Science and Christ*, p.199.

55   Ibid., p.202.

56   Teilhard, *How I Believe*, trans. R. Hague, London: Collins, 1969, p.23.

57   Teilhard, *The Appearance of Man*, p.245.

58   Teilhard, *Letters to Two Friends, 1926–1952*, p.108.

59   Teilhard, *The Appearance of Man*, p.244.

60   Teilhard, *The Phenomenon of Man*, pp.18–19.

61   Teilhard, *The Appearance of Man*, p.246.

62   S.J. Gould, *Hen's Teeth and Horse's Toes*, p.249.

63 G.G. Simpson, 'Review of the Phenomenon of Man' in *Scientific American*, April 1960, pp.204–206.

64 Teilhard, *The Appearance of Man*, p.252.

65 Ibid., p.255.

66 Teilhard, *The Future of Man*, p.227.

67 Ibid., p.97.

68 Teilhard, *The Future of Man*, p.116.

69 Teilhard, *Christianity and Evolution*, trans. R.Hague, London: Collins, 1971, p.229.

70 Teilhard, *The Appearance of Man*, p.230. 'There *must* undoubtedly *be* "other inhabited worlds"'

71 Teilhard, *The Appearance of Man*, p.229.

72 Teilhard, *The Appearance of Man*, p.230.

73 Teilhard, *The Appearance of Man*, p.230.

74 Teilhard, *Letters from a Traveller*, trans. R. Hague et al., London: Collins, 1962, p.355.

CHAPTER EIGHT

SIN AND EVIL IN TEILHARD'S EVOLUTIONARY WORLD

If, as the result of some interior revolution, I were to lose in succession my faith in Christ, my faith in a personal God, and my faith in spirit, I feel that I should continue *to believe* invincibly in *the world*. The world (its value, its infallibility and its goodness)—that, when all said and done, is the first, the last, and the only thing in which I believe. It is by this faith that I live. And it is to this faith, I feel, that at the moment of death, rising above all doubts, I shall surrender myself.

—Teilhard de Chardin, *How I Believe*

The sort of religion that has been foretold with such warmth and brilliance by my friend Julian Huxley: to which he has given the name of 'evolutionary humanism'.

—Teilhard de Chardin, *The Heart of Matter*

It is not the intention of this chapter to deal with the many aspects of Teilhard's theology but to show how his evolutionary views changed his estimate of Christ's role. 'It would do no harm', the foremost Catholic theologian of our time remarks, 'for a present-day Christology'—the theology and mission of Christ—'to take up the ideas of a Teilhard de Chardin and to elaborate them with more precision and clarity, even if in his work it is not easy to find an intelligent and orthodox connection between Jesus of Nazareth and the cosmic Christ, the Omega Point of evolution'[1]. A fellow evolutionist, George Gaylord Simpson, refers to Teilhard's claim that his vision is not only compatible with Christianity but is its true interpretation[2].

Evolution and the development of Christian doctrine

Although Teilhard regarded his views on evolution as scientific, his prime concern was to recast all knowledge in the mould of evolution. 'One might well become impatient', he writes in *The Phenomenon of Man*,

or lose heart at the sight of so many minds (and not mediocre ones either) remaining today still closed to the idea of evolution ...For many, evolution is still only transformism, and transformism is only an old

Darwinian hypothesis as local and dated as Laplace's conception of the
solar system or Wegener's Theory of Continental Drift. Blind indeed
are those who do not see the sweep of a movement whose orbit
infinitely transcends the natural sciences and has successively invaded
and conquered the surrounding territory—chemistry, physics,
sociology and even mathematics and the history of religions.[3]

The area of human thought which primarily concerns Teilhard is
theology, and he firmly believes that for theology to be 'thinkable
and true' it must incorporate the 'scientific fact' of evolution. Teilhard
in keeping with his biological evolutionary views describes 'the
Kingdom of God' as 'a prodigious biological operation—that of the
Redeeming Incarnation' (p.293). What does Teilhard mean? In 'Christ
the Evolver [Le Christ évoluteur], or a Logical development of the
Idea of Redemption'[4], written in 1942 when he was sixty one,
Teilhard calls for a 'readjusting' of 'the fundamental lines of our
Christology to a new universe' (p.139) in the light of evolution.
....'Here, if I am not mistaken, is the core of the modern religious
problem, and the starting point, it may well be, of a new theology'
(p.144).

The problem, Teilhard claims, is an outdated Christology based
on a static view of mankind. On this view, mankind

remains in a state of equilibrium, and includes no cycle more extensive
than that of individual lives. Understood in this way, mankind would
perpetuate itself on earth, and even extend itself, throughout the ages,
but without any change in its level. ....As seen by modern
anthropology, the human group no longer forms a static aggregate of
juxtaposed elements, but constitutes a sort of super-organism, subject
to a global and well-defined law of growth. Man (and in this he
resembles every other living thing) was born not only as an individual,
but *as a species*. It is appropriate, accordingly, to recognize and study in
him, beyond the cycle of the individual, *the cycle of the species*. (p.140)

Teilhard admits that 'Scientists are still a long way from reaching
agreement about the particular nature of this higher cycle'. He
continues, 'I do not think that I would be mistaken, however, in
saying that the idea is gaining ground in scientific circles, and will
soon be generally accepted, that the biological process now taking
place in mankind consists, specially and essentially, in the progressive development of a collective human consciousness'. (p.141)
Undaunted that the biological foundation upon which he proceeds to
build his new Christology has no consensus in its favor, Teilhard

undertakes to reformulate traditional Christology as if he had a scientific warrant for it:

> If scientific views on humanisation are carried to their logical con-
> clusion they assure the existence at the peak of anthropogenesis of an
> ultimate centre or focus of personality or consciousness, which is
> necessary to control and synthesize the genesis in history of spirit.
> Surely this 'Omega Point' (as I call it) is the ideal place from which to
> make the Christ we worship radiate—a Christ whose supernatural
> domination, we know, is matched by a physical power which rules the
> natural spheres of the world. 'In quo omnia constant' (In him all things
> hold together'. Col.1: 17). We have here an extraordinary confluence,
> indeed, of what is given to us by faith and what is arrived at by reason.
> What used to appear to be a threat becomes a magnificent
> reinforcement. Far from conflicting with Christian dogma, the
> boundless dimensional augmentation man has just assumed in nature
> would thus have as its result (if carried to its ultimate conclusion) a
> new access of immediacy and vitality to contribute to traditional
> Christology. (p.143)

If the scientific existence of point Omega is rejected the remainder of his argument of course becomes irrelevant. But even allowing the existence at the peak of anthropogenesis 'of an ultimate centre or focus of personality' there remains the theological claim that this centre 'is the ideal place from which to make the Christ we worship radiate'. Teilhard, while affirming the scientific existence of Omega Point, admits a theological difficulty.

> At this point, however, we meet a basic difficulty, which contains the
> exact point I am commending to the earnest consideration of the
> professionals for whom I am writing.
>
> Regarded *materially* in their nature as 'universal centres', the Omega
> Point of science and the revealed Christ coincide—as I have just said.
> But considered *formally*, in their mode of action, can they truly be
> identified with one another? (p.143)

The essay, 'Christ the Evolver, or a Logical Development of the Idea of Redemption', is devoted to proving their coincidence in mode of action. From a biological evolutionary viewpoint, according to Teilhard, mankind reaches perfection at point Omega. He refers to the process as 'humanisation by evolution'. On the other hand he sees the traditional action of Christ as being a 'humanisation by redemption'. He then asks the question, 'can one, without distorting the Christian attitude, pass from the notion of 'humanisation by redemption' to that of 'humanisation by evolution''.

He sets about showing that the transition is legitimate, contending that there is a creative aspect to redemption. In the development of Christian doctrine, he says, what once appeared subordinate in Christian teaching sometimes assumes a primary importance. His example is that earlier teaching on marriage gave a primary role to the duty of procreation, while now the tendency is to place 'increasing emphasis on the mutual spiritual fulfilment of husband and wife'. Likewise:

> For obvious historical reasons, Christian thought and piety have hitherto given *primary* consideration in the dogma of the redemption to the idea of expiatory reparation. Christ was regarded *primarily* as the Lamb bearing the sins of the world, and the world *primarily* as a fallen mass. In addition, however, there was from the very beginning another element in the picture—a positive element, of reconstruction or re-creation. (p.145)

Teilhard does not indicate what the 'obvious historical reasons' were for the Christian emphasis on expiatory reparation in the dogma of redemption. The term 'fallen mass' in referring to the world would imply in *Teilhard's* eyes an unavoidable failure, prior to evolutionary theory, to understand that the creative process of necessity involves imperfection. 'Is it not now happening', Teilhard asks,

> that (in line with the mechanism of dogmas) these two elements, the positive and the negative, of the Christian influence, may be reversing their respective values, or even their natural order, in the outlook and the piety of the faithful, under the guidance of the spirit of God? (p.145)

While one can not deny that in Christian thought there is a creative aspect to redemption, to label the expiatory sacrifice of Christ as a negative element in Christianity, whose value is historically conditioned because it was formulated at a time of scientific infancy (i.e. ignorance of evolution), would make nonsense of the Christian tradition. And needless to say, Teilhard makes out no exegetical case for the identification of the evolutionary process with the re-creation referred to by St. Paul—'For the creation waits with eager longing for the revealing of the sons of God; for the creation was subjected to futility, not of its own will but by the will of him who subjected it in hope; because the creation itself will be set free from its bondage to decay and obtain the glorious liberty of the children of God' (Romans, 8:19–21).

Teilhard assimilated Christ-the-Redeemer to Christ-the-Evolver, that is, he gave primary emphasis to the creative aspect of Christ's role rather than to the redemptive aspect. In support of this reversal, he appeals to the Early Church of Alexandria. He remarks that, 'In the first century of the Church, Christianity made its definitive entry into human thought by boldly assimilating the Christ of the gospel to the Alexandrian Logos' [Au 1er siècle de l'Église, le Christianne a fait son entrée définitive dans la pensée humaine en assimilant hardiment le Jésus de l'Évanglie au Logos alexandrin]. Teilhard is adamant that a continuation of the same tactics, with an assurance of some success, is awaiting us. This time, however, the assimilation will not be to the static Logos 'of the stable Greek cosmos', but to 'the neo-Logos of modern philosophy—the evolutive principle of a universe in movement'[5]. Etienne Gilson commented on an error in Teilhard's citation of the Alexandrian Fathers. The Alexandrian Fathers to whom he appealed in support of his theological position had assimilated the Logos to the Redeemer—not, as Teilhard claimed, the other way about.[6]

Newman's name appears several times in Teilhard's letters[7] during the First World War, and he had a deep influence on Teilhard's thinking during this crucial period of his life when his evolutionary ideas were being formed. Teilhard was reading him constantly during the whole of 1916, and was well aware of Newman's attempt to distinguish a doctrinal development from a doctrinal corruption. In the *Development of Christian Doctrine* (1845) Newman[8] lists seven marks of a true development, among which is conservative action upon the past, that is, the developed doctrine does not contradict or reverse previous development. Teilhard's own admission that his view is a reversal of the relative values of the two elements, expiation and re-creation, and contrary to the 'natural order' suggests that his view is a theological corruption, judged by the criterion Newman extracted from the history of doctrine. Since Teilhard does not elaborate on the meaning he attaches to the expression 'natural order' one cannot say much more about this odd admission. One clue, however, emerges from his remark immediately afterwards. He refers to the 'irresistible rise of a Christian optimism' associated with this reversal, 'which without in any way rejecting the dark side of creation prefers to emphasize its luminous aspect'. So it appears that the sole reason for preferring to emphasize the importance of the re-creation aspect of Christ's work is that it is more in keeping with the optimistic ethos surrounding his interpretation of the advance of scientific knowledge. While admitting that there is no scriptural warrant for the reversal he wishes to see —'there is no explicit mention in the gospel'— Teilhard claims in a footnote that 'Christ has foretold it: 'I have many yet many things to say to you, but you cannot bear them now. When the Spirit of truth comes, he will guide you into all truth''.

Evolution's goal

The cross, the central symbol of Christianity, in Teilhard's cosmic Christology is 'the symbol of the arduous labour of evolution—rather than the symbol of expiation'[9]. The remark aptly expresses Teilhard's belief the evolution saves us. Elsewhere in different language the saving power of evolution is taken up again—the image of the Lamb of God bearing the burden of the world's progress (p.146).

In answer to the question 'Can biology taken to its extreme limit, enable us to emerge into the transcendent?'[10] (the title of a note dated 1951) Teilhard replies that 'we must answer that it can'. The 'extreme limit' is point Omega, and for Teilhard this is not only the limit of perfection of the human species but also an irreversible state from which humankind can no longer lapse.

> By becoming reflective the evolutionary process *can continue only if it sees that it is irreversible, in other words transcendent*: since the complete irreversibility of a physical magnitude, in as much as it implies escape from the conditions productive of disintegration which are proper to time and space, is simply the biological expression of transcendence. Evolution, the way out towards something that escapes total death, is the hand of God gathering us back to himself.[11]

One could imagine how evolution might reach an irreversible state, in the sense that it reaches a stage from which it no longer proceeds or lapses, but why should what it produces escape death? Teilhard feels that death is somehow eliminated at point Omega, along with the elimination of space and time. In this context irreversibility *is* transcendence, for it appears to possess all the characteristics of transcendence, that is, it is no longer confined by space and time, and death is no more. But can Teilhard's Point Omega be truly labeled as 'the biological expression of transcendence'?

Evolution's movement is towards a perfect human species, according to him, but in that case what happens to the myriad failures, 'the unfit', along the way? According to the traditional view Christ's redeeming work extends to all creation, including 'the dross' of the evolutionary process. In his teleological view, perfection at the end of the process is assured; however, 'the unfit' are necessarily discarded in order that Point Omega may be reached. It is difficult to see how 'the unfit' can participate in the final perfection. The only satisfaction for 'the unfit' appears to lie in their being assured that they are part of Teilhard's evolutionary process. Such a theological position offers them no salvation. For the crux of Teilhard's theology is that evolution saves us. This assertion, Teilhard claims, is a consequence of the Christian position that there is a creative aspect to redemption. But can one move logically from the traditional position of a creative aspect of redemption to Teilhard's claim that creation by evolution has a saving aspect? In other words, can the terms in the expression, redemption is creative, be reversed to read, creation (by evolution) is redemptive? Teilhard appears to be making such a transposition.

The unreality of the claim for the saving power of evolution is seen in his attitude to 'the unfit', 'the dross' of humanity in the First World War. For Teilhard 'the dross' of humanity must of biological necessity be discarded in his evolutionary scheme.

Here we come to the crucial aspect of Teilhard's theology of salvation. Teilhard envisages biological perfection of the human species at Point Omega, the culmination of evolution, and as a consequence its salvation. Accepting his mechanism of evolution, perfection of the human species is conceivable.

Original Sin

An area in which the division between Teilhard and traditional Christianity appears most marked is in the understanding of sin and evil. His views on this topic depend very much on his reformulated

Christology. The traditional Catholic doctrine of 'Original sin' within the context of a world in evolution was of particular concern to him. As the result of the Fall, human nature is estranged from God. This state of estrangement is 'Original sin'. It is sin by analogy, contracted but not committed. Because of 'Original sin' humanity is oppressed by sin and death.

In *Le Milieu Divin* (1927), Teilhard still espoused to some extent the traditional Catholic doctrine.

> Above all, by revealing an original fall, Christianity provides our intelligence with a reason for the disconcerting excess of sin and suffering at certain points.[12]

Also in the appendix to *The Phenomenon of Man*, 1948, entitled, 'Some Remarks on the Place of Evil in a World in Evolution', he refers to 'some catastrophe or primordial deviation'. But in his two essays on the topic, 'Note on Some Possible Historical Representations of Original Sin'[13] (1922) and 'Reflections on Original Sin'[14] (1947) as well as an appendix to his important theological essay 'Christ the Evolver', Teilhard completely rejects the idea of an original fall. The appendix is significant because it shows that he regarded the doctrine of 'Original sin' as needing to be reformulated as a necessary consequence of Christ's new role as the motive force of evolution. Not only does Teilhard's Christology require a different understanding of 'Original sin' in a world in evolution, but of all sin and evil.

The fullest account of his views is found in his 1947 essay, 'Reflections on Original Sin'. He begins by stating that for conclusive scientific and theological reasons original sin 'belongs to the trans-historic order'[15]. If this view is accepted, Teilhard claims, 'the conflict between original sin and modern thought disappears so completely that a dogma, at present such an intellectual brake, is suddenly seen to allow us an inner freedom of flight'[16]

Teilhard argues that since the bringing of death is ascribed to sin in traditional doctrine, it forces a dating of the Fall prior to any known fossil, that is, in the Pre-Cambrian period, for only after that time was death observed. But says Teilhard:

> Taken in the widest and most fundamental sense of the word, death (that is, disintegration) begins in truth to become apparent as early as the atom. Being built into the very physico-chemical nature of matter,

all it does is to express in its own way the structural atomicity of the universe. ...Located and tracked down in nature by its specific effect, death, original sin cannot therefore be assigned to any particular place or time. What it does do ...is to affect and infect the whole of time and space. If there is an original sin in the world, it can only be and have been everywhere in it and always, from the earliest of the nebulae to be formed as far as the most distant. This is what science tells us; and, by a most reassuring coincidence, this is what is even now being confirmed (if we carry them to their logical conclusion) by the most orthodox requirements of Christology.[17]

In a footnote Teilhard explains that although Man's death is the only death in question in regard to original sin, 'man could not have been alone in a system of essentially mortal animals in escaping organic decomposition'. It is noteworthy that he considers only physical death in his discussion of the traditional account of original sin and makes no mention of the more important spiritual death which separates man from God, the source of life. Teilhard identifies original sin with the tendency to physical death, that is disintegration, of all matter from man to the atom, whereas in the traditional view death is a consequence of the primordial sin. 'Original sin', Teilhard claims, 'expresses ...the perennial and universal law of imperfection which operates in mankind in virtue of its being 'in fieri' (in the process of becoming)'[18]. It is not the result of a human act, but the consequence of the manner in which God chose to create.

But what of the claim that this interpretation is in accord with 'the most orthodox of requirements of Christology'? Teilhard reduces to 'one point' the 'criterion of Christian orthodoxy'. It is that Christ is held to be *'the measure of and the head of creation'* (p.190).

Teilhard argues that even if there was a primordial sin committed towards the end of the tertiary period (when he estimates Man first appeared) 'in one corner of the planet earth':

It would mean obviously, that, *directly, organically* and *formally*, Christ's power could not extend beyond, could not fill more than, one short slender fibre in the universe which envelopes us. In legal title—juridically—Christ could still, it is true, be declared (in virtue of his divine dignity) master of the other cosmic factors; but he would no longer be, in the full physical sense intended by Saint Paul, he 'in quo omnia constant' [the one in whom all things hold together. Colossians 1:17] ...What we now have to investigate is how it [the Fall] might be conceived or imagined, not as an isolated fact, but as a general condition affecting the whole of history. (p.190)

Can Teilhard's claim be justified that St. Paul intended a 'physical sense' by the 'in quo omnia constant'? Firstly, what does 'physical sense' mean? What can it mean except the evolutionary role Teilhard assigns to Christ as the driving force of the evolutionary process. Does the traditional view of the primordial sin as a historic event somehow give Christ only 'legal title' as master of the cosmos and consequently fail to fulfill the physical role supposedly intended by St. Paul? The same argument could also be leveled against Christ's incarnation and redemptive death on the cross, occurring at a particular place and time.

'The *instantaneous* creation of the first Adam', Teilhard writes,

> seems to me an incomprehensible type of operation—unless the word simply covers the absence of any attempt at explanation. [And], if we accept the hypothesis of a *single perfect* being put to the test *on only one occasion*, the likelihood of the Fall is so slight that one can only regard the Creator as having been extremely unlucky. (p.193)

Teilhard's most serious objection to the traditional doctrine of original sin is that it implies the instantaneous creation of a man[19]. This is not unexpected in view of his evolutionary gradualism; yet he insists with particular vigor on the sudden birth of intelligence.

> The birth of intelligence corresponds to a turning in upon itself, not only of the nervous system, but of the whole being. What at first sight disconcerts us, on the other hand, is the need to accept that this step could only be achieved *at one single stroke*. ....In the case of human ontogeny we can slur over the question at what moment the new-born child may be said to achieve intelligence and become a thinking being, for we find a continuous series of *states* happening in the same individual from the fertilised ovum to the adult. ...It is quite different in the case of phyletic embryogenesis in which each stage or each state is represented by a *different being*, and we have no means at our disposal for evading the problem of discontinuity. If the threshold of reflection is really (as its physical nature seems to require, and as we have ourselves admitted) a critical transformation, a mutation from zero to everything, it is impossible for us to imagine an intermediary at this precise level. Look at it as we will, we cannot avoid the alternative—either thought is made unthinkable by a denial of its psychical transcendence over instinct, or we are forced to admit that it appeared *between* two individuals.
>
> The terms of this proposition are disconcerting, but they become less bizarre, and even less offensive, if we observe that, from a rigorously

scientific attitude, nothing prevents us supposing that intelligence might (or even must) have been as little visible externally at its phyletic origin as it is to-day to our eyes in every new-born child at the ontogenetical stage. ....let us nevertheless keep hold of one idea—that the access to thought represents a threshold which had to be crossed at a single stride.[20]

With such an admission Teilhard's objection to the instantaneous creation of the first man carries less persuasive force, as the characteristic separating man from the animals, intelligence, appeared in an instant 'between two individuals' in evolution. It would have been relatively easy for Teilhard to accept that upon the birth of intelligence man used it to disobey his creator. But Teilhard's account does not at any stage involve an act of human disobedience. God creates in an evolutionary manner—'the creative act is comprehensible only as a gradual process of arrangement and unification'—and so creation necessarily involves suffering, error and sin. But 'the primordial multiple' from which all material beings are formed,

is in no way directly sinful; on the other hand, since its gradual uni-fication entails a multitude of tentative probings in the immensities of space-time, it cannot escape (from the moment it ceases to be 'nothing') being permeated by suffering and error. Statistically, in fact, in the case of a system which is in the process of organization, it is absolutely inevitable ('fatalistically determined'): (1) that local disorders appear during the process ..., and (2) that, from level to level, collective states of disorder result from these elementary disorders (because of the organically interwoven nature of cosmic stuff). Above the level of life, this entails suffering, and, starting with man, it becomes sin.[21]

To avoid the accusation that God is responsible for evil, Teilhard declares the initial matter, 'the primordial multiple', to be 'in no way directly sinful'.

In the essay 'Reflections on Original Sin' (1947) Teilhard claims that his explanation of original sin respects both the evidence of science and the theology of salvation: 'the experiential background of dogma coincides with that of evolution' (p.196). 'It is true', he writes, that in his explanation

original sin ceases to be an isolated act and becomes a state (affecting the human mass as a whole, and as a result of an endless stream of transgressions punctuating mankind in the course of time). Yet even this, far from weakening the dogmatic characteristics of the Fall, intensifies them. In the first place, redemption is indeed universal, since it corrects a state of affairs (the universal presence of disorder) which is tied up with the basic structure of the universe in process of creation. Secondly, individual baptism retains, and in an even more emphatic form, its full justification. Looked at in this way, each new soul wakening into life is integrally contaminated by the totalized influence of all transgressions, past, present, and still to come, which by statistical necessity are inevitably spread throughout the human whole as it proceeds towards sanctification. In each soul there is something which needs to be purified. (p.196-7)

The traditional doctrine sees original sin as a defacing of creation, whereas Teilhard sees it as a necessary by-product of a creation which will not stop short of perfection.

Sin and evil in an evolutionary world

In the same essay Teilhard claims that in an evolutionary universe the intellectual problem of evil disappears.

The problem (intellectual problem) of evil disappears. In this picture, physical suffering and moral transgressions are inevitably introduced into the world not because of some deficiency in the creative act but by the very structure of participated being: in other words they are introduced as the *statistically inevitable by-product* of the unification of the multiple. In consequence they contradict neither the power of God nor his goodness. Is the game worth the candle? Everything depends on the final value and beatitude of the universe—a point on which we may well trust to God's wisdom. ....This amounts to saying that the problem of evil, insoluble in the case of a static universe, no longer arises in the case of an evolutive universe. It is strange that so simple a truth should be so little perceived and stated.[22]

Even if Teilhard had successfully argued that evil is inevitable in an evolutionary world there is something further that would have to be done to get rid of the problem of evil. Omnipotence can do anything of which the description is not self-contradictory[23]. Teilhard would have to show (or at least give grounds for thinking that) self-contradiction is involved in supposing creation in any other way than by evolution. Although Teilhard does not attempt that, he does in one place bring omnipotence up against what it is powerless to alter:

Our analysis has led to the conclusion that *not through inability*, but by the *very structure of the nil* [en vertu de la *structure même du Néant*] to which he stoops, God can proceed to creation *in only one way*: he must arrange, and, under his magnetic influence and using the tentative operation of enormous numbers, gradually unify an immense multitude of elements. Initially, these are infinite in number, extremely simple, and hardly conscious—then gradually become fewer, more complex, and ultimately endowed with reflection. What, then, is the inevitable counterpart to every success gained in the course of such a process, if not that it has to be paid for by a certain amount of wastage? So we find physical discords or decompositions in the pre-living; suffering in the living; sin in the domain of freedom.[24]

Just prior to this passage he refers to 'the creatable nil, which is pure nothing—and which nevertheless, by passive potentiality of arrangement (that is to say, of union), is a possibility of being, a prayer for being' (p.194). Nothing in what he calls his 'analysis', and nothing in the content of what he refers to as the 'creatable nil' helps at all in the elucidation of these statements.

How did Teilhard come by the idea that in order to create, God had to manipulate nothingness? Only one possibility suggests itself. The idea was touched in his mind by the doctrine of creation *ex nihilo*, creation from nothingness. But nothingness, of course, is not a kind of stuff that might be recalcitrant even to omnipotence. It isn't anything. The doctrine of creation from nothingness rules out the supposition that in creating God worked on anything. Once again one comes up against the meaning of omnipotence. Teilhard would have to show that it would be self-contradictory to create from nothingness other than evolutively.

Creation and the inevitability of evil

The editor of Teilhard's essay, 'Reflections on Original Sin', claims that Teilhard's comment that 'above the level of life', evolution 'entails suffering, and starting with man, it becomes sin', avoids the ambiguity of certain expressions which might result in evil appearing to be in man the pure statistical result of a process of evolution[25]. This is a strange comment in view of Teilhard's statement on the very next page of his essay: 'Physical suffering and moral transgressions are inevitably introduced into the world ...as the *statistically inevitable by-*

product of the unification of the multiple'. If moral transgressions are 'inevitable' what role is there for free-will?

De Lubac, the eminent Jesuit theologian, in *The Religion of Teilhard de Chardin*[26] defends Teilhard against the charge of seeing moral transgressions 'as the statistical inevitable by-product' of evolution and quotes *Le Milieu Divin*, where Teilhard refers to moral evil as 'the wrong use of our freedom' (p.82). But *Le Milieu Divin* (1927) is not a reliable source of Teilhard's mature theological views, for there he accepts a Fall which he completely rejects in his later writings.

In a later book, *The Faith of Teilhard de Chardin* (1964), de Lubac is at pains to defend Teilhard's statistical approach to moral evil. He begins by quoting Teilhard's 'postage' example[27] to illustrate how evil in an evolutionary world, both physical and moral, is a statistical necessity. In this example de Lubac[28] begins by accepting Teilhard's claim that 'statistical necessity does not imply obligation or do away with sin'. The example runs as follows: 'It is statistically necessary that when a large number of letters are posted, some mistakes will occur, stamps forgotten, wrong addresses, etc. At the same time everyone who sends a letter is free not to make a mistake'. This is a strange example to illustrate the inevitability of moral evil, as it does not capture the phenomenon of sin at all. With some justification it could be argued that the postage example could make sense of physical evil. But sin is not an inadvertent mistake; it involves the will. At least one can say that Teilhard held mutually contradictory views on the nature of sin and evil.

Morality of balance and morality of movement

In Chapter 7 the two moralities were discussed with a view to ascertaining Teilhard's vision of the ideal human being for the purpose of genetic engineering; in this chapter the emphasis is on their theological significance. As mentioned previously, Teilhard was indebted to Bergson for the concept of open and closed morality. In his essay 'The Phenomenon of Spirituality' (1937) Teilhard opposes traditional morality, which he calls the morality of balance, to his evolutionary morality, the morality of movement. The discovery of evolution, he claims, has forced upon mankind a new morality. 'For us who see the development of consciousness as the essential phenomenon of nature', he writes,

> things appear in a very different light. If indeed as we have assumed the world culminates in a thinking reality, the organization of personal energies represents the supreme stage of cosmic evolution on earth; and morality is consequently nothing less than the higher development of mechanics and biology. The world is ultimately constructed by moral forces; and reciprocally, the function of morality is to construct the world: an entirely new valuation leading to an altered programme of morality.[29]

It would be idle effort to work at the words 'morality is consequently nothing less than the higher development of mechanics and biology' to get any clarity of meaning out of them. The general drive of the passage is clear, that morality is to be shaped by the stage of cosmic evolution that has been reached on earth. The morality of balance, the morality of a static universe, Teilhard says,

> has until now been understood as a fixed system of rights and duties intended to establish a static equilibrium between individuals, and at pains to maintain it by a *limitation* of energies, that is to say of force. ....Now the problem confronting morality is no longer how to preserve and protect the individual, but how to guide him so effectively in the direction of his anticipated fulfillments that the 'quantity of personality' still diffuse in humanity may be released in fullness and security' (p.106).

Teilhard wants a change in emphasis from the protection of the individual to co-operation with the evolutionary process which for Teilhard is a development of consciousness.

Of some importance to the question of the relation of ethics to biological evolution are the opposing views of Julian Huxley and his grandfather T. H. Huxley which are juxtaposed in *Evolution and Ethics 1893–1943*[30]. Teilhard and Julian Huxley were close friends and shared similar views on the subject. Julian Huxley dismisses Thomas Huxley's 'antithesis' between ethics and evolution as false, because, he asserts, it is based on a limited definition of evolution and a static view of ethics. Teilhard concurred, as he wished to replace static morality with a dynamic morality based on biological evolution. Along with Julian Huxley, he extended the notion of evolution to encompass all reality. Julian Huxley claimed that 'we can obtain from the past history of the evolution of life not only reassurance as to the basis of some of our ethical beliefs, but also ethical guidance for the future' (p.198).

How does the past history of evolution provide a basis for ethics? 'Evolutionary ethics', Julian Huxley asserts,

> must be based on a combination of a few main principles: that it is right to realize ever new possibilities in evolution, notably those which are valued for their own sake; that it is right both to respect human individuality and to encourage its fullest development; that it is right to construct a mechanism for further social evolution which will satisfy these prior conditions as fully, efficiently, and as rapidly as possible. (p.124)

An example of what can be derived from Julian Huxley's evolutionary approach to ethics is the answer to the question: was Gaugin morally right in leaving his wife and devoting himself to painting? Here there is a conflict between the full development of a special talent (sanctioned by evolutionary principles) and the duty to wife and family. Evolutionary ethics supports the view that 'wherever there is a genuine and informed sense of vocation, this will be sufficient ethical sanction' (p.129). Julian Huxley readily admits that many moralists will disagree. But,

> evolutionary standards socialize morality and enlarge the scope of its values. Thus art and science, music and philosophy, all have their ethical aspect, since they provide new possibilities of experience of value in and for themselves, and this is a desirable evolutionary outcome. (p.129)

Julian Huxley concedes that ethics in an evolutionary context does not have any absolute value: 'While to the evolutionist ethics can no longer be regarded as having any absolute value, yet their relativity is neither chaotic nor meaningless: ethics are relative to a process which is both meaningful and of indefinitely long duration—that of evolutionary progress' (p.234). It follows that evolutionary ethics favors 'the most desirable direction of evolution', a direction which has culminated in the appearance of man and human society. On the principle of 'the most desirable direction of evolution' Julian Huxley develops his second claim that evolutionary considerations can provide 'ethical guidance for the future'. For the course of 'greatest moral rightness' lies in a reconciliation of the claims of the present and the future.

The minimum claim of the future is that our direction of evolution (which on the human level means the direction of social change) should leave the door open for further advance towards still higher levels of organization and yet unrealized possibilities; the maximum claim is that the future possibility should take precedence over present realization. The course of greatest moral rightness lies somewhere between these two extremes'. (p.125)

For Julian Huxley it is the 'desirable direction of evolution which provides the comprehensive (though least specific) external standards for our ethics' (p.126). From this premiss he draws the conclusion that 'a static stability [of social organization] is undesirable, and a complete or static certitude of ethical belief itself is unethical'. There is, however, 'an optimum rate of change above which stability is endangered and the sacrifices of the present are excessive, [and] below which the advance is so slow the welfare of future generations is needlessly impaired.'

T. H. Huxley is prepared to concede that 'cosmic evolution may teach us how the good and evil tendencies of man come about; but, in itself, it is incompetent to furnish any better reason why what we call good is preferable to what we call evil than we had before' (p.80). It does not follow from the fact that biological evolution proceeds by natural selection, 'the survival of the fittest', that 'men in society, men as ethical beings, must look to the same process to help them towards perfection'. On the contrary the evolutionary principle evident in nature, 'the strongest, the most self assertive, tend to tread down the weaker', is opposed to our ethical norms.

Social progress means a checking of the cosmic process at every step and the substitution for it of another, which may be called the ethical process ....the practice of that which is ethically best—what we call goodness or virtue—involves a course of conduct which, in all respects, is opposed to that which leads to success in the cosmic struggle for existence. In place of ruthless self-assertion it demands self-restraint; in place of thrusting aside, or treading down, all competitors, it requires that the individual shall not merely respect, but shall help his fellows; its influence is directed, not so much to the survival of the fittest, as to the fitting of as many as possible to survive. Laws and moral precepts are directed to the end of curbing the cosmic process and reminding the individual of his duty to the community. (pp.81-82)

Julian Huxley charges T.H. Huxley with accepting a static view of ethics. But his Romanes lecture does not give that impression. From his historical perspective T.H. Huxley recalls that the struggle to make life more humane has been long and tedious: 'Ethical nature may count upon having to reckon with a tenacious and powerful enemy as long as the world lasts' (p.84).

Teilhard's shares Julian Huxley's view that ethics are relative to the evolutionary process. In the 'The Phenomenon of Spirituality' (1937) the dynamic morality advocated by Teilhard is 'to try everything and force everything in the direction of human consciousness'. He gives a biological evolutionary reason for this approach to morality: 'These perspectives will appear absurd to anyone who does not see that ever since its beginnings life has been groping, an adventure, a risk'[31]. Teilhard holds that in biological evolution there is an advancing wing of humanity, which must be encouraged (See Chapter 7).

According to Teilhard many things seemingly allowed by the morality of balance are forbidden by the morality of movement. For example, 'money morality was dominated by the idea of exchange and fairness', but in the morality of movement 'riches only become good to the extent that they *work* for the benefit of the spirit'. Teilhard's explanation does not add much to our understanding. He says, in future the morality of the individual 'will forbid him a neutral and 'inoffensive' existence, and compel him strenuously to free his autonomy and personality to the uttermost'. This suggests something other than that usually advocated by the proponents of Christianity. Correlatively, many things seemingly forbidden by the morality of balance are not only permitted but even obligatory in the morality of movement. Teilhard does not give a specific example here, but elsewhere he does.

His preference for a supposed furtherance of the evolutionary process over the keeping of 'rules' is evident in his attitude to sexuality. In his essay 'The Evolution of Chastity' (1934) Teilhard refers to two opposing theories of chastity in the following terms:

> Fundamentally, there is a confrontation between two opposing theories of chastity—two ideas of purity. One side says, 'Above all, break no rule—even at the cost of some loss of richness.' The other side says, 'Above all, increase your richness, even at the cost of some contamination.' I need hardly say that, to my mind, it is the latter who have hold of the truth and will be vindicated by the future.[32]

One can only surmise what Teilhard means by 'contamination' in reference to chastity, but his reference to 'rule' in a Christian context can only mean the Commandments. Elsewhere in the essay he measures 'the moral value of actions by the spiritual impulse they provide'.

> Fundamentally, is not this spiritual use of the flesh precisely what men of genius, men who have been true creators, have instinctively found and adopted, without asking the moralists for their approval? And is it not from these allegedly impure sources that a life has been drawn which here and now sustains those of us to whom conservation is of prime importance? (p.81)

He quotes with approval the words of the heroine of a Russian novel; 'we shall in the end find another way of loving'. He takes this to mean that as evolution progresses spiritual fecundity (accompanying material fecundity ever more closely) will 'ultimately become the sole justification of union. Union for the sake of the child—but why not union for the sake of the work, for the sake of the idea?'

Following the same line of thought Teilhard concludes his autobiographical essay 'The Heart of Matter' (1950) with a proposal for a 'third way' for formalizing sexual energy. The first way is in marriage, which is ordered to having children. In the second way the separation of the sexes has given rise to religious life. But 'there can be no doubt', Teilhard says, 'that we lack a third road between the two. I do not mean a *middle* road, but a higher road ...no longer retreating (by abstinence) from the unfathomable spiritual powers that lie still dormant under the mutual attraction of the sexes, but of conquering them by sublimation'[33]. Teilhard followed the 'third way' in his own life as a Jesuit priest. He had deep relationships with several women, in particular Lucile Swan, the sculptor, and Rhoda de Terra, who had been divorced from his long time paleontologist colleague, Helmut de Terra. The intensity of his relationship with Lucile Swan, who was in China with him and typed *The Phenomenon of Man*, is evident from their recently published correspondence.[34] Teilhard was true to his vows of celibacy, even though he was tempted. 'Thank you once again', he wrote to Lucile, 'for what you give me so richly. God help us to conquer the fire'[35]. Two years after Teilhard's death Pedro Arrupe, the then General of the Jesuits, was asked whether young Jesuits seeking personal growth might follow the 'third way'. The editors of Lucile Swan's correspondence with

Teilhard report that 'in a letter of December 12, 1967, Arrupe, appealing to the texts of the Second Vatican Council and the statutes of the Society, said that the 'third way' (understood as the cultivation of an exclusive and intimate relationship with a woman similar to marriage but without conjugal privileges) cannot be justified or approved for Jesuits'[36]

The religion of tomorrow

The expression 'the religion of tomorrow' is Teilhard's and appears in his important essay, 'The Christic'[37], written just a month before his death. It is his last attempt to express his synthesis of science and theology. 'Today, after forty years of continuous thought', he writes, 'it is still the same fundamental vision that I feel I must present, and enable others to share in its matured form—for the last time.'(p.83)

Teilhard summarizes the three characteristics of the incarnate God which he perceives as now of the utmost importance for the rejuvenation of the Church: 'tangibility', which seems to mean Christ's entry into the very process of evolution by his birth; 'expansibility', Christ's standing at the culmination of evolution by virtue of his resurrection; and finally 'assimilative' power, point Omega integrating the human race in the unity of a single body, a hyperpersonality. Teilhard admits that this vision may be seen as an

> apparently illogical mixture of primitive 'anthropomorphism', mythical marvel and gnostic extravagance. But the remarkable fact remains—let me emphasize this—that, however strange the combination of the three factors may appear, *it holds good—it works*—and that you have only to diminish the reality (or even the realism) of a single one of the three confronting components for the flame of Christianity to be immediately extinguished. (p.89)

He offers no evidence in support of these claims.

Teilhard continues, 'I am completely convinced that the great spiritual edifices of tomorrow can be constructed (and will in fact be constructed) only if we start from this new element ("sense of evolution") and use it as our foundation'. But he doubts whether 'left to itself, our consciousness (however intense it may be in each one of us) of sharing in a planetary Flux of co-reflection is capable of building up the sort of religion that has been foretold with such warmth and brilliance by my friend Julian Huxley: to which he has given the name of "evolutionary humanism"'.

Julian Huxley in 1959 at the centennial celebration of the publication of *The Origin of Species* gave the following expression to his 'evolutionary humanism'.

> Future historians will perhaps take this Centennial Week as epitomizing an important critical period in the history of this earth of ours—the period when the process of evolution, in the person of inquiring man, began to be truly conscious of itself. ...This is one of the first public occasions on which it has been frankly faced that all aspects of reality are subject to evolution, from atoms to fish and flowers to human societies and values—indeed, that all reality is a single process of evolution. ....the evolution of mind or sentiency is an extremely rare event in the vast meaningless of the insentient universe. ...In the evolutionary pattern of thought there is no longer either need or room for the supernatural. The earth was not created, it evolved. So did ...our human selves, mind and soul as well as brain and body. So did religion ....Finally, the evolutionary vision is enabling us to discern, however incompletely, the lineaments of the new religion that we can be sure will arise to serve the needs of the coming era ...it gives man a potent incentive for fulfilling his evolutionary role.[38]

This may be compared with the following passage from Teilhard:

> A Religion of Evolution: that, when all said and done, is what Man needs ever more explicitly if he is to survive and 'super-live'....'*In a system of cosmo-noo-genesis, the comparative value of religious creeds may be measured by their respective power of evolutive activation.*' If we use this criterion, where, among the various currents of modern thought, can we find, if not the fulness at least the germ of what may be regarded as the Religion of tomorrow?....As I said before, it is still, and will always be, Christianity: but a 're-born Christianity, as assured of victory tomorrow as it was in its infancy—because it alone (through the double power, *at last fully understood*, of its Cross and Resurrection) is capable of becoming the Religion whose specific property it is to provide the driving force in Evolution.[39]

Both writers see evolution as the key to understanding all reality and the basis for the religion of the future. Julian Huxley, however, sees no place for the supernatural in evolutionary thought and so his 'religion' has no place for the supernatural. Teilhard's view that Christianity's specific property is to provide the driving force of evolution downplays its supernatural role.

Only a religion of the kind he preaches, Teilhard maintains, is capable of providing the 'spiritual activation' necessary to-day. Nonetheless, finding no other to share his vision, doubt comes over him, 'Am I, after all, simply the dupe of a mirage in my own mind?' But every time he begins to doubt 'three successive waves of evidence rise up from deep within me to counter that doubt'[40].

Firstly, the vision introduces a '*coherence* into the underlying depths of his mind and heart'. Even so he is a little disturbed that 'my faith does not produce in me as much real charity, as much calm trust, as the catechism still taught to children produces in the humble worshipper kneeling beside me'. While it is surprising that he makes such an admission for the very first time in his writings, and that only weeks before his death, he immediately rejects it. 'Nevertheless I know, too, that this sophisticated faith, of which I make such poor use, is the only faith I can tolerate, the only faith that can satisfy me—and even (of this I am certain) the only faith that can meet the needs of the simple souls, the good folk, of tomorrow'.

Secondly, there is the *contagious power* of his message. Once again he makes an unexpected admission. 'It would be impossible for me, as I admitted earlier, to quote a single 'authority (religious or lay) in which I could claim fully to recognize myself, whether in relation to my "cosmic" or "Christic' vision". As before he consoles himself with the observation that his ideas are becoming more widely accepted 'in the pulsation of countless people who are all—ranging from the border-line of unbelief to the depths of the cloister—thinking and feeling, or at least beginning vaguely to feel, just as I do'.

Finally, he points to the *superiority* of his vision to what he has been taught, and he adds 'even though there is at the same time an *identity* with it'. Teilhard claims to be the bearer of what amounts to a new revelation. He is fully aware of the audacity of his claim. In the final paragraph of the essay, as if in an effort to counter any objection, he declares that he and he alone, as the result of 'the new spiritual atmosphere created by the appearance of the idea of evolution', has 'the two essential components of the 'Ultra-human' in a state of extreme mutual sensitivity, love of God and faith in the world'.

> These two components are everywhere 'in the air'; generally, however, they are not strong enough, *both at the same time*, to combine with one another *in one and the same subject*. In me, it happens by pure chance (temperament, upbringing, background) that the proportion of the one

to the other is correct, and the fusion of the two has been effected spontaneously—not as yet with sufficient force to spread explosively—but strong enough nevertheless to make it clear that the process is possible—and that *sooner or later there will be a chain-reaction.* This is one more proof that Truth has to appear only once, in one single mind, for it to be impossible for anything ever to prevent it from spreading universally and setting everything ablaze[41].

NOTES

1　K. Rahner, *Theological Investigations*, trans. H.M. Riley, London: Darton, Longman and Todd, 1988, p.227.

2　G.G. Simpson, *Scientific American*, April 1960, p.201.

3　Teilhard, *The Phenomenon of Man*, pp.218–9.

4　Teilhard, *Christianity and Evolution*, trans. R. Hague, London: Collins, 1969 p.138

5　Teilhard, *Christianity and Evolution*, p.181. / *Comment je crois*, Paris: Éditions du Seuil, 1969, p.211.

6　R. Speaight, *Teilhard de Chardin, A Biography*, London: Collins, 1967, p.326.

7　Teilhard, *The Making of a Mind*, pp.93–4, 114, 148, 167.

8　J.H. Newman, *Development of Christian Doctrine*, London: Longmans, 1845.

9　Teilhard, *Writings in Time of War*, p.71.

10　Teilhard, *Science and Christ*, trans.R. Hague, London: Collins, 1965, p.212.

11　Teilhard, *Science and Christ*, p.212.

12　Teilhard, *Le Milieu Divin*, p.102.

13　Teilhard, *Christianity and Evolution*, p.45.

14　Ibid., p.187.

15　Ibid., p.188.

16　Ibid., p.189.

17　Ibid., pp.189–190.

18　Ibid., p.51

19　Ibid., p.193.

20　Teilhard, *The Phenomenon of Man*, p.171.

21　Teilhard, *Christianity and Evolution*, p.195.

22   Ibid., p.196.

23   Thomas Aquinas, *Summa Theologiae*, Part 1, Question 25, Articles 1–6.

24   Teilhard, *Toward the Future*, p.197. / *Les Directions de l'avenir*, Paris: Éditions du Seuil, 1973, p.212.

25   Teilhard, *Christianity and Evolution*, p.195.

26   H. de Lubac, *The Religion of Teilhard*, p.117.

27   Teilhard, 'La pensé du Père Teilhard de Chardin, par lui-même' in *Les Études Philosophiques* [Paris] 10, no. 4, p.581, (1955). A facsimile appears in Schmitz-Moormann, vol. X, p.4568.

28   De Lubac, *The Faith of Teilhard de Chardin*, trans. René Hague, London: Burns and Oates, 1964, p.103.

29   Teilhard, *Human Energy* London: Collins, 1969 p.105

30   T.H. Huxley and Julian Huxley, *Evolution and Ethics 1893–1943*, London: The Pilot Press, 1947.

31   Teilhard, *Human Energy*, p.108.

32   Teilhard, *Toward the Future*, p.78.

33   Teilhard, *The Heart of Matter*, pp. 59-60.

34   T.M. King and Mary Wood, *The Letters of Teilhard and Lucile Swan*, Washington: Georgetown University Press, 1993.

35   Ibid., p.64.

36   Ibid., p.295.

37   Teilhard, *The Heart of Matter*, p.83.

38   J. Huxley, The Evolutionary Vision in *Evolution after Darwin*, (Tax and Callender eds.) Vol 3 Chicago: University of Chicago Press, 1960, pp.249, 252, 260, 261.

39   Teilhard, *The Heart of Matter*, pp.97–99.

40   Teilhard, *The Heart of Matter*, p.100.

41   Ibid., p.102.

CHAPTER NINE

COSMIC OPTIMISM

> Get behind me all Godless pessimists *and* all Christian pessimists.
> —Teilhard de Chardin, *Letters from a Traveller*

> 'Human hopes' have been discussed without any attempt to look at the question that must be answered first: what is man justified in hoping for, *objectively*, leaving aside any emotional, philosophical, or mystical considerations, but viewed bio-cosmically?
> —Teilhard de Chardin, in C. Cuénot, *Teilhard de Chardin*

> Between these alternatives of absolute optimism or absolute pessimism, there is no middle way because by its very nature progress is all or nothing.
> —Teilhard de Chardin, *The Phenomenon of Man*

When the times through which Teilhard lived are considered—the world wars, the Nazi concentration camps, the atom bomb, and the Stalinist terror—one is astonished at Teilhard's optimism about what is to be expected. This optimism is in marked contrast to the anxiety that beset his childhood and which resurfaced in his old age. 'I am not yet out of my period of 'anxieties', he writes in 1953, 'an evil of which I can find traces in my childhood'[1]. His close friend and fellow Jesuit Pierre Leroy attributed Teilhard's life-long anxiety to a sense of impermanence, which led him in his childhood to 'a desperate search for the hardest matter'[2]. In the autobiographical essay *The Heart of Matter* (1950) Teilhard describes this search from the age of six. This need for something incorruptible led him to '*worship* in a real sense of the word, a fragment of metal (the lock-pin of a plough)'[3]. He answers the question, Why iron?, and in particular, Why one special piece of iron? It had to be, he says, as thick and massive as possible. Later he substituted quartz for iron, which ultimately led him to the study of geology and fossils. This deep need for permanence is reflected in a diary entry about his earliest memories:

> A Memory? My very first! I was five or six. My mother had snipped of[f] a few of my curls. I picked one up and held it close to the fire. The hair was burnt up in a fraction of a second. A terrible grief assailed me; I had learnt that I was perishable...What used to grieve me as a child? This insecurity of things. And what used I to love? My genie of iron!

With a plowhitch I believed myself, at seven years, rich with a treasure
incorruptible, everlasting. And then it turned out that what I possessed
was just a piece of iron that rusted. At this discovery I threw myself on
the lawn and shed the bitterest of tears of my existence.[4]

The loss of seven of his ten siblings while he was still a child, and
the strange attitude of his mother, who refused consolation, may
have aggravated his sense of insecurity. Raph Greenson, a psychia-
trist, in a symposium devoted to Teilhard, remarks that 'It is not
surprising that a little boy with this touching childhood history might
become concerned with searching for a world with other than
fearsome changes, and would become interested in durability,
deathlessness, and perfection'[5]

There is a further background point to be made: Teilhard's concerns in his study of paleontology for the past and for the future of
humanity led him to a comparative neglect of the present. The
important words in Teilhard's writings are the 'past' and the 'future'.
Such an attitude, with its focus always on the past or the future made
it easier for Teilhard to feel optimistic in spite of the present state of
things. We shall be returning to these personal considerations later.

The nineteenth century into which Teilhard was born was char-
acterized by a faith in the unfailing progress of humanity. Typical of
writers in that period was Herbert Spencer. 'Progress', Spencer said
in *Social Statics*[6], 'is not an accident, but a necessity ...the things we
call evil and immorality must disappear; ...man must become perfect'
(p.80). The reason Spencer gives for this proposition is that 'all evil
results from the non-adaptation of constitution to conditions' (p.73).
Moral evil in present-day society, he held, arises from a conflict
between the characteristics that adapted human beings for their
primitive state, namely that they should sacrifice the welfare of other
beings to their own, and those characteristics that are now required,
that they should not do so. 'All sins of men against each other',
Spencer writes, 'from cannibalism of the Carrib to the crimes and
venalities that we see around us ...have their cause comprehended
under this generalization'. From this principle flows the Spencerian
dictum that 'Belief in human perfectibility merely amounts to the
belief, that in virtue of the process [adaptation to the new conditions
of human society] man will eventually become completely suited to
his mode of life' (p.78).

Theologians of the late nineteenth and early twentieth century
tended to share Spencer's belief in a new age for mankind. Adolf

Harnack gave expression to this belief in a series of celebrated lectures at the University of Berlin in 1899–1900. These lectures were subsequently published as *Das Wesen des Christentums* (English translation: *What is Christianity?*[7])—thanks to an ardent listener who took down the extempore lectures in shorthand. Harnack is highly critical of the established churches because they—in particular the Roman Catholic Church—have surrendered the simplicity of the Gospel for 'doctrine'. The Church had betrayed the Gospel in its struggle with Gnosticism by putting 'its teaching, its worship, and its discipline, into fixed forms and ordinances', and then excluding 'everyone who would not yield to them' (p.207). 'The real difficulties in the way of the religion of the Gospel remain the old ones', Harnack says, not 'modern ideas' (p.300). He urges us to 'look at the course of mankind's history, follow its upward development, and search, in strenuous and patient service, for the communion of minds in it' (p.301). His ideal society is a 'communion of minds' animated by a belief in what he saw as early Christianity.

The former Jesuit George Tyrell, in his posthumous work *Christianity at the Cross-Roads* (1910), was looking for a new universal religion of which Christianity was but the germ: 'Is it not the very growth of the spirit that is straining the old categories and forms and seeking a better embodiment—and this more especially in Catholicism?'[8]. But he did not see the future universal church as conforming to Harnack's ideas: 'The Christ that Harnack sees, looking back through nineteen centuries of Catholic darkness, is only the reflection of a Liberal Protestant face, seen at the bottom of a deep well'[9]. Yet both writers were imbued with the optimism of the age.

Chadwick in *The Secularization of the European Mind in the Nineteenth Century* (1975) notes that in the latter part of the nineteenth century 'something happened to religious people which affected their attitude to the world'[10]. Part of change was due to the theory of evolution. 'After 1864', Chadwick writes, 'the word *evolution* was not quite a neutral word. It was quite near the word progress'.

By the close of the First World War, however, the mood changed. Among theologians Karl Barth's *Der Römerbrief* (*The Epistle to the Romans*[11]) (1918) signaled a change to a more somber and realistic analysis of humanity's religious possibilities. Poets, notably of course T.S. Eliot, reflected the changed mood in such poems as 'The Waste Land' (1922). Likewise, the philosopher of history, Oswald Spengler, captured something of the mood of the times in *The Decline of the*

West (1918). Teilhard, however, exuded an optimism, 'malgré les apparences', to the contrary. Both Teilhard (1881–1955) and Barth (1886–1968) lived through the same period and one cannot but be amazed at their different attitudes to the same historical events, in particular to the First World War. Barth saw in the War the bankruptcy of the theology of the time and the titanic impulse of humanity to storm the heights and 'build a city and a tower with its top in the heavens'. 'Christianity watches with some discomfort', he writes, 'the building of these eminent towers ...for it detects therein the menace of idolatry' (p.463). Barth opposed what he saw as the mere cultural religion of the recent past that knew no Fall, no original sin, but only development: 'Christianity is uneasy when it hears men speaking loudly and with confidence about "creative evolution", when it marks their plans for perfecting the development of pure and applied science, of art, of morals and of religion, of physical and spiritual health, of welfare and of well-being' (p.462). Many theologians became Barthian-minded between the two World Wars, among them Dietrich Bonhoeffer.

But there was also a liberal element that was still making itself felt, represented in particular by F.R. Tennant, who was strongly influenced by the theory of biological evolution. In *Philosophical Theology* (1930) Tennant disagrees with A.R. Wallace, the co-proposer with Darwin of the theory of natural selection to account for biological evolution, 'that, inasmuch as natural selection cannot account for the origin of the higher moral sentiments, resort to a supernatural cause is necessary'[12]. Tennant maintains that naturalism can supply an explanation for the emergence of 'higher moral sentiments' without appeal to an intervening divine cause.

> Just as a bodily organ, developed in response to environment so as to fulfil a certain function, often proves, when acquired, to be capable of performing other functions also, and becomes a starting-point for developments in new directions, so may a mental functioning once sufficiently developed to possess utility in the struggle for existence, be able of itself, or without further evocation from the environment, to develop to higher levels, which from nature's point of view are superfluous. (p.94)

Though some theological optimism survived the Great War, the predominant mood after the War was dark. But with the advent and in the aftermath of the Second World War a surprising change took place, typified by Teilhard. When one might have expected an even more pessimistic attitude to prevail among theologians, one finds the exact opposite, an optimism about humanity's future.

Between the end of the Second World War and his death Teilhard was particularly severe in his attitude to Karl Barth. As mentioned in Chapter 7, Teilhard dismisses contemporary scientific essays which 'postulate that human nature is definitely unchangeable and imperfectible'; and likewise the theologian Karl Barth for his view that 'Men have never been good, they are not good, they will never be good'[13]. In *What the World is looking for in the Church* (1952) Teilhard opposes the spirit of the times to Barthian pessimism. 'In spite of the froth', Teilhard writes,

> of existentialism and Barthianism which has been smothering us during recent years, the basic current in the world at this moment is not heartsick pessimism (whether atheist or religious) but a conquering optimism (as evidenced by the rapid rise of Marxism). It is not only self-centered, grasping ambition directed towards 'well-being'; it is also a collective drive towards 'fuller-being', expected and sought for in the direction of the fulfilment of the zoological group to which we belong.[14]

This quotation also gives a clue to the reason for the optimistic mood among intellectuals generally after the Second World War, compared to the deep pessimism after the First. Part of the explanation for this optimism lies in a certain admiration for Russia's part in the war. Among intellectuals, worldwide, this admiration was coupled with a deep sympathy with Marxism and a belief that Marxism enshrined genuine human values. Max Charlesworth is typical of such intellectuals. In his essay, *Catholics and Communists* (1968) Charlesworth observes with approval that 'the possibility of communication between Catholics and Communists has been in the air since the end of the last war'[15]. He argues that dialogue is possible with Communism but not with Nazism because Nazism enshrines 'values' which are all anti-human, and 'one cannot make any real distinction between the essential values of Nazism and the abuses and corruptions that may have affected those values' (p.111). Whereas, he thinks, this is not the case with communism: 'the abuses of communism are like the abuses of Christianity' in that the abuses do not pertain to the essentials of either. Within Teilhard's own order, the Jesuits, there were theologians who were beginning to apply Marxist theory to social situations. There was also a long tradition in French life of sympathy with Marxist ideas. The French Marxist Roger Garaudy wrote a preface for the Russian translation of Teilhard's *The Phenomenon of Man* in 1965 and a sympathetic study, 'Perspectives de L'Homme', of Teilhard's ideas[16]

Although Teilhard condemned Communism in *The Phenomenon of Man* (1940) as 'ghastly fetters' (p.257), later in life he was of the belief that Marxism was capable of being Christianized. In the essay 'The Christian Phenomenon' (1950) he refers to 'neo-humanist Marxism' as 'destined to become Christianized', and even voices the view that the gospel message permeates the most Stalinist materialism: 'Could anyone, for example, say to what extent the gospel message, not only in a potential form but as a legacy, permeates the most Stalinist materialism?'[17]. Teilhard was well aware of the situation under Stalin; for mention has already been made of Gabriel Marcel's consternation on hearing Teilhard brush aside the extermination of millions in Soviet slave labor camps as a mere episode in a march towards a glorious future.

Delfgaauw includes a short section on Teilhard's and Marx's view of history in his book *Evolution, The Theory of Teilhard de Chardin* (1961). He remarks that Teilhard's view of history reminds us in many respects of Karl Marx. Delfgaauw contrasts their attitude to science with the comment that 'with Marx science is a means of discovering the determined course of history' (p.54), whereas for Teilhard science does not fulfill that role. This is wide of the truth. For Teilhard the science of paleontology reveals the direction of evolution which he then identified with that of human history.

Marxism a sign of a 'Conquering Optimism'

What was it that convinced Teilhard after the Second World War that the rise of Marxism was a sign of a 'conquering optimism'? This is an important question because it takes us to the foundations of Teilhard's optimism. In 'The Heart of the Problem' (1949) Teilhard says that 'for some obscure reason something has gone wrong between Man and God *as in these days He is represented to Man*'[18]. Teilhard sees this as the heart of the religious problem. He remarks on his unique background as a Jesuit priest, and as one who has had the good fortune 'to live in close and intimate professional contact, in Europe,

Asia and America, with what was and still is most humanly valuable, significant and influential—"seminal" one might say—among people of many countries' (p.261). This is the 'cry of one who thinks he sees'.

The discovery of biological evolution means, for Teilhard, that Man is still evolving. Teilhard admits that 'Many biologists, and not the least eminent among them (all being convinced that Man, like everything else emerged by evolutionary means) undoubtedly still believe that the human species has reached an upper organic limit beyond which it cannot develop' (p.262). But his confidence is unshaken. He maintains that the mistake of Christianity, and other religions, has been to seek for 'the Higher Life, the Union, the long dreamed-of consummation ...*Above*, in the direction of some kind of transcendency': should we not rather look for it', Teilhard says, '*Ahead*, in the prolongation of the inherent forces of evolution? Above or ahead—or both? ....This is ... the vital question, and the fact that we have left it unconfronted is the root cause of all our religious troubles' (p.263).

Teilhard claims that there is a state of conflict which appears almost 'irreconcilable' between the two kinds of faith in the heart of modern Man: faith in evolution and the traditional faith of religious worship. To render 'the problem more concrete' he equates Marxism with faith in evolution. For he sees both faith in evolution and Marxism as 'faith in Man'. In the essay 'Faith in Man' (1947) he defines 'Faith in Man' as the 'fervent conviction that Mankind as an organic and organized whole possesses a future: a future consisting not merely of successive years but of higher states to be achieved by struggle. Not merely survival, let us be clear, but some form of higher life or super-life'[19]. Later in the essay he considers the two extremes of 'Faith in Man', Christianity and Marxism. He says that it is

> incontestable, a matter of every day experience, that each of these [the Christians and the Marxists], to the extent that he believes (and sees the other believe) in the future of the world, feels a basic human sympathy for the other—not for any sentimental reason, but arising out of the obscure recognition that both are going the same way, and despite all ideological difference they will eventually, in some manner, come together on the summit. (p.192)

The ideological differences are less important for Teilhard than the 'obscure recognition' that both are headed in the same direction.

Teilhard's attitude to Marxism goes a considerable way towards explaining his optimism following the Second World War.

Teilhard and Bonhoeffer

The phenomenon of a theological optimism mis-matched with the times had another exemplification in the thought of Dietrich Bonhoeffer (1906–1945), who was murdered by the Nazis. In his *Letters and Papers from Prison* he grapples with the problem of presenting the Gospel to 'a world come of age'. 'As in the scientific field, so in human affairs generally,' Bonhoeffer writes, '"God" is being pushed more and more out of life, losing more and more ground'[20]. Bonhoeffer accepts the course the world is taking in spite of 'false developments and failures ...even an event like the present war is no exception'. He denounces 'The attack by the Christian apologetic on the adulthood of the world' and calls it pointless, ignoble and unchristian—pointless, because it is an attempt 'to put a grown-up man back into adolescence'; ignoble, because it is an attempt to exploit man's weakness for purposes that are alien to him; 'unchristian, because it confuses Christ with one particular stage in man's religiousness'. Whatever one makes of these comments, they are a sign of an optimism out of keeping with the circumstances.

Teilhard and Bonhoeffer faced the same problem, that of presenting the Gospel to an increasingly secularized world. They tackled it in different ways. Bonhoeffer saw secularization as a sign of a 'world come of age', whereas Teilhard rejected secularization at its strongest point, science. Each offered different grounds for a boundless optimism. Bonhoeffer viewed in the Second World War only a 'false development' which must not make 'the world doubt the necessity of the course it is taking, or of its development'[21]. This attitude is remarkably similar to Teilhard's (see Chapter 6). 'Since the great conflict', Teilhard writes at the conclusion of the First World War, 'from which we are emerging has enabled us in the end to understand our vocation and to feel the vigour of our youth, we must not grieve at the cruelty of war nor the anticlimax of peace'[22].

Bonhoeffer concurs with Teilhard, but for different reasons, that theology's attempt to take 'up arms against Darwinism' is misguided (p.188). Teilhard saw this attempt as misguided because he believed that Darwinism was a naive theory of evolution which ignored the 'within' of things; whereas Bonhoeffer accepted Darwinism as a scientific account of the evolution of human beings, outside the scope of theology, and indicative of a 'world come of age'.

In the forward to *Comment Je Crois* (1969, published in English as *Christianity and Evolution*, (1971)) N. M. Wildiers, who edited many of Teilhard's writings, suggests as a key Teilhard's analysis of the problem of 'secularity'. Wildiers defines 'secularity' as recognition of the value inherent in the earth and in humanity's earthly activity. 'Secularism', on the other hand, he defines as every attitude or teaching which stresses exclusively the values of earthly life at the expense of any religious or metaphysical consideration.

Wildiers describes Teilhard's analysis of the problem of secularity as extremely original in form and dimension. He had no doubts about Teilhard's diagnosis of the malaise of modern society: 'The crisis we are suffering to-day does indeed consist in the conflict between a religion of transcendence and a secularized world'[23], or as Teilhard expressed it, a conflict between the 'God of the Above' and the 'God of the Ahead', between 'a religion of heaven' and a 'religion of the earth'. Having defined the problem, what solution does Teilhard offer to resolve the conflict? Humanity's labor acquires a peculiar virtue, Teilhard claims, when earthly work is linked to a world in evolution. 'In a static world', Wildiers writes,

> the dignity of human labour does not qualify for expression in the same terms as it does in a world in evolution. It is precisely because we live in a world which is in the process of construction that our labour takes on a new value and a capital importance. Man's task coincides exactly with the duty to carry out the great work of evolution and to guide it to completion.

Wildiers links Teilhard's answer to the problem of secularity with that of Bonhoeffer's. Teilhard spoke of a 'holy love of earth' as Bonhoeffer spoke of 'holy secularity' (heilige Weltlichkeit). No-one familiar with Teilhard's writings could deny that Wildiers has captured Teilhard's thought on the value of human work. And if human work in the light of Teilhard's view of evolution 'takes on a new value and a capital importance', it is only natural that it should be accompanied by optimism, as the end result is assured. But how humanity is to co-operate with the evolutionary process is not made clear by Teilhard, apart from a general appeal to devote more effort to scientific research, which will become the chief pleasure of all human beings—'not only the restricted band of paid research workers, but also for the man in the street, the day's ideal would be the wresting of another secret or another force from corpuscles, stars, or organized matter. ...That, on an estimate of the forces engaged, is what is being relentlessly prepared around us'[24].

Psychological background to Teilhard's optimism

De Lubac refers to the legend 'fairly commonly believed' that the 'optimistic' views Teilhard taught

> are the fantasies of a man who paid little attention to the hard facts of life, or were the fruit of a happy temperament, or the effusion of a noble soul that could not bear to look evil in the face: unless, indeed, they were unconsciously dictated to him by memories, too hastily transposed to a new context, of his religious training'[25]

Now de Lubac is correct in saying that Teilhard's optimistic views were not the fruit of a happy temperament. As noted at the beginning of the chapter Teilhard was plagued by anxiety from his childhood. Another Jesuit scientist and life-long friend of Teilhard, Pierre Leroy, also refers to Teilhard's 'great optimism': 'He was indeed an optimist, in his attribution to the universe of a sense of direction in spite of the existence of evil and in spite of appearances; but in daily life that concerned him personally, he was far from being an optimist ...how often in intimate conversation have I found him depressed and with almost no heart to carry on ...he was at times prostrated by fits of weeping, and he appeared to be on the verge of despair'[26]. Leroy returns to this strange double aspect of Teilhard's personality in an international meeting to celebrate the centenary of Teilhard's birth. 'The last time I saw him was in New York; it was nearing Christmas 1954', Leroy reminisces:

> He was as sad as I had ever seen him. His face had changed: there was not much left in him which would remind me of the vigour and enthusiasm with which he had so many times illuminated and strengthened my soul, and those of many others he had charmed with his endearing ways. He returns to his gloomiest hours of 1925, the date of his exile into China. ...Here was an utterly depressed man.

It is notable that Leroy twice in the space of a few pages refers to Teilhard's fits of depression and weeping. How is this to be reconciled with Teilhard's optimism? Many writers comment on Teilhard's optimism but make no reference to his alternation between exhilaration and fits of deep depression. Only a very close friend would be aware of it. What caused these violent changes in mood? Leroy gives us a clue in the following remark: 'He keeps asking himself whether he may not have shown a wrong course'[27]. Teilhard gave indirect expression to his misgivings just one month before his death, in 'The Christic' (March 1955):

> How is it, then, that as I look around me, still dazzled by what I have seen, I find that I am almost the only person of my kind, the only one to have *seen*? And so I cannot, when asked, quote a single writer, a single work, that gives a clearly expressed description of the wonderful 'Diaphany' that has transfigured everything for me?[28]

Part of that wonderful diaphany was his cosmic optimism.

Evolution and cosmic optimism

To turn now to the *theoretical* foundation of Teilhard's optimism, Midgley argues that evolutionary theories by their very nature spawn beliefs which oscillate between being optimistic and pessimistic: 'the two emotional responses which belong most naturally to evolutionary speculation—on the one hand, optimistic, joyful wonder at the profusion of nature, and on the other, pessimistic, sombre alarm at its wasteful cruelty'[29].

What was it in Teilhard's evolutionary theory that especially gave rise to optimism? Teilhard's search was for a source of hope. He saw evolution as a growth in complexity and consciousness, but the optimism is due more to the belief that human beings, both biologically and spiritually, are bound for perfection.

It was in a posthumous publication, 'The Antiquity and World Expansion of Human Culture' (1956), that Teilhard, for the first time in his writings, acknowledged that it is possible that humanity may not become better or happier in the course of the process of evolution[30]. De Lubac concedes that Teilhard appears 'sometimes over-optimistic, or to come too close to views that were in fact a long way from his own'[31]. He ascribes this optimism to a readiness to accept what was positive in the thought of others, even when they themselves did not realize all its implications. De Lubac, however, admits that Teilhard's view of the future 'was not entirely free from illusion' (p.121). It has been noted in Chapter 6 that he saw the First World war as a critical stage in mankind's understanding of the 'cosmic current' carrying it along. He finishes the essay, 'The Promised Land' (1919), with the words: 'from the mountain peak, I have seen *The Promised Land*'.

Teilhard saw evolution as the foundation of his optimism. 'At last we see', he exclaimed in 'The Mechanism of Evolution' (1951), *'the emergence as a scientific fact* of a generalized and optimistic sense of history'[32]. This optimistic view of history arises, Teilhard thought, from his discovery of the law of complexity-consciousness and the convergent nature of evolution. In combination they were, he thought, 'the greatest discovery ever bequeathed to the natural sciences since that other discovery of the existence of *an* evolution' (p.308). 'If the scientific reality of this massive phenomenon', Teilhard writes, '(as massive, in truth, as, at the other extreme of things, the expansion of the universe) were to be definitively confirmed, a great light would certainly dawn over the world of tomorrow' (p.308). The 'massive phenomenon' is the dual process of increasing complexity-consciousness and subsequent convergence of the evolutionary process. The 'great light' would arise because hominisation 'would *be given a direction*' (p.309).

A fellow Jesuit, Robert O'Connell, shares Teilhard's vision. 'Teilhard's view of reality', O'Connell writes, is 'as strange and shocking as their hearers found Copernicus' proposal, or Darwin's, or Freud's.'[33].

Evolution and human history

Teilhard reacted angrily to those who did not share his view that mankind's ground for hope is the evolutionary process. 'What is man justified in hoping for, *objectively*,' Teilhard writes,

> leaving aside any emotional, philosophical or mystical considerations (but viewed bio-cosmically[34])? ...In other words, what, in evolutionary terms, now, in 1951, is the *probable* human potential? I shall protest until my dying breath against all the stupidities of pseudo-existentialism and a pseudo-Christianity: that's where the whole problem lies.[35]

Mankind's reason for hope is its probable human potential, viewed bio-cosmically. It is only from an 'evolutionary viewpoint' that human potential should be viewed; mankind is still objectively young and therefore full of energy for the future, and thus has grounds for hope. Teilhard draws the same conclusion in *The Phenomenon of Man*. 'If progress is a myth', he writes,' ...our efforts will flag. With that the whole of evolution will come to a halt—because we are evolution'[36]. In the section immediately following, entitled 'The Dilemma and the Choice', Teilhard draws the conclusion, without giving any reason for it, that 'Between these alternatives of absolute optimism or absolute pessimism, there is no middle way because by its very nature progress is all or nothing'. His choice is 'absolute optimism'.

Teilhard laments the fact that natural history and human history have far too long been separate disciplines. Even though historians such as Toynbee and Spengler have treated the social evolution *'in a biological way* ' it still remains 'outside and separate from biology'. 'The domain of zoology and the domain of culture', Teilhard writes,

> are still two compartments, mysteriously alike, maybe, in their laws and arrangement, but nevertheless two different worlds. The most organically aware of historians seem definitely to have halted at that dualism—without, moreover, any apparent surprise or uneasiness.[37]

Teilhard is intent on removing this traditional dualism, that of human history and biology. Surprised that historians balk at removing this dualism, he gives hints, elsewhere, as to why it is resistant to removal. In *The Phenomenon of Man* he says that 'taking advantage of the immense duration it has still to live, then mankind has immense possibilities before it'[38]. The potential of mankind in its infancy, with the enormous span of time and the immense possibilities before it, constitutes the realm of evolution. The 'if', the uncertainty about whether the possibilities are to be realized, constitutes the realm of history.

Again in *The Mechanism of Evolution* (1951) he shows disappointment that 'minds as acute as Spengler and Toynbee' reduce history to a periodic function, without beginning or end, 'whereas the problem in understanding man is to discover some basic current beneath the superficial oscillations' (p.305). The 'basic current' is 'the *combined* increase of complexity and consciousness' (p.308).

In a series of letters published as *Letters from a Traveller*, Teilhard shows clearly his conflation of evolution and human history. In a letter to a friend in 1935 he writes:

> It is almost as though, for reasons arising from the progress of my own science, the past and its discovery had ceased to interest me. *The past has revealed to me how the future is built* and pre-occupation with the future tends to sweep everything else aside. It is precisely that I may be able to speak with authority about the future that it is essential for me to establish myself more firmly than before as a specialist on the past.[39]

The end of the world and optimism

In *The Phenomenon of Man* Teilhard envisages two possibilities for the end of the world. Firstly he dismisses 'all pessimistic representations of the earth's last days—whether in terms of cosmic catastrophe, biological disruptions or simply arrested growth or senility'[40]. ('Yet perhaps anything', he says as an aside, 'would be better than long-drawn-out senility'.) Such predictions, he says, are drawn from characteristics of individual human beings, who are subject to accident, disease and senility, and then extended, '*without correction*, to life as a whole'—in short, 'Accident, disease and decrepitude spell the death of men; and therefore the same applies to mankind'. Teilhard denies that this is a valid extrapolation, because the loss of the individual is not irreparable from the point of view of the continuation of life.

One could begin by objecting to Teilhard's premiss that all such representations of the earth's last days are drawn from the fate of individuals. Because of Man's evolutionary uniqueness, Teilhard argues, 'however improbable it might seem, *he* must *reach his goal*, not necessarily, doubtless, but infallibly [non pas nécessairement, sans doute, mais infailliblement]'[41]. So what we should expect is an ultimate perfection 'coming at its biologically appointed hour'. Only in this direction can we get a glimpse of the end of the world.

Two points need to be noted. Teilhard concedes that mankind's goal might seem improbable. Why does he make this remark? Secondly, what does he see as the goal? The answer to the first question seems to be that the conditions of the individual, subject to accident, sickness and disease, and possible cosmic catastrophe or arrested growth, are more serious than he originally was prepared to admit. But his major fear is arrested human growth or senility. The reason for this fear is that such a situation would be a falsification of the evolutionary progress of mankind. The goal of mankind is evolution's goal, the climax of the evolutionary process. Teilhard identifies this goal with the end of human history and also with the Christian parousia when all things will be gathered under the headship of Christ. There is a double identification here: the identification of evolution with human history, and also with 'salvation history'. (The latter identification was discussed in Chapter 8.) It is no wonder, then, that Teilhard is so optimistic—mankind *'must reach the goal'*.

Teilhard outlines 'two almost contradictory suppositions about the physical and psychical state [of] our planet ...as it approaches maturation'[42]. The first envisages that 'disease and hunger will be conquered by science ...evil on the earth will be reduced to a minimum ...and ...hatred and internecine struggles will have disappeared in the ever-warmer radiance of Omega'. He sees this as the one towards which 'we ought in any case to turn our efforts as to an ideal'. But there is another possibility: 'Obeying a law from which nothing in the past has ever been exempt, evil may go on growing alongside good, and may attain its paroxysm at the end in some specifically new form'. Teilhard is aware that this is in keeping with traditional Christian thinking, but he rejects it because it is not in conformity with his evolutionary views and would sap mankind's 'zest for life'.

Teilhard as at pains to point out that although the final convergence of the noosphere upon itself will take place *'in peace'*, yet because a critical point is being approached—point Omega—it will be in a state of *'extreme tension'*. His reason for this comment is that he wishes to dissociate his perspective from 'the old millenary dreams of a terrestrial paradise at the end of time'. Teilhard makes it clear that the supposition that evil will be reduced to a minimum, disease and hunger will be conquered, and hatred and war will disappear as the end of the world approaches, 'would conform most harmoniously with [his] theory'. Given the scientific probability 'that life has before it long periods of geological time in which to develop', the success of the forces of evolution 'is the only acceptable assumption'. At this juncture he makes the transition from evolution to human history. 'Taking advantage of the immense duration it has still to live, mankind has enormous possibilities before it'. The enormous possibilities constitute the realm of evolution, the realization of those possibilities constitutes the realm of human history.

Earlier in life, Teilhard was inclined to the supposition that evil will go on increasing and reach its paroxysm at the end of the world, as a passage in 'My Universe' (1924) shows. 'When the end of time is as at hand', he writes,

> a terrifying spiritual pressure will be exerted on the confines of the real, built up by the desperate efforts of souls tense with longing to escape the earth. This pressure will be unanimous. Scripture, however, tell us that at the same time it will be infected by a profound schism. ....It is then, we may be sure, that the Parousia will be realized in a creation that has been taken to the climax of its capacity for union[43].

If this second supposition is accepted Teilhard's theory would collapse.

The real problem with the two suppositions is that the first sees human history as a continuing of evolution, while the second denies this.

Evolution as an ethical blindfold

There are reasons for thinking that Teilhard's ground for hope, the probable human potential over a great span of time, acted as an ethical blindfold in his reaction to the human tragedies that occurred around him in his lifetime. As the German theologian Jürgen Moltmann observed:

> Teilhard did not merely consider that natural catastrophes have a point in the interests of the greater evolution. With the help of the evolutionary idea, he continually also tried to wring a meaning out of the experiences of human catastrophes. In the letters he wrote during the First World War to friends shattered by the senselessness of the massacre, he tried to convert them to a positive view of the war, as a noble contribution to natural evolution.[44]

A particularly strong expression of his cosmic optimism, in the face of the human catastrophe of the First World War, appeared in his 'The Great Monad' (1918) which has already been mentioned in Chapter 6.

> When the Great War broke out which at one blow brought crashing
> down the whole structure of a decrepit civilisation ...As though every
> greater order has not always emerged from the ruins of the lesser! ...as
> if a new and fresh surface did not force its way up through the tattered
> fragments of the old crust![45]

Surprisingly, the editor of this essay does not see these words as
wringing meaning out of human tragedy but as 'vindicating'
Teilhard's 'faith in the World' (p.192). In the same essay Teilhard
while extolling peace—'for which the nations long (as I do myself,
more than anyone)'—says that 'When peace comes, everything will
once more be overlaid by the veil of the former melancholy and
trivialities. ...Happy, perhaps, will those be whom death has taken in
the very drama and atmosphere of war' (pp. 178–179).

Teilhard expressed the same feelings in his attitude to the Second
World War and the development of the atomic bomb. Referring to
this war, he describes 'his inability to take sides'[46] and says the 'true
enemies are those who deny progress'[47]. The dropping of the atomic
bomb on the two Japanese cities brought this response: 'The quicker
ending of the War, the vast sums of money spent—what did such
things matter when the worth of science was on trial'[48]

An important paper by Teilhard, 'Fossil Men: Recent Discoveries
and Present Problems' (1943), originally published in English and
delivered to the Catholic University of Peking, illustrates Teilhard's
optimism. As mentioned in Chapter 3 this paper was translated into
French and included in Teilhard's collected works, published by
Éditions du Seuil[49]. In the original English paper, which appears as a
facsimile in Schmitz-Moormann, Teilhard unhesitatingly opts for the
continued evolution of human beings. But he goes much further and
sees in the fossil record 'scientific ground' for 'our hopes and
expectations for human progress'[50]. But the sentence following
appears to question this hope with its comment: *'provided*, however,
that *we stick to the same line of march as our forerunners'*. Although he
fleetingly entertains the possibility of human beings refusing the
direction of evolution offered to them, he rejects such a possibility
because it would be a denial of the law of complexity-consciousness:
'a definite and universal process, persistently carrying a certain part
of cosmic material from highly disintegrated and apparently
inanimate elements towards more and more amazingly complex and
more and more manifestly consciousness units'[51]. 'This', he concludes, 'is the only type of evolution in which the development of

Man, (as disclosed by prehistory) can be placed without physical distortion or even contradiction'[52].

Moral and physical evil in a world of cosmic optimism

Teilhard's cosmic optimism arises in no small part from his understanding of physical and moral evil. In Chapter 8 this aspect of his thought was considered. Teilhard gives succinct expression to this understanding in his autobiographical essay 'The Heart Of Matter' (1950). 'From the point of view of the convergent Evolution', he writes,

> to which sixty years of varied experience and of thought have introduced me ...the whole cosmic Event may be reduced in its essence to one single process of arrangement, whose mechanism (that is, the use of the effects of Large Numbers and the play of Chance) is governed by statistical necessity: so that every moment it releases a given quantity of events that cause distress (failures, disintegrations, death ...)[53]

As noted in Chapter 8, Teilhard's 'postage' example'[54] to illustrate how evil in an evolutionary world is a statistical necessity does not capture the phenomenon of moral evil at all. Moral evil is not an inadvertent mistake; it involves the will.

Teilhard also believed that already in the animal kingdom we find a distant analogy with what, in Man, will be strictly sin. 'See how the animals behave', Teilhard writes in a letter of 2 January 1925, '(monkeys, for example, or even certain insects): we see them doing things that are materially culpable, and only need the emergence of a fuller consciousness to become fully reprehensible'[55]. But Teilhard did not follow up this line of thinking. De Lubac concedes that on the matter of sin as a statistical necessity Teilhard's 'thought is still incomplete—much more so, indeed, than he seems to have realized'. De Lubac has retreated from his earlier unequivocal defense of Teilhard's view of moral evil[56]. Quite generally, even Teilhard's most ardent admirers became aware of his defective understanding of moral evil. This defective understanding of moral evil acts as ethical blinkers to play down the significance of evil in the world, allowing concentration on the distant goal of the evolutionary process. To a large extent it is Teilhard's acceptance of the 'statistical necessity' of all evil, which enables him to maintain his cosmic optimism.

Teilhard's evolutionary optimism: Humanist or Christian?

In spite of what many writers suggest, Teilhard's optimism was not due to his thinking as a Christian. 'Between these alternatives of absolute optimism or absolute pessimism', Teilhard writes,

> there is no middle way because by its very nature progress is all or nothing. We are confronted accordingly with two directions and only two: one upwards and the other downwards, and there is no possibility of finding a half-way house.

> On neither side is there any tangible evidence to produce. Only in support of hope, there are rational invitations to an act of faith.[57]

Robert O'Connell rightly asks the question: What are these 'rational invitations'? 'Humanity', he answers, is 'evolution's finest achievement'...'We need courage to live up to evolution's often stark demands on us; but even more fundamentally, we need "faith" in the "supreme value of evolution" and in the "magnificent cause" which it embodies'[58].

Delfgaauw notes that 'Teilhard belongs to the relatively small number of paleontologists who persist in regarding evolution as progress. In this his position is the same as that of Julian Huxley'. But astonishingly he remarks that 'behind Teilhard's conviction lies the fact that he is a Christian'[59]. What has that fact to do with Teilhard's evolutionary optimism? Being a Christian might well underwrite belief in an optimistic consummation of things ('all shall be well, and all shall be well, and all manner of things shall be well'—Julian of Norwich said[60]); it could do nothing to underwrite the prospects held out by a particular theory of evolution. And the remark is at odds with Teilhard's claim that the prospects he holds out draw nothing from religion or metaphysics, but are scientifically based.

In his major work *The Phenomenon of Man* (1940) Teilhard found it necessary to answer those critics who claimed that he had ignored the existence of sin and evil in the world. 'Throughout the long discussions we have been through, Teilhard writes, 'one point may perhaps have intrigued or even shocked the reader. Nowhere, if I am not mistaken, have pain or wrong been spoken of'[61]. The appendix written eight years later in 1948 occupies only three pages. On 'the disconcerting excess of sin and suffering' which he had accepted in *Le Milieu Divin*[62] as due to 'an original fall', he now says that 'I do not feel that I am in a position to take a stand'.

In 'Christ the Evolver' (1942) Teilhard asserts that there is a Christian optimism stemming from the theory of evolution. 'Under the pressure of to-day's events', he writes,

> and the evidence we now have, the tangible world and its future developments are certainly taking on an increasing interest for the followers of the gospel. This is producing a 'humanist' revival in religion, which without in any way rejecting the dark side of creation prefers to emphasize its luminous aspect. We are even now witnessing, and taking part in, the irresistible rise of a Christian optimism.[63]

In this essay, as we saw (Chapter 8), Teilhard proposes a new role for Christ and reinterprets many Christian beliefs. So although his optimism proceeds from his theory of evolution, he thinks that he finds in it warrant for a new 'Christian optimism'. In 'The God of Evolution' (1953) he finds confirmation of his view in 'a most revealing correspondence between the pattern of the two confronting Omegas:

> that postulated by modern science and that experienced by Christian mysticism. A correspondence—and one might say a parity! For Christ would not still be the Consummator so passionately described by St. Paul if he did not take on precisely the attributes of the astonishing cosmic pole already potentially (if not as yet explicitly) demanded by our new knowledge of the world: the pole at whose peak the progress of evolution must finally converge.[64]

What can be called with any specificity 'Christian mysticism'—the experiences, for example, of St. Teresa of Avila—have nothing in common with what Teilhard is talking about.

Cosmic convergence and the Parousia

Point Omega, for Teilhard, the culmination of the evolutionary process, and the Parousia, for the Christian the future return of Christ in glory, will coincide. How could they not? 'How can these two super-entities', he writes:

the one 'supernatural', the other natural, fail to come together and harmonise in Christian thought; the critical point of maturation envisaged by science being simply the physical condition and experimental aspect of the critical point of the Parousia postulated and awaited in the name of Revelation'[65]

In conclusion, Teilhard's grounds for optimism arise in the main from an identification of his particular understanding of the evolutionary process with human history and with 'salvation history'. His understanding of the evolutionary process was bolstered by an extraordinary confidence in his own views. He saw his principle of 'convergence' in biological evolution, which arose initially from his involvement with Piltdown Man, as perhaps 'the greatest discovery bequeathed to the natural sciences'[66] since the discovery of evolution. He had the most exalted sense of his religious mission. In a letter to Ida Treat in 1937, shortly before he began writing *The Phenomenon of Man*, he wrote: 'When it comes to trying to decide how to carry out my aspirations truthfully I see no other course ...than to continue as intensively as possible to hasten a Christian renaissance (revolution?)'. He continues by indicating the importance of his task. 'To advance this work', he exclaims, 'I admit, there might in fact be a necessary gesture, different from but comparable to those of Christ or Saint Francis' [67].

NOTES

1   Teilhard, *Letters from a Traveller*, p.338.

2   L. Zonneveld and R. Muller, *The Desire to be Human*, Netherlands: Mirananda, 1983, p.250.

3   Teilhard, *The Heart of Matter*, p.18.

4   C. Cuénot, *Teilhard de Chardin*, A Biographical Study, trans. Vincent Colimore (London: Burns and Oates, 1965), p.3.

5   Browning et al. (eds.), *Teilhard de Chardin: In Quest of the Perfection of Man*, p.193.

6   H. Spencer, *Social Statics; or, The Conditions Essential to Human Happiness*, London: Williams and Norgate, 1850, (American reprint, 1868).

7   A. Harnack, *What is Christianity?*, trans. T.M.Saunders, London, Oxford and New York: Williams and Norgate, 1901.

8   G. Tyrrell, *Christianity at the Cross-Roads*, London: Longmans, Green and Co., 1910, p.280.

9   Ibid., p.44.

10 O. Chadwick, *The Secularization of the European Mind in the Nineteenth Century*, Cambridge: Cambridge University Press, 1975, p.258.

11 K. Barth, *The Epistle to the Romans*, sixth ed., trans. E.C. Hoskyns, London: Oxford University Press, 1932.

12 R. Tennant, *Philosophical Theology*, Vol. II, Cambridge: Cambridge University Press, 1930, reprinted 1968, p.94.

13 Teilhard, *The Appearance of Man*, p.252.

14 Teilhard, *Christianity and Evolution*, p.215.

15 M. Charlesworth, *Church, State, and Conscience*, St. Lucia: University of Queensland Press, 1973, p.100.

16 Delfgaauw, *Evolution, The Theory of Teilhard de Chardin*, p.50.

17 Teilhard, *Christianity and Evolution*, p.199.

18 Teilhard, *The Future of Man*, p.260.

19 Ibid., p.185.

20 Dietrich Bonhoeffer, *Letters and Papers from Prison*, trans. R. Fuller et al., 3rd ed., London: SCM Press, 1967, p.178.

21 Ibid., p.178.

22 Teilhard, *Writings in Time of War*, p.287.

23 Teilhard, *Christianity and Evolution*, p.11.

24 Teilhard, *The Phenomenon of Man*, p.280.

25 De Lubac, *The Religion of Teilhard de Chardin*, p.36.

26 Teilhard, *Letters from a Traveller*, pp.35–36.

27 L. Zonneveld and R. Muller, *The Desire to be Human*, Netherlands: Mirananda, 1983, p.250.

28 Teilhard, *The Heart of Matter*, p.100.

29 Midgley, *Evolution as a Religion*, pp. 4–5.

30 Schmitz-Moormann, Vol. X, p.4587.

31 De Lubac, *The Faith of Teilhard de Chardin*, trans. R.Hague, London: Burns and Oates, 1964, p.106

32 Teilhard, *Activation of Energy*, p.305.

33 O' Connell, *Teilhard's Vision of the Past: The Making of a Method*, New York: Fordham University, 1982, p.128.

34 This phrase has been omitted from the English translation. See C. Cuénot, *Teilhard de Chardin*, Paris, Libraire Plon, 1958, p.316. 'On a parlé d' "espérances humaines" sans songer à la question préalable et préjudicielle de savoir ce que l'Homme (objectivement—en dehors de toute sentimentalité, philosophie et mystique) est en droit, bio-cosmiquement, d'espérer.'

35 C. Cuénot, *Teilhard de Chardin*, p.260.

36 Teilhard, *The Phenomenon of Man*, p.232.

37 Teilhard, *Man's Place in Nature*, p.86.

38 Teilhard, *The Phenomenon of Man*, p.285.

39   Teilhard, *Letters from a Traveller*, pp.207–208. Italics were inserted by the French editor.

40   Teilhard, *The Phenomenon of Man*, p.275.

41   Ibid., p.276. and *Le Phénomène humain*, Paris, Éditions du Seuil, 1955, p.307.

42   Ibid., p.288.

43   Teilhard, *Science and Christ*, p.84.

44   J. Moltmann, *The Way of Jesus Christ*, pp. 294-295.

45   Teilhard, *The Heart of Matter*, p.184.

46   Teilhard, *Letters to Two Friends, 1926-1952*, p.99.

47   Teilhard, *Letters to Two Friends, 1926-1952*, p.160.

48   Teilhard, *The Future of Man*, p.143.

49   Both the French translation and the English translations based on it, delete all references to the Piltdown skull (apart from one oversight: Piltdown skull or Eoanthropus still appears in Figure 12).

50   Schmitz-Moormann, Vol. IX, p.3935.

51   Ibid., p.3935.

52   Ibid., Vol. IX, p.3935.

53   Teilhard, *The Heart of Matter*, p.51.

54   Teilhard, *'La pensé du Père Teilhard de Chardin, par lui-même'* in Les Études Philosophiques [Paris] 10, no. 4, p.581, (1955). A facsimile appears in Schmitz-Moormann, vol. X, p.4568.

55   De Lubac, *The Faith of Teilhard de Chardin*, p.103.

56   Ibid., p.117.

57   Teilhard, *The Phenomenon of Man*, p.233.

58   O'Connell, *Teilhard's Vision of the Past*, pp.115–116.

59   Delfgaauw, *Evolution, The Theory of Teilhard de Chardin*, p.73.

60 Julian of Norwich, *Revelations of Divine Love*, (1373), London: Burns and Oates, 2nd ed., 1952, p.49.

61 Teilhard, *The Phenomenon of Man*, p.311.

62 Teilhard, *Le Milieu Divin*, p. 102.

63 Teilhard, *Christianity and Evolution*, p.145.

64 Ibid., p.242.

65 Teilhard, *The Future of Man*, pp. 223–24.

66 Teilhard, *Activation of Energy*, p.308.

67 Teilhard, *Letters to Two Friends, 1926–1952*, p.94.

INDEX OF NAMES

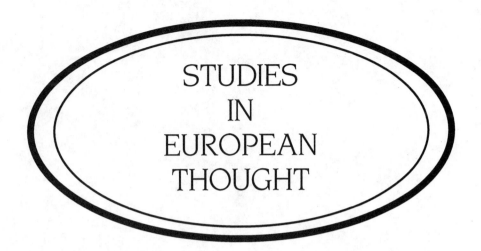

STUDIES
IN
EUROPEAN
THOUGHT

This series of monographs, translations, and critical editions covers comparative and interdisciplinary topics of significance from the early eighteenth century to the present. Volumes, both published and projected, include a collection of essays on German drama, a study of the Künstlerroman, and a study on the aesthetics of the double talent of Kubin and Herzmanovsky-Orlando.

For additional information about this series or for the submission of manuscripts, please contact:

Peter Lang Publishing
Acquisitions Dept.
516 N. Charles St., 2nd Floor
Baltimore, MD 21201

To order other books in this series, please contact our Customer Service Department at:

800-770-LANG (within the U.S.)
(212) 647-7706 (outside the U.S.)
(212) 647-7707 FAX

or browse online by series at:

www.peterlang.com